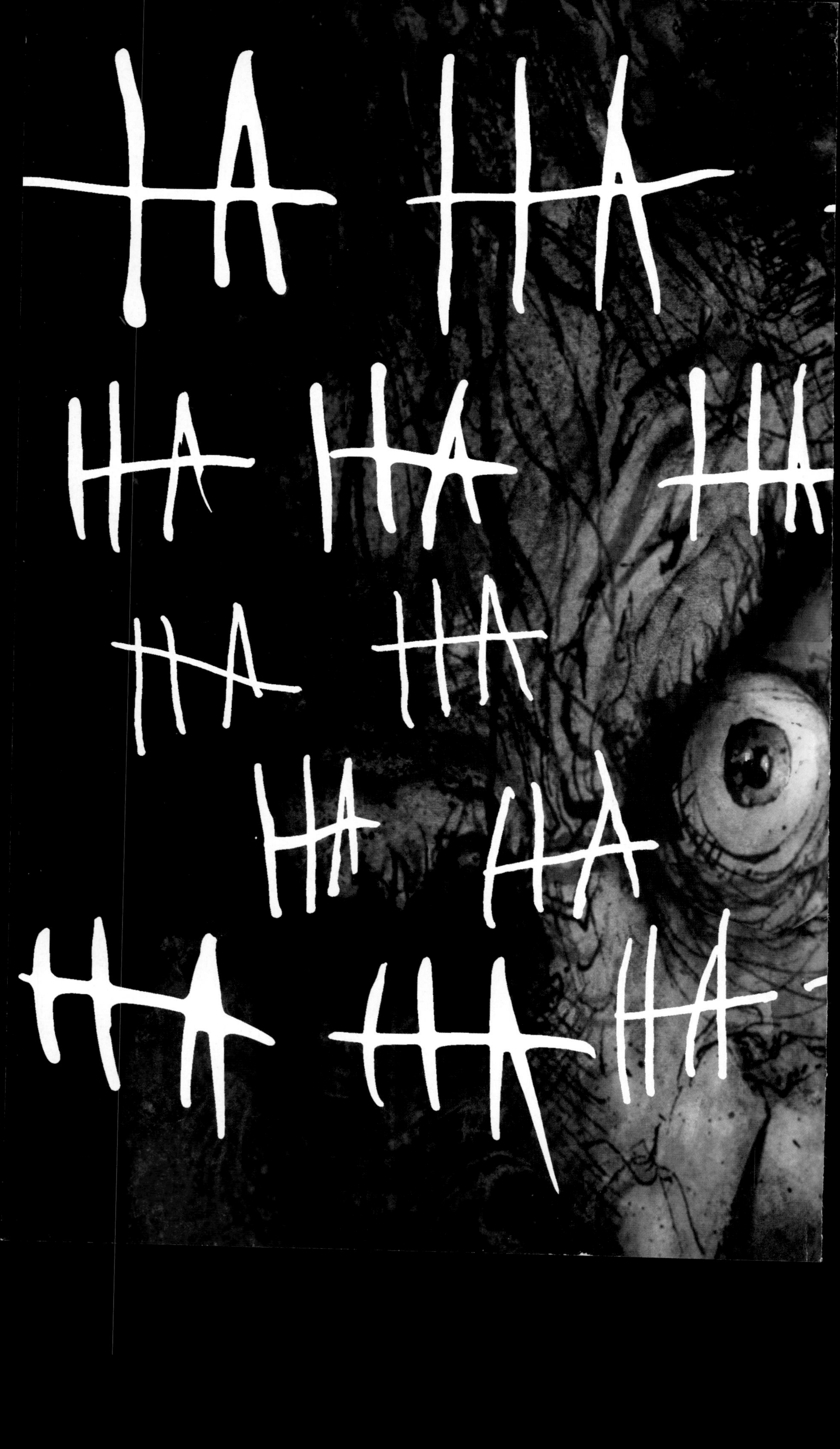
HA HA
HA HA HA
HA HA
HA HA
HA HA HA

# Arkham Asylum
## MADNESS

Written and drawn by
**Sam Kieth**

Colors by Michelle Madsen
and Dave Stewart

Painted pages by Sam Kieth

Letters by Steve Wands

Batman created by Bob Kane

Michael Siglain  Editor
Harvey Richards  Assistant Editor
Robbin Brosterman  Design Director-Books
Louis Prandi  Art Director

DC COMICS
Diane Nelson  President
Dan DiDio and Jim Lee  Co-Publishers
Geoff Johns  Chief Creative Officer
Patrick Caldon  EVP-Finance and Administration
John Rood  EVP-Sales, Marketing and Business Development
Amy Genkins  SVP-Business and Legal Affairs
Steve Rotterdam  SVP-Sales and Marketing
John Cunningham  VP-Marketing
Terri Cunningham  VP-Managing Editor
Alison Gill  VP-Manufacturing
David Hyde  VP-Publicity
Sue Pohja  VP-Book Trade Sales
Alysse Soll  VP-Advertising and Custom Publishing
Bob Wayne  VP-Sales
Mark Chiarello  Art Director

ARKHAM ASYLUM: MADNESS
Published by DC Comics, 1700 Broadway, New York, NY 10019.
Copyright © 2010 by DC Comics. All rights reserved. All characters,
the distinctive likenesses thereof and all related elements, are trademarks
of DC Comics.  The stories, characters and incidents mentioned in this
book are entirely fictional. DC Comics does not read or accept unsolicited
submissions of ideas, stories or artwork.  Printed by RR Donnelley,
Salem, VA, USA. 5/26/10 . First Printing. DC Comics, a Warner Bros.
Entertainment Company.
HC ISBN: 978-1-4012-2337-3
SC ISBN: 978-1-4012-2554-4

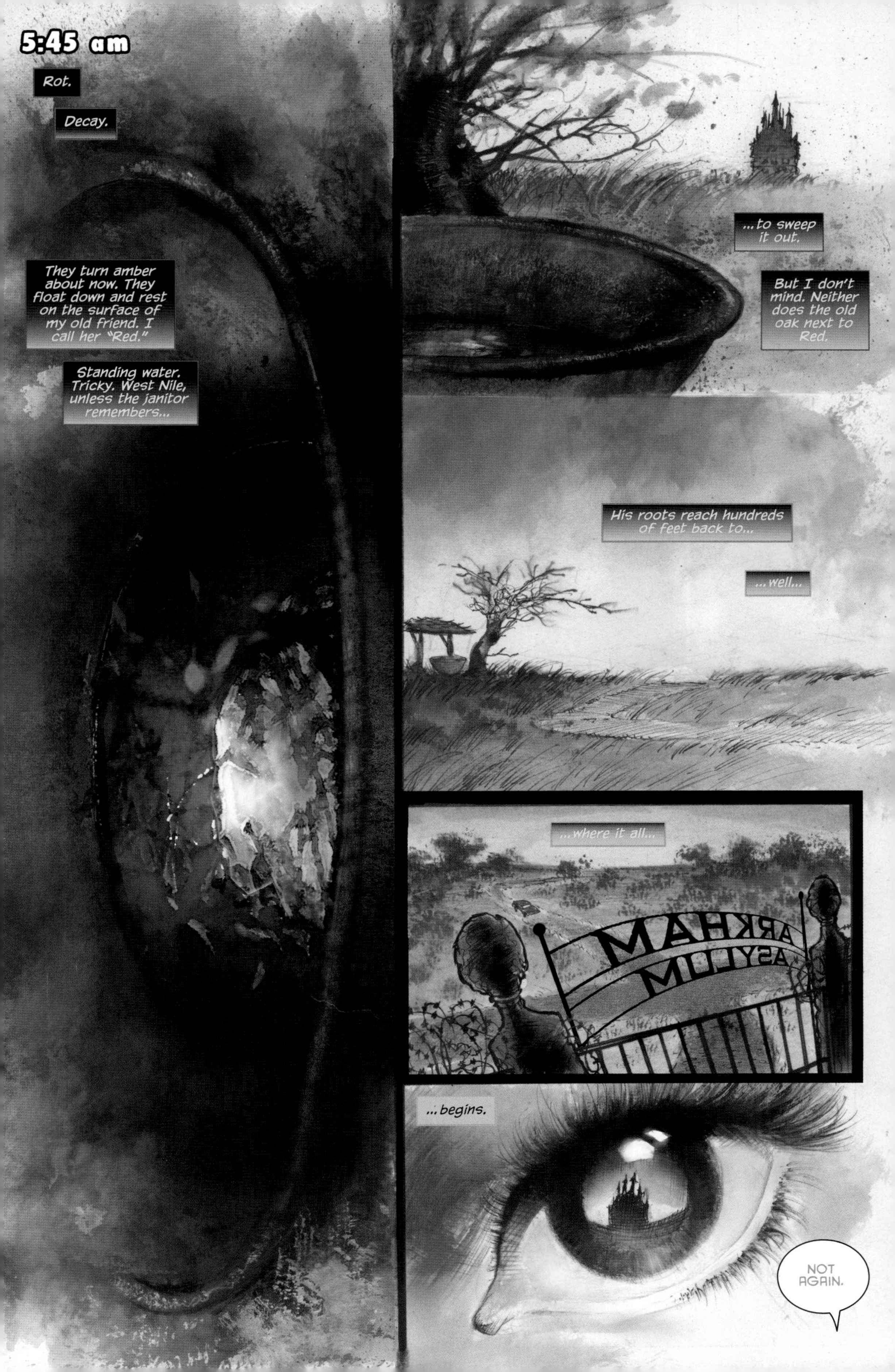
5:45 am
Rot.
Decay.
They turn amber about now. They float down and rest on the surface of my old friend. I call her "Red."
Standing water. Tricky. West Nile, unless the janitor remembers...
...to sweep it out.
But I don't mind. Neither does the old oak next to Red.
His roots reach hundreds of feet back to...
...well...
...where it all...
ARKHAM
ASYLUM
...begins.
NOT AGAIN.

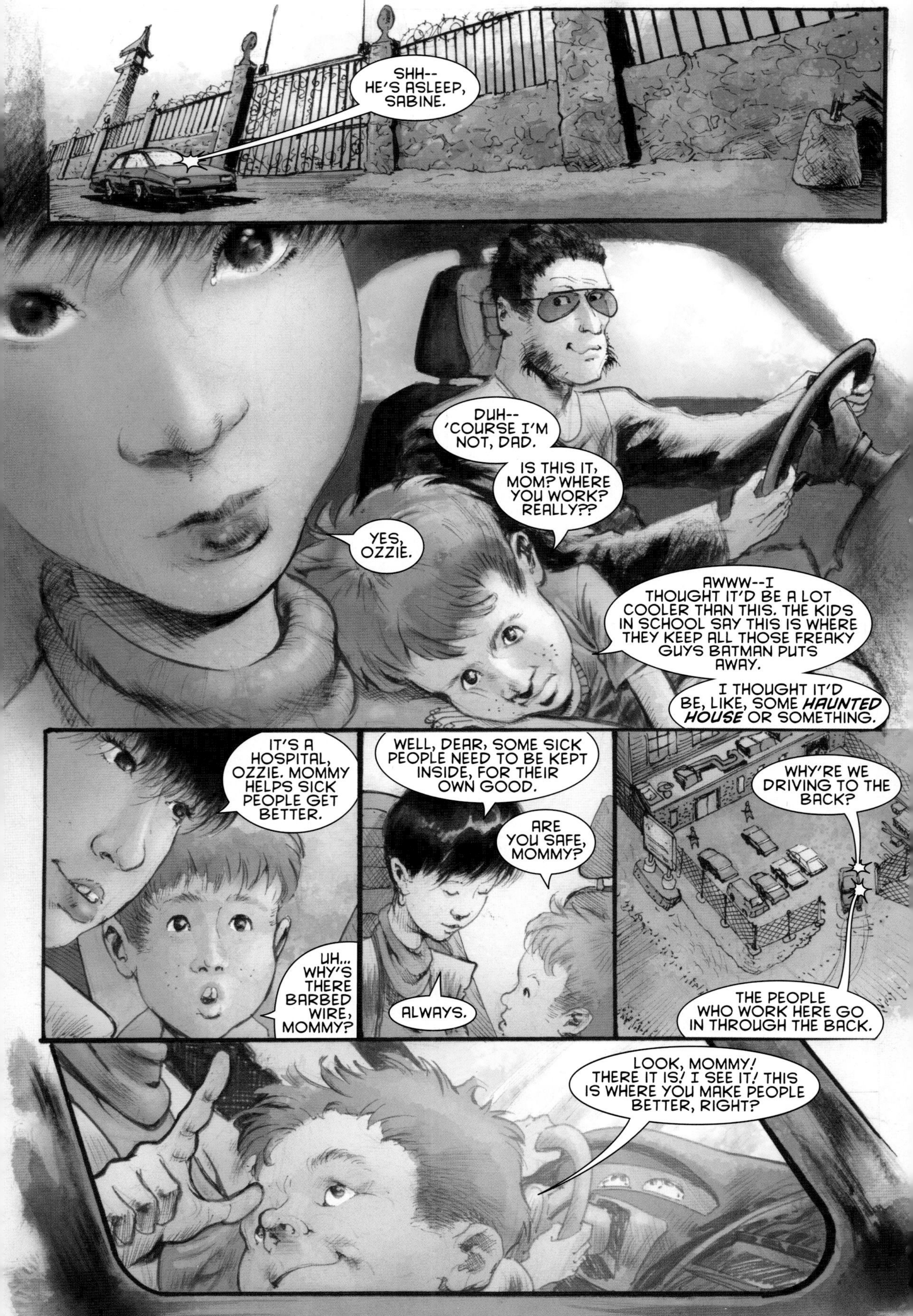
SHH--
HE'S ASLEEP, SABINE.
DUH-- 'COURSE I'M NOT, DAD.
IS THIS IT, MOM? WHERE YOU WORK? REALLY??
YES, OZZIE.
AWWW--I THOUGHT IT'D BE A LOT COOLER THAN THIS. THE KIDS IN SCHOOL SAY THIS IS WHERE THEY KEEP ALL THOSE FREAKY GUYS BATMAN PUTS AWAY.
I THOUGHT IT'D BE, LIKE, SOME *HAUNTED HOUSE* OR SOMETHING.
IT'S A HOSPITAL, OZZIE. MOMMY HELPS SICK PEOPLE GET BETTER.
UH... WHY'S THERE BARBED WIRE, MOMMY?
WELL, DEAR, SOME SICK PEOPLE NEED TO BE KEPT INSIDE, FOR THEIR OWN GOOD.
ARE YOU SAFE, MOMMY?
ALWAYS.
WHY'RE WE DRIVING TO THE BACK?
THE PEOPLE WHO WORK HERE GO IN THROUGH THE BACK.
LOOK, MOMMY! THERE IT IS! I SEE IT! THIS IS WHERE YOU MAKE PEOPLE BETTER, RIGHT?

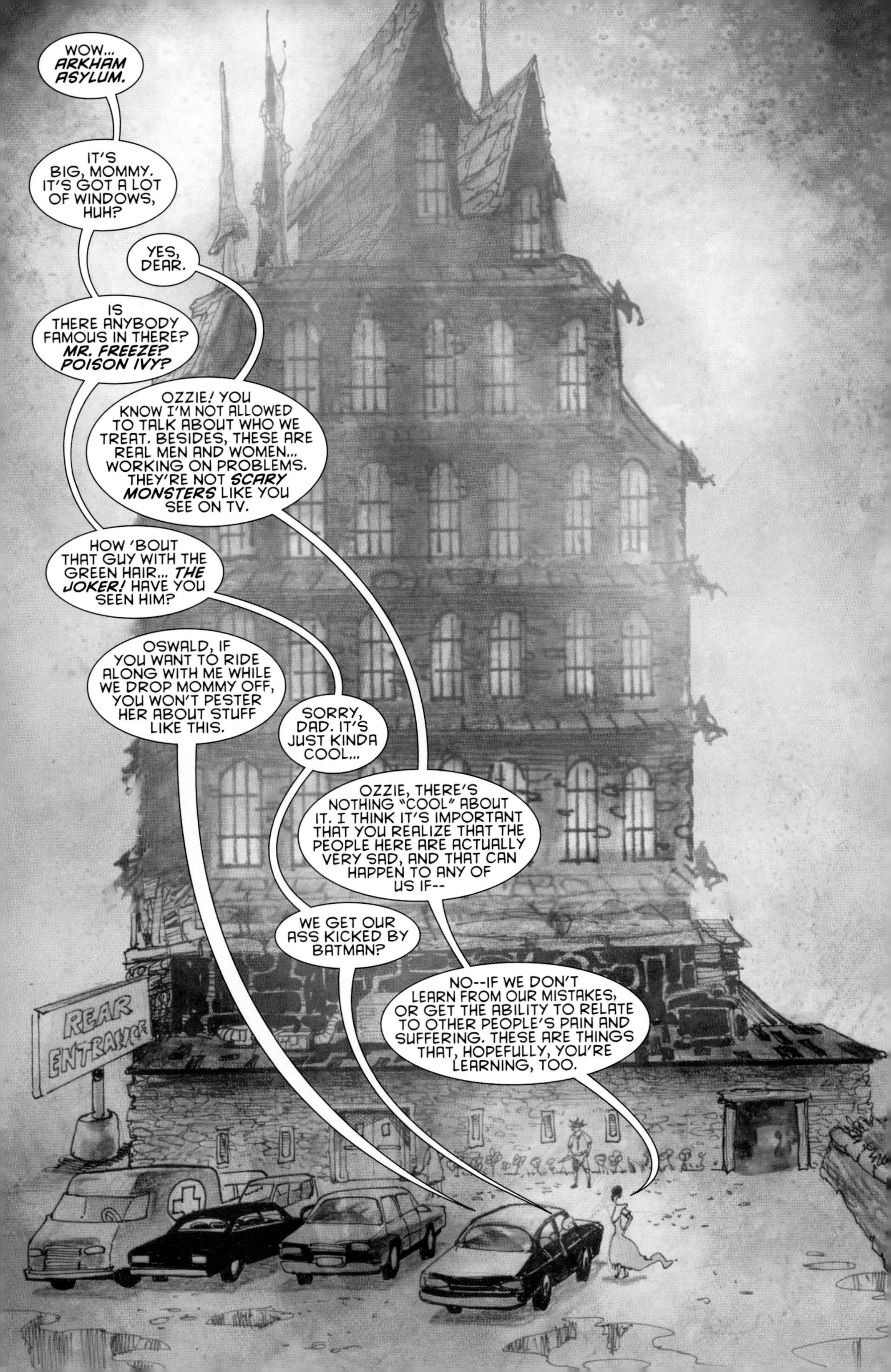
WOW... *ARKHAM ASYLUM.*
IT'S BIG, MOMMY. IT'S GOT A LOT OF WINDOWS, HUH?
YES, DEAR.
IS THERE ANYBODY FAMOUS IN THERE? *MR. FREEZE? POISON IVY?*
OZZIE! YOU KNOW I'M NOT ALLOWED TO TALK ABOUT WHO WE TREAT. BESIDES, THESE ARE REAL MEN AND WOMEN... WORKING ON PROBLEMS. THEY'RE NOT *SCARY MONSTERS* LIKE YOU SEE ON TV.
HOW 'BOUT THAT GUY WITH THE GREEN HAIR... *THE JOKER!* HAVE YOU SEEN HIM?
OSWALD, IF YOU WANT TO RIDE ALONG WITH ME WHILE WE DROP MOMMY OFF, YOU WON'T PESTER HER ABOUT STUFF LIKE THIS.
SORRY, DAD. IT'S JUST KINDA COOL...
OZZIE, THERE'S NOTHING "COOL" ABOUT IT. I THINK IT'S IMPORTANT THAT YOU REALIZE THAT THE PEOPLE HERE ARE ACTUALLY VERY SAD, AND THAT CAN HAPPEN TO ANY OF US IF--
WE GET OUR ASS KICKED BY BATMAN?
NO--IF WE DON'T LEARN FROM OUR MISTAKES, OR GET THE ABILITY TO RELATE TO OTHER PEOPLE'S PAIN AND SUFFERING. THESE ARE THINGS THAT, HOPEFULLY, YOU'RE LEARNING, TOO.
REAR ENTRANCE

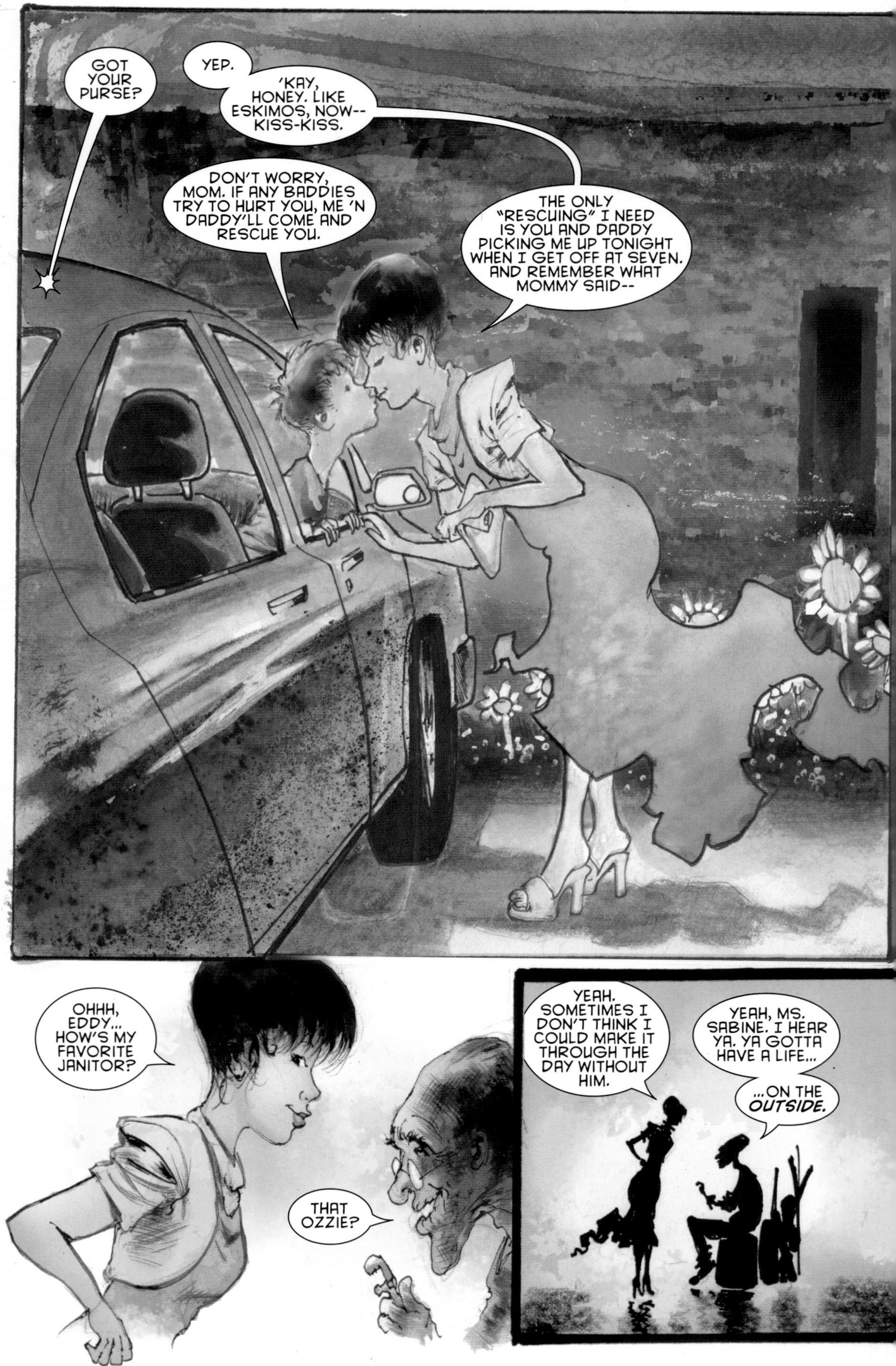
GOT YOUR PURSE?
YEP.
'KAY, HONEY. LIKE ESKIMOS, NOW-- KISS-KISS.
DON'T WORRY, MOM. IF ANY BADDIES TRY TO HURT YOU, ME 'N DADDY'LL COME AND RESCUE YOU.
THE ONLY "RESCUING" I NEED IS YOU AND DADDY PICKING ME UP TONIGHT WHEN I GET OFF AT SEVEN. AND REMEMBER WHAT MOMMY SAID--
OHHH, EDDY... HOW'S MY FAVORITE JANITOR?
THAT OZZIE?
YEAH. SOMETIMES I DON'T THINK I COULD MAKE IT THROUGH THE DAY WITHOUT HIM.
YEAH, MS. SABINE. I HEAR YA. YA GOTTA HAVE A LIFE...
...ON THE *OUTSIDE.*

--MOMMY WORKS IN A NICE PLACE. SHE HELPS PEOPLE GET BETTER. WE NEED TO LEARN COMPASSION FOR THE PEOPLE MOMMY HELPS.

'KAY, MOM. 'BYE.

HEY, IS THAT THE PRETTIEST NURSE AT ARKHAM?

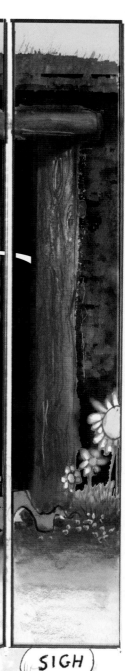

Nice, hypocrite. But what *can* I say?

CLAK CLAK CLAK CLAK CLAK CLAK CLAK

He's a child.

Arkham Sign-i-

| | Time In |
|---|---|
| Sunday | |
| Monday | |
| Tuesday | X |
| Wednesday | |
| Thursday | |
| Friday | |
| Saturday | |

And with one stroke of lead...

SIGH

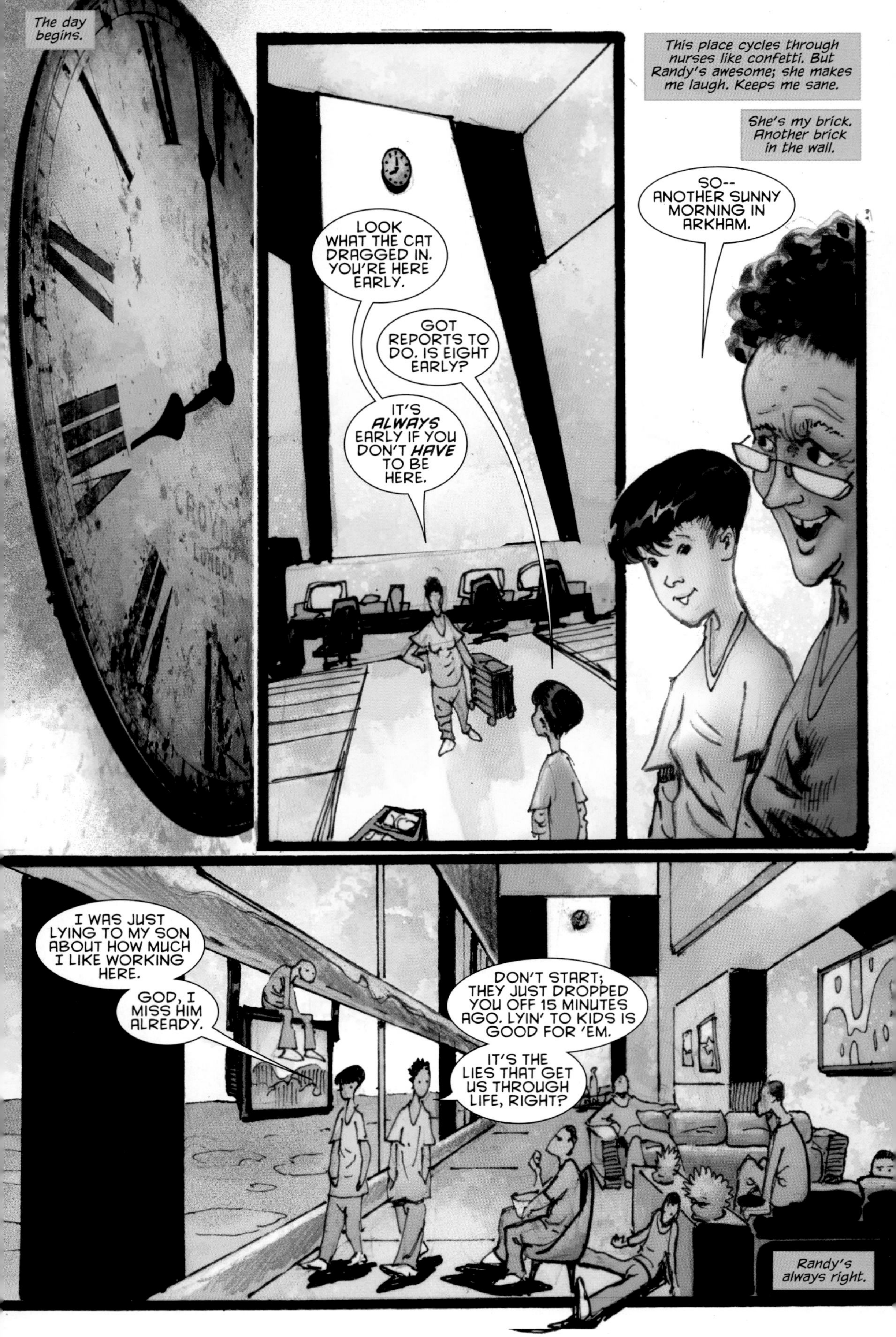
The day begins.
LOOK WHAT THE CAT DRAGGED IN. YOU'RE HERE EARLY.
GOT REPORTS TO DO. IS EIGHT EARLY?
IT'S *ALWAYS* EARLY IF YOU DON'T *HAVE* TO BE HERE.
This place cycles through nurses like confetti. But Randy's awesome; she makes me laugh. Keeps me sane.
She's my brick. Another brick in the wall.
SO-- ANOTHER SUNNY MORNING IN ARKHAM.
I WAS JUST LYING TO MY SON ABOUT HOW MUCH I LIKE WORKING HERE.
GOD, I MISS HIM ALREADY.
DON'T START; THEY JUST DROPPED YOU OFF 15 MINUTES AGO. LYIN' TO KIDS IS GOOD FOR 'EM.
IT'S THE LIES THAT GET US THROUGH LIFE, RIGHT?
Randy's always right.

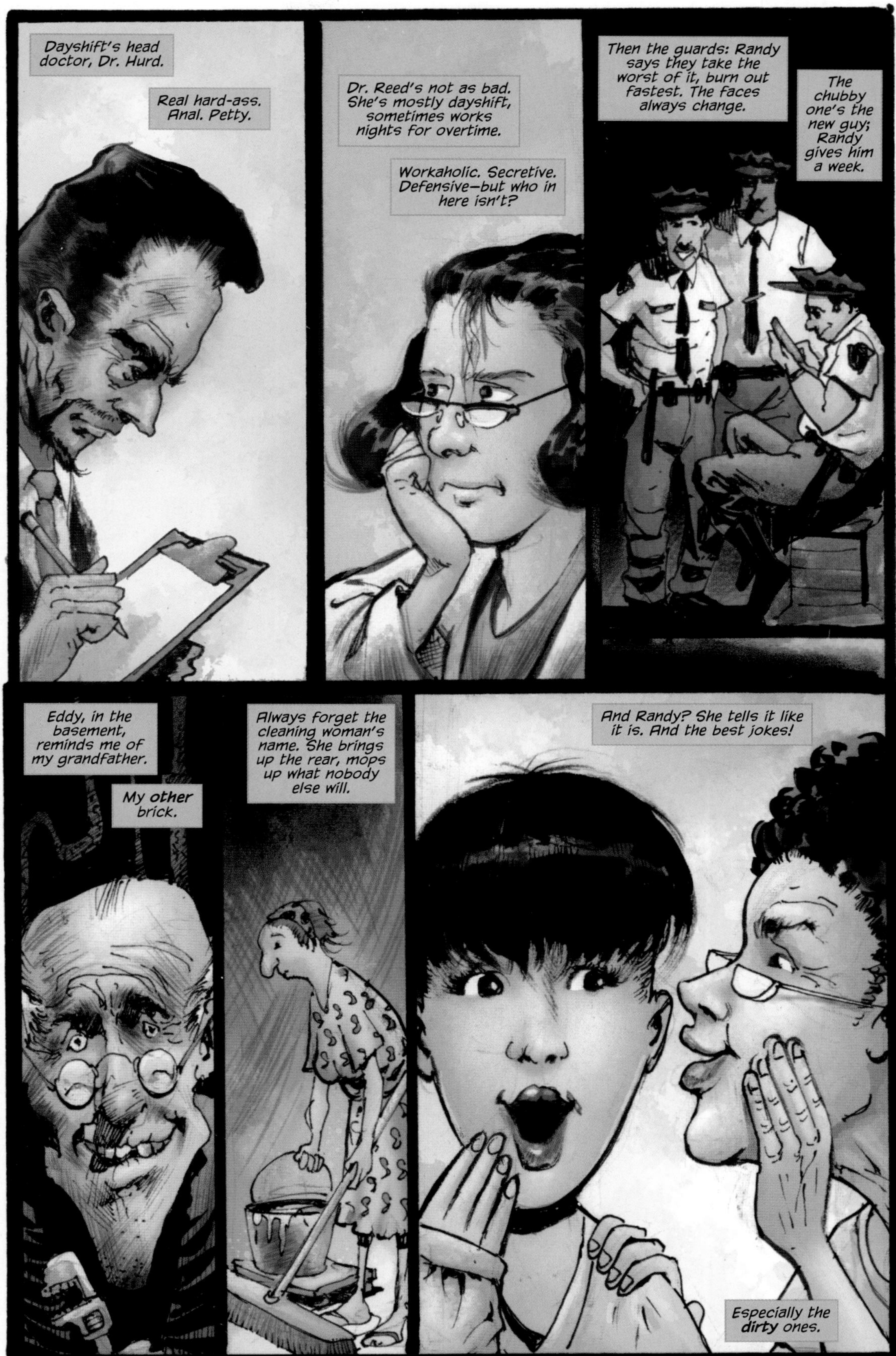
Dayshift's head doctor, Dr. Hurd.
Real hard-ass. Anal. Petty.
Dr. Reed's not as bad. She's mostly dayshift, sometimes works nights for overtime.
Workaholic. Secretive. Defensive—but who in here isn't?
Then the guards: Randy says they take the worst of it, burn out fastest. The faces always change.
The chubby one's the new guy; Randy gives him a week.
Eddy, in the basement, reminds me of my grandfather.
My **other** brick.
Always forget the cleaning woman's name. She brings up the rear, mops up what nobody else will.
And Randy? She tells it like it is. And the best jokes!
Especially the **dirty** ones.

**8:30 am**

*It's moist up here. Sticky. Humid. Stifling.*

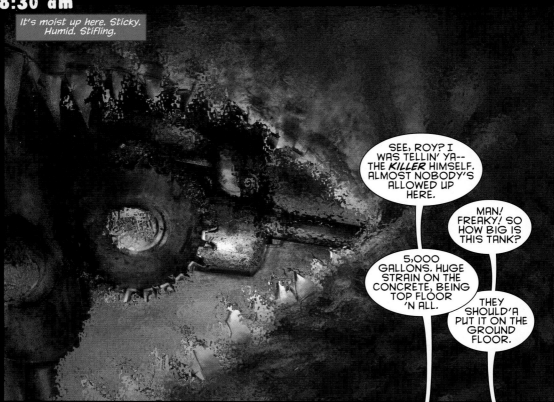

SEE, ROY? I WAS TELLIN' YA-- THE *KILLER* HIMSELF. ALMOST NOBODY'S ALLOWED UP HERE.

MAN! FREAKY! SO HOW BIG IS THIS TANK?

5,000 GALLONS. HUGE STRAIN ON THE CONCRETE, BEING TOP FLOOR 'N ALL.

THEY SHOULD'A PUT IT ON THE GROUND FLOOR.

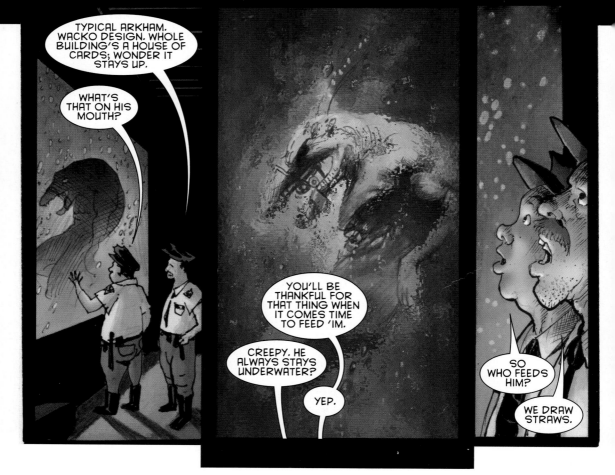

TYPICAL ARKHAM. WACKO DESIGN. WHOLE BUILDING'S A HOUSE OF CARDS; WONDER IT STAYS UP.

WHAT'S THAT ON HIS MOUTH?

YOU'LL BE THANKFUL FOR THAT THING WHEN IT COMES TIME TO FEED 'IM.

CREEPY. HE ALWAYS STAYS UNDERWATER?

YEP.

SO WHO FEEDS HIM?

WE DRAW STRAWS.

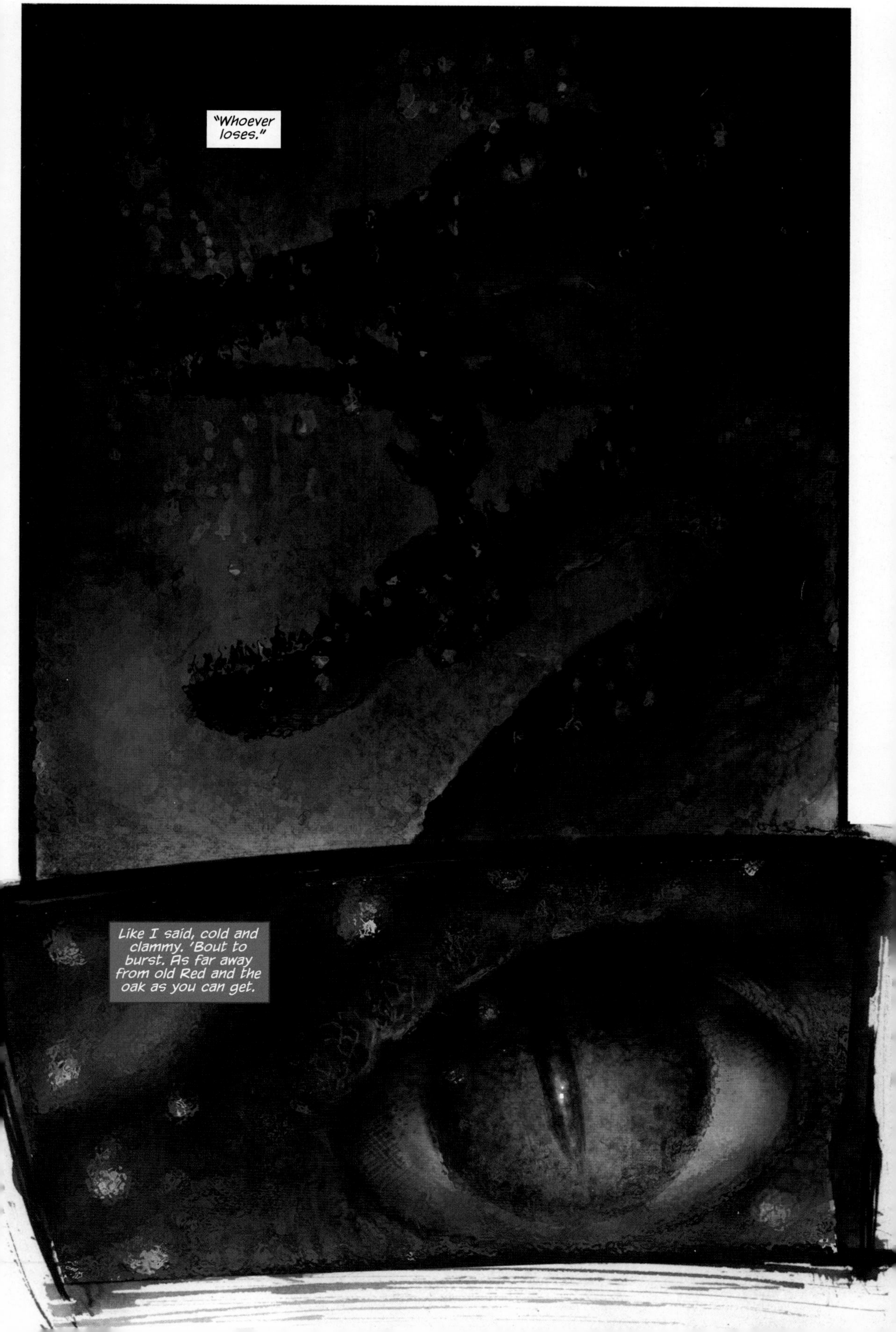
"Whoever loses."
Like I said, cold and clammy. 'Bout to burst. As far away from old Red and the oak as you can get.

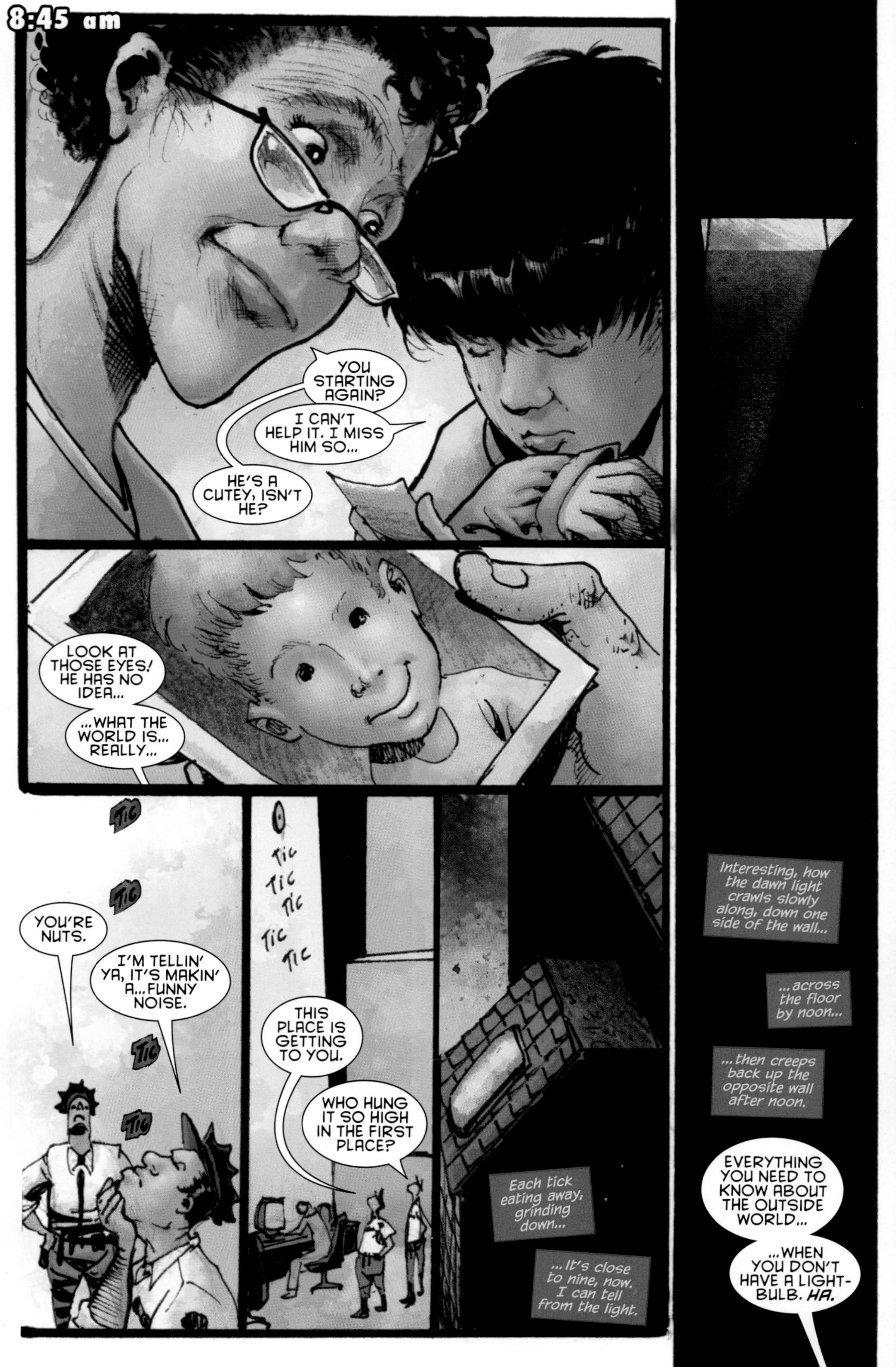
8:45 am
YOU STARTING AGAIN?
I CAN'T HELP IT. I MISS HIM SO...
HE'S A CUTEY, ISN'T HE?
LOOK AT THOSE EYES! HE HAS NO IDEA...
...WHAT THE WORLD IS... REALLY...
TIC
TIC
YOU'RE NUTS.
I'M TELLIN' YA, IT'S MAKIN' A...FUNNY NOISE.
TIC
TIC
TIC TIC TIC TIC TIC
THIS PLACE IS GETTING TO YOU.
WHO HUNG IT SO HIGH IN THE FIRST PLACE?
Each tick eating away, grinding down...
...It's close to nine, now. I can tell from the light.
Interesting, how the dawn light crawls slowly along, down one side of the wall...
...across the floor by noon...
...then creeps back up the opposite wall after noon.
EVERYTHING YOU NEED TO KNOW ABOUT THE OUTSIDE WORLD...
...WHEN YOU DON'T HAVE A LIGHT-BULB. HA.

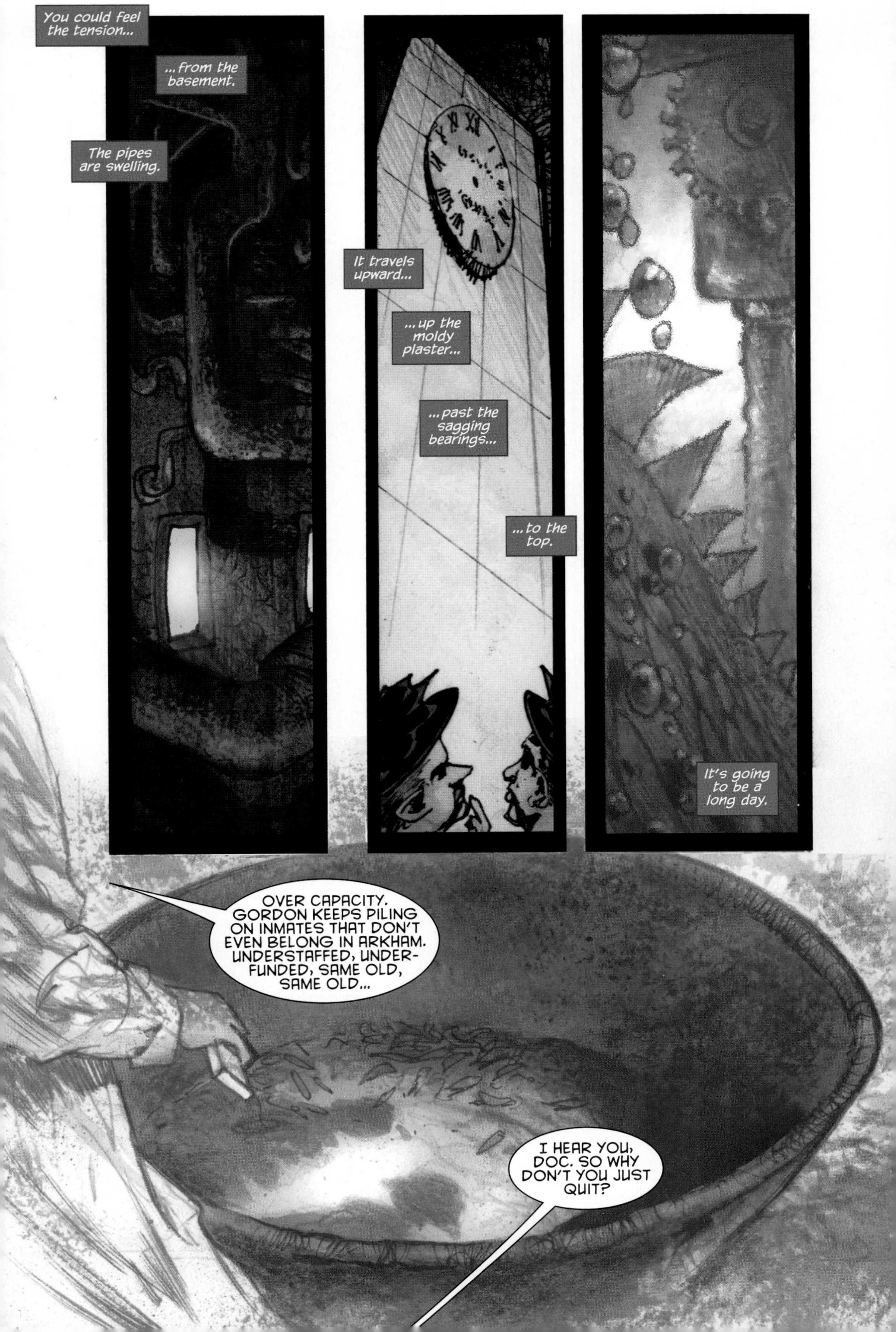
You could feel the tension...
...from the basement.
The pipes are swelling.
It travels upward...
...up the moldy plaster...
...past the sagging bearings...
...to the top.
It's going to be a long day.
OVER CAPACITY. GORDON KEEPS PILING ON INMATES THAT DON'T EVEN BELONG IN ARKHAM. UNDERSTAFFED, UNDER-FUNDED, SAME OLD, SAME OLD...
I HEAR YOU, DOC. SO WHY DON'T YOU JUST QUIT?

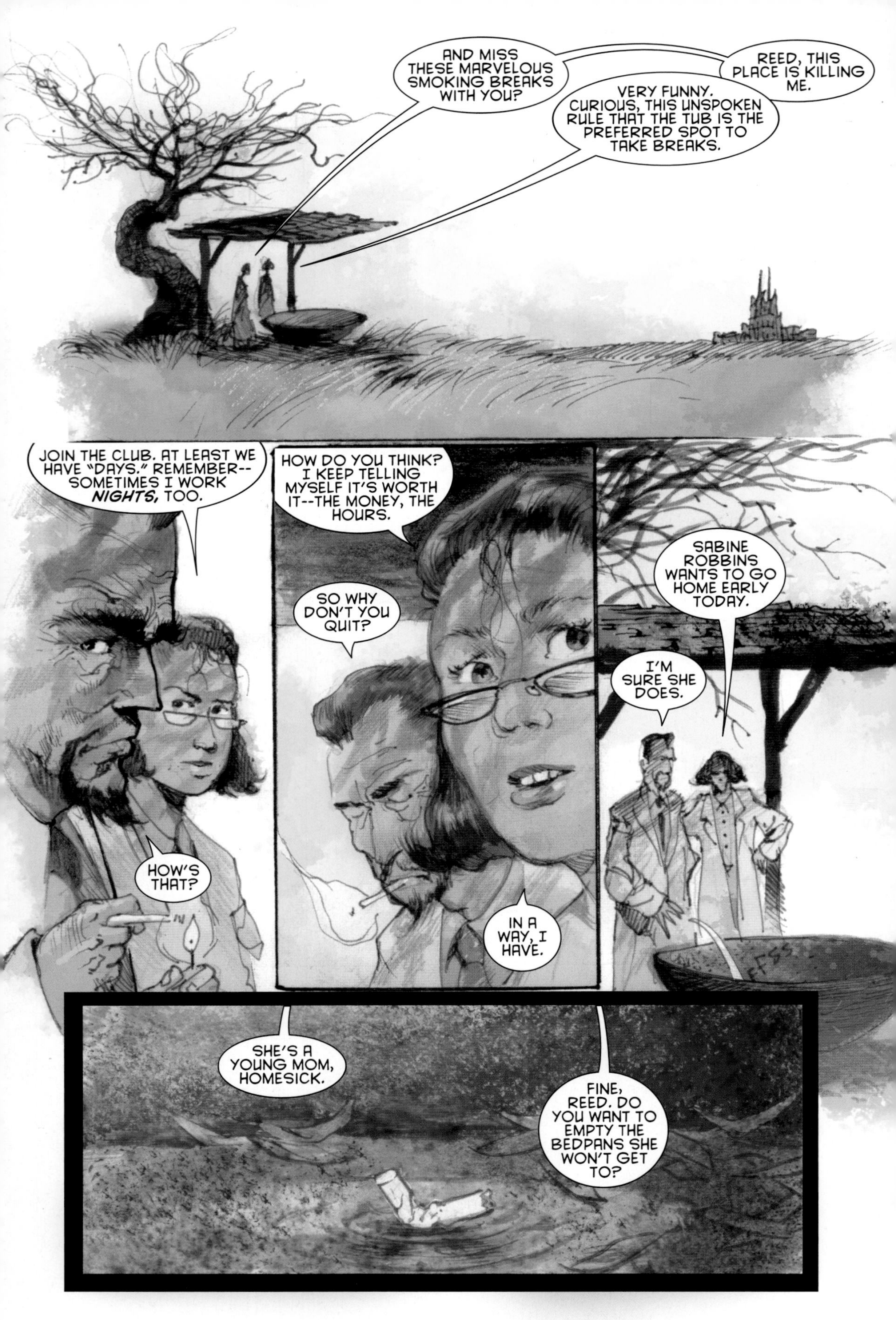
REED, THIS PLACE IS KILLING ME.
AND MISS THESE MARVELOUS SMOKING BREAKS WITH YOU?
VERY FUNNY. CURIOUS, THIS UNSPOKEN RULE THAT THE TUB IS THE PREFERRED SPOT TO TAKE BREAKS.
JOIN THE CLUB. AT LEAST WE HAVE "DAYS." REMEMBER-- SOMETIMES I WORK *NIGHTS,* TOO.
HOW'S THAT?
HOW DO YOU THINK? I KEEP TELLING MYSELF IT'S WORTH IT--THE MONEY, THE HOURS.
SO WHY DON'T YOU QUIT?
IN A WAY, I HAVE.
SABINE ROBBINS WANTS TO GO HOME EARLY TODAY.
I'M SURE SHE DOES.
SHE'S A YOUNG MOM, HOMESICK.
FINE, REED. DO YOU WANT TO EMPTY THE BEDPANS SHE WON'T GET TO?

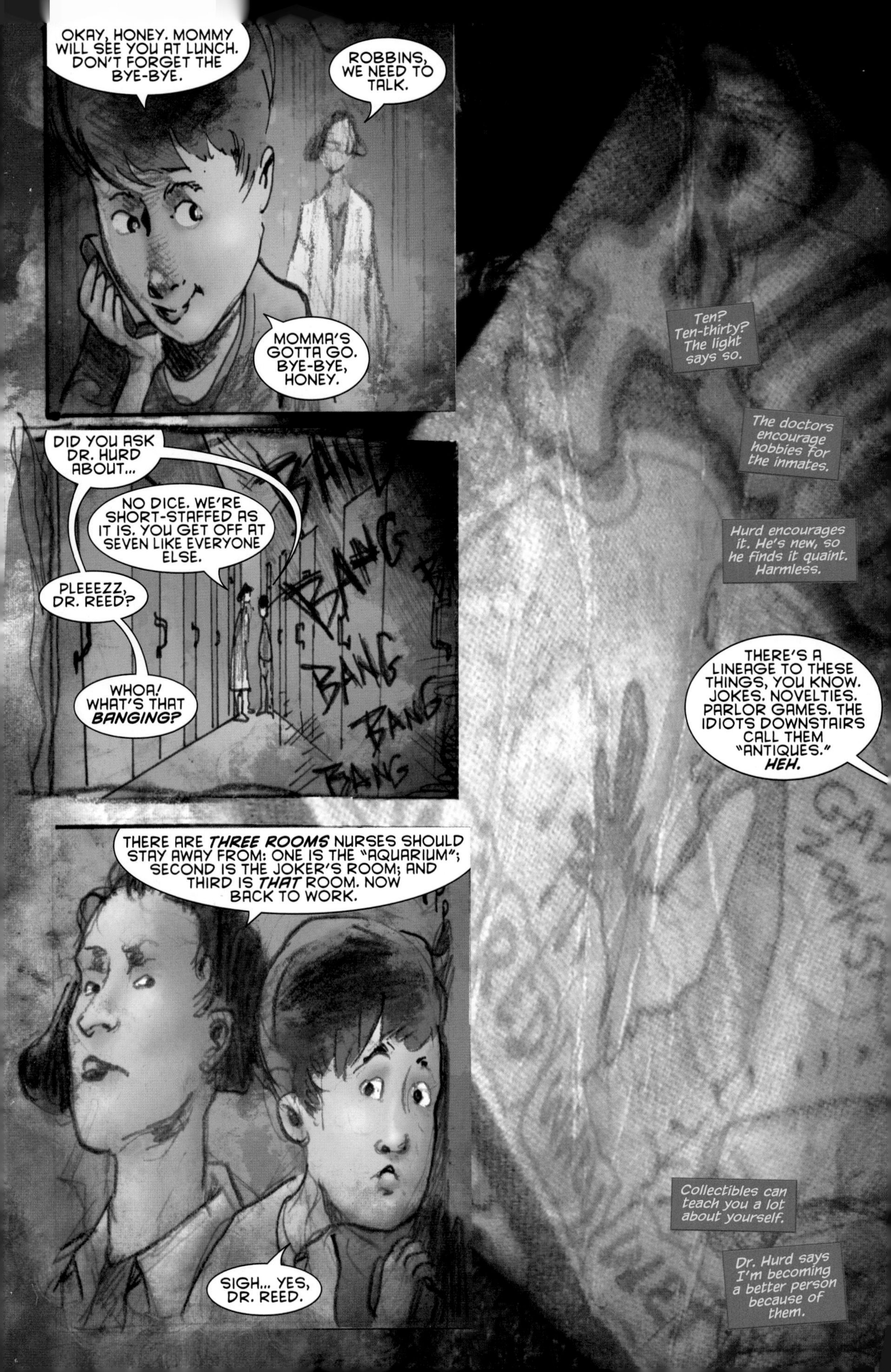
OKAY, HONEY. MOMMY WILL SEE YOU AT LUNCH. DON'T FORGET THE BYE-BYE.
ROBBINS, WE NEED TO TALK.
MOMMA'S GOTTA GO. BYE-BYE, HONEY.
Ten? Ten-thirty? The light says so.
The doctors encourage hobbies for the inmates.
DID YOU ASK DR. HURD ABOUT...
NO DICE. WE'RE SHORT-STAFFED AS IT IS. YOU GET OFF AT SEVEN LIKE EVERYONE ELSE.
PLEEEZZ, DR. REED?
WHOA! WHAT'S THAT BANGING?
BANG
BANG
BANG
BANG
BANG
Hurd encourages it. He's new, so he finds it quaint. Harmless.
THERE'S A LINEAGE TO THESE THINGS, YOU KNOW. JOKES. NOVELTIES. PARLOR GAMES. THE IDIOTS DOWNSTAIRS CALL THEM "ANTIQUES." HEH.
THERE ARE THREE ROOMS NURSES SHOULD STAY AWAY FROM: ONE IS THE "AQUARIUM"; SECOND IS THE JOKER'S ROOM; AND THIRD IS THAT ROOM. NOW BACK TO WORK.
SIGH... YES, DR. REED.
Collectibles can teach you a lot about yourself.
Dr. Hurd says I'm becoming a better person because of them.

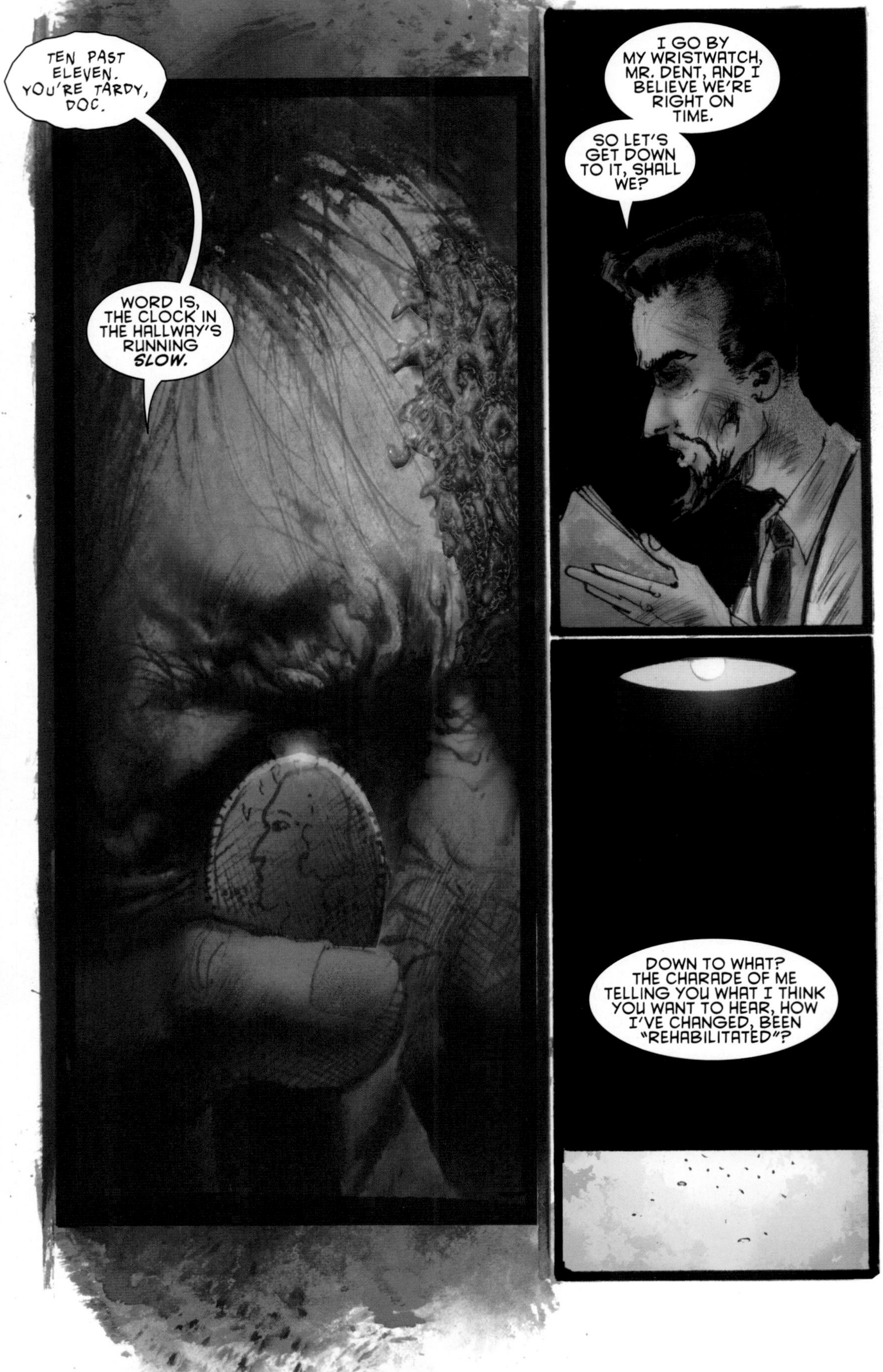
TEN PAST ELEVEN. YOU'RE TARDY, DOC.
WORD IS, THE CLOCK IN THE HALLWAY'S RUNNING *SLOW.*
I GO BY MY WRISTWATCH, MR. DENT, AND I BELIEVE WE'RE RIGHT ON TIME.
SO LET'S GET DOWN TO IT, SHALL WE?
DOWN TO WHAT? THE CHARADE OF ME TELLING YOU WHAT I THINK YOU WANT TO HEAR, HOW I'VE CHANGED, BEEN "REHABILITATED"?

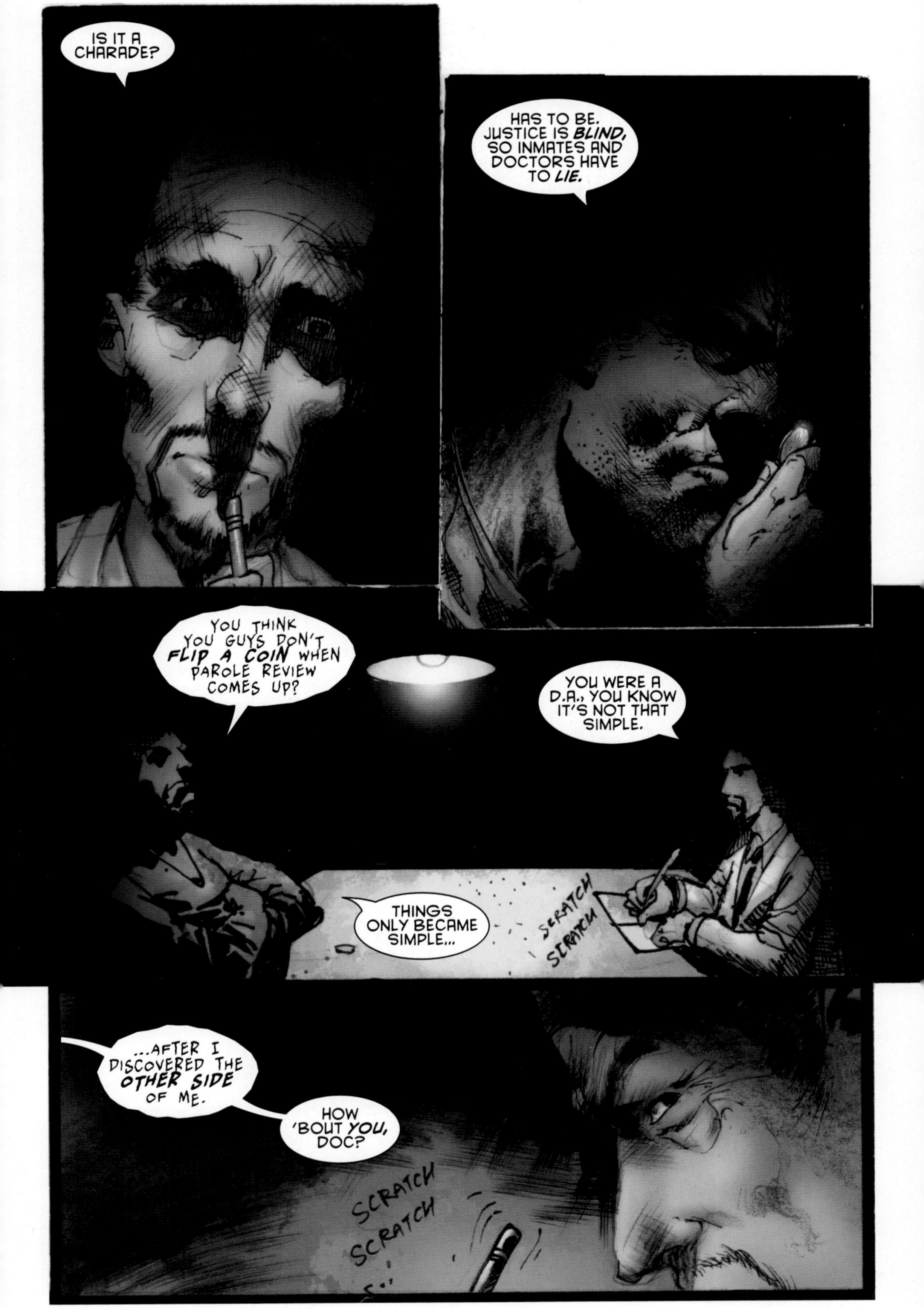
IS IT A CHARADE?
HAS TO BE. JUSTICE IS BLIND, SO INMATES AND DOCTORS HAVE TO LIE.
YOU THINK YOU GUYS DON'T FLIP A COIN WHEN PAROLE REVIEW COMES UP?
YOU WERE A D.A., YOU KNOW IT'S NOT THAT SIMPLE.
THINGS ONLY BECAME SIMPLE...
SCRATCH
SCRATCH
...AFTER I DISCOVERED THE OTHER SIDE OF ME.
HOW 'BOUT YOU, DOC?
SCRATCH
SCRATCH

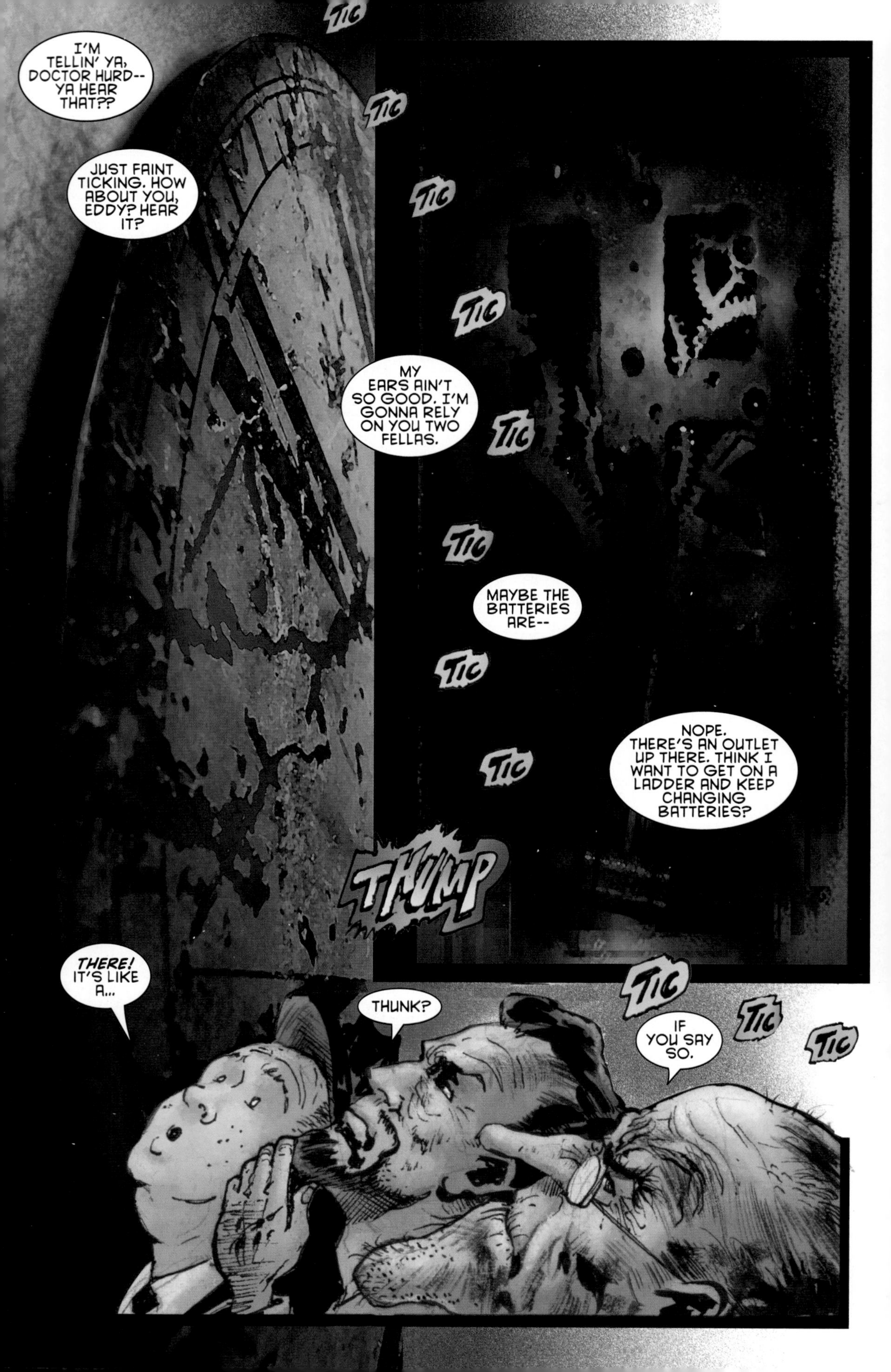
TIC
I'M TELLIN' YA, DOCTOR HURD-- YA HEAR THAT??
TIC
JUST FAINT TICKING. HOW ABOUT YOU, EDDY? HEAR IT?
TIC
TIC
MY EARS AIN'T SO GOOD. I'M GONNA RELY ON YOU TWO FELLAS.
TIC
TIC
MAYBE THE BATTERIES ARE--
TIC
TIC
NOPE. THERE'S AN OUTLET UP THERE. THINK I WANT TO GET ON A LADDER AND KEEP CHANGING BATTERIES?
THUMP
THERE! IT'S LIKE A...
THUNK?
IF YOU SAY SO.
TIC
TIC
TIC

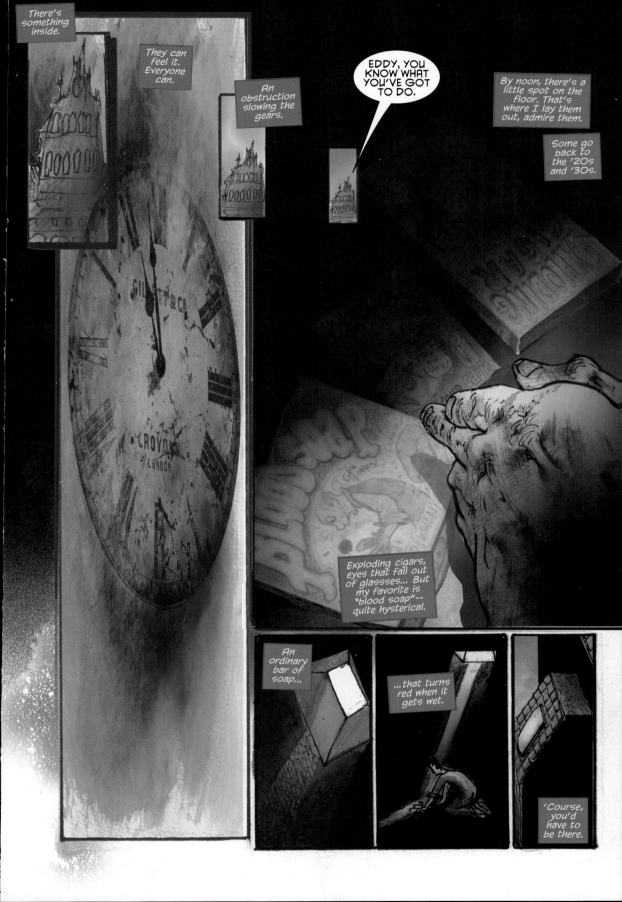

There's something inside.

They can feel it. Everyone can.

An obstruction slowing the gears.

EDDY, YOU KNOW WHAT YOU'VE GOT TO DO.

By noon, there's a little spot on the floor. That's where I lay them out, admire them.

Some go back to the '20s and '30s.

Exploding cigars, eyes that fall out of glassses... But my favorite is "blood soap"-- quite hysterical.

An ordinary bar of soap...

...that turns red when it gets wet.

'Course, you'd have to be there.

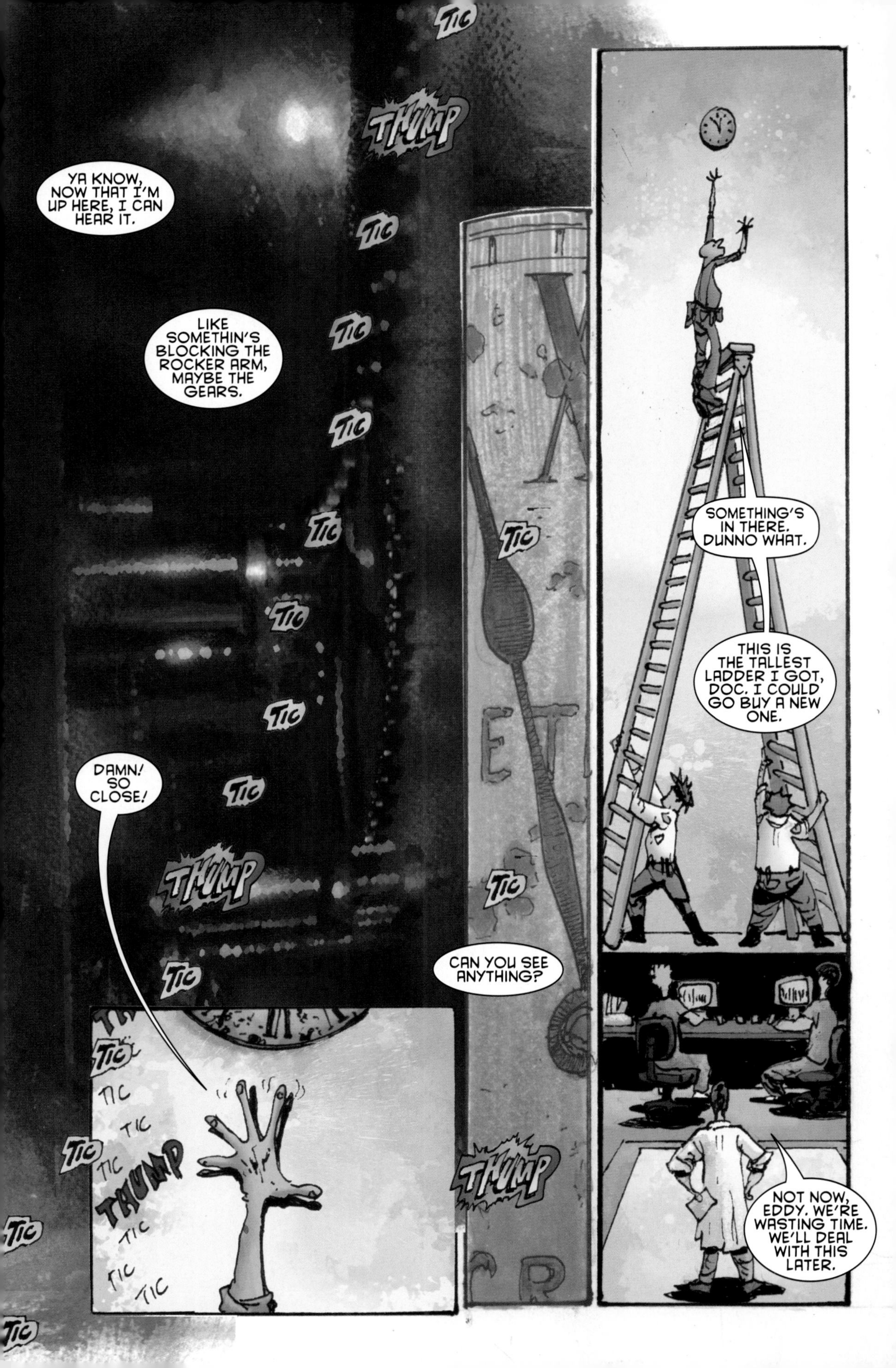
TIC
THUMP
YA KNOW, NOW THAT I'M UP HERE, I CAN HEAR IT.
TIC
LIKE SOMETHIN'S BLOCKING THE ROCKER ARM, MAYBE THE GEARS.
TIC
TIC
TIC
TIC
TIC
TIC
DAMN! SO CLOSE!
THUMP
TIC
TIC
TIC
TIC
TIC
THUMP
TIC
TIC
TIC
TIC
TIC
TIC
CAN YOU SEE ANYTHING?
THUMP
SOMETHING'S IN THERE. DUNNO WHAT.
THIS IS THE TALLEST LADDER I GOT, DOC. I COULD GO BUY A NEW ONE.
NOT NOW, EDDY. WE'RE WASTING TIME. WE'LL DEAL WITH THIS LATER.

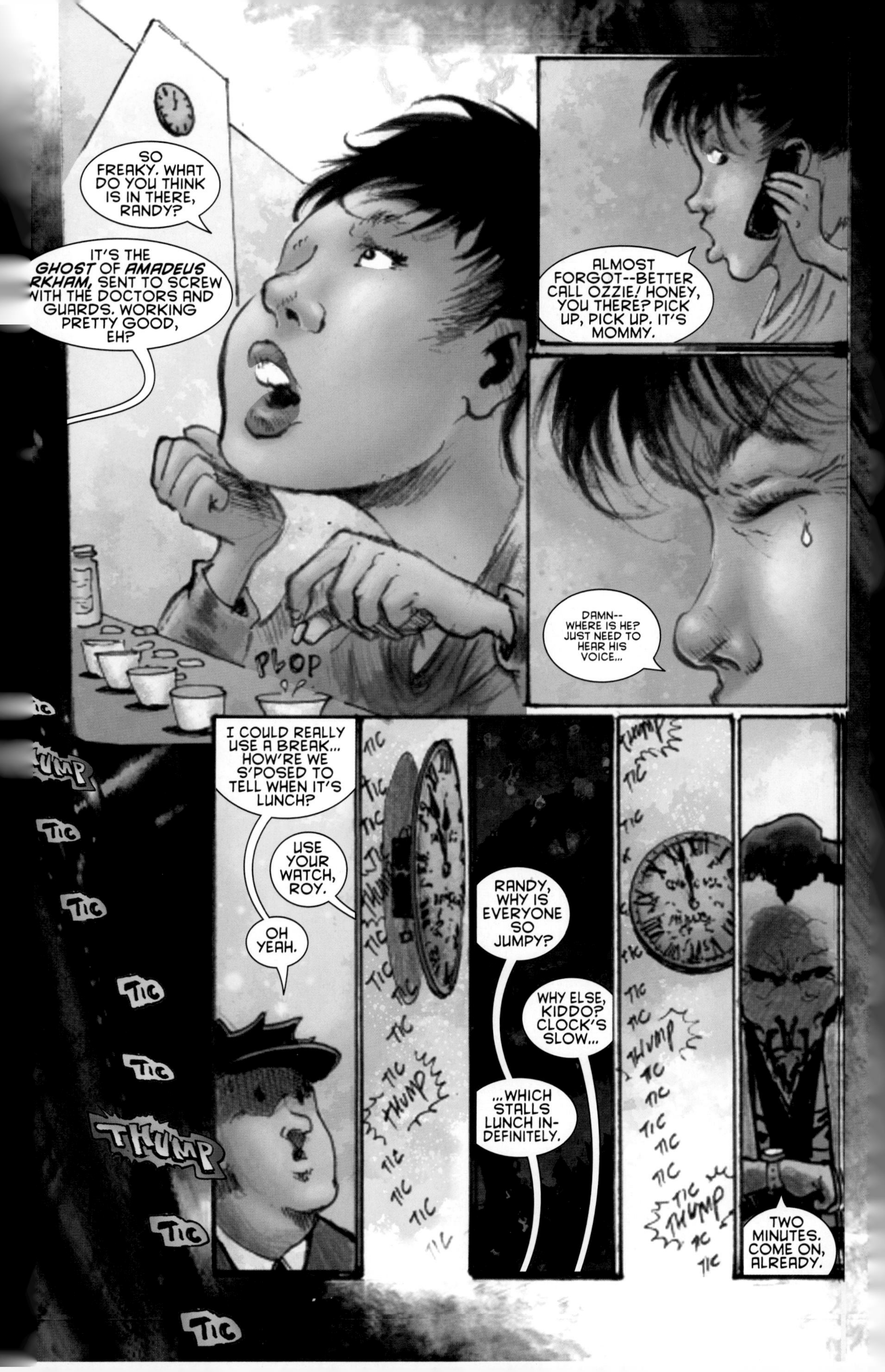
SO FREAKY. WHAT DO YOU THINK IS IN THERE, RANDY?
IT'S THE GHOST OF AMADEUS ARKHAM, SENT TO SCREW WITH THE DOCTORS AND GUARDS. WORKING PRETTY GOOD, EH?
PLOP
ALMOST FORGOT--BETTER CALL OZZIE! HONEY, YOU THERE? PICK UP, PICK UP. IT'S MOMMY.
DAMN-- WHERE IS HE? JUST NEED TO HEAR HIS VOICE...
I COULD REALLY USE A BREAK... HOW'RE WE S'POSED TO TELL WHEN IT'S LUNCH?
USE YOUR WATCH, ROY.
OH YEAH.
RANDY, WHY IS EVERYONE SO JUMPY?
WHY ELSE, KIDDO? CLOCK'S SLOW...
...WHICH STALLS LUNCH INDEFINITELY.
TWO MINUTES. COME ON, ALREADY.
TIC
THUMP
TIC
TIC
TIC
TIC
THUMP
TIC
TIC

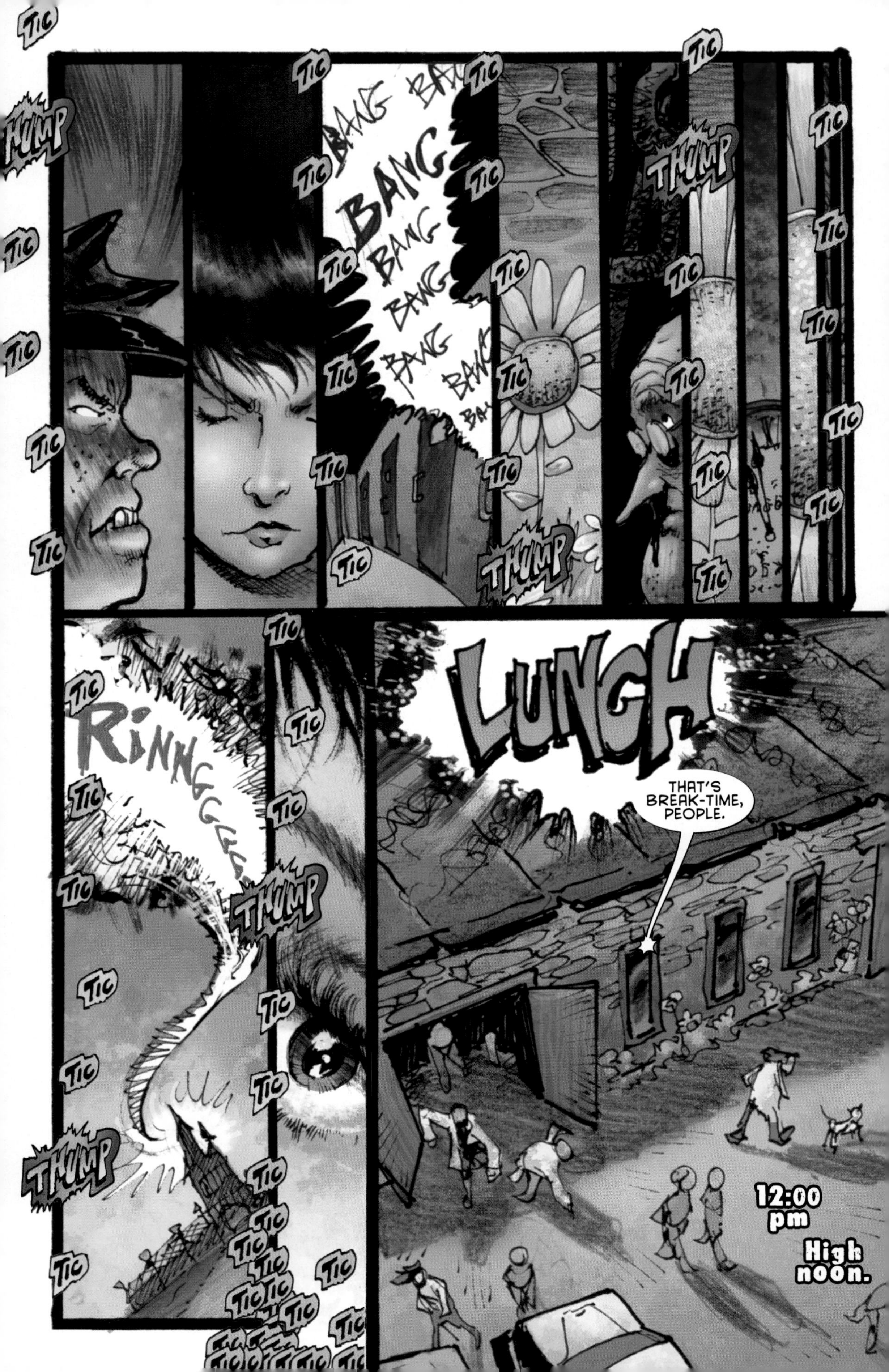

TIC
THUMP
BANG BANG
BANG
BANG
BANG
BANG
BANG
BANG
BANG
THUMP
THUMP
RINNGGG
THUMP
THUMP
LUNCH
THAT'S BREAK-TIME, PEOPLE.
12:00 pm
High noon.

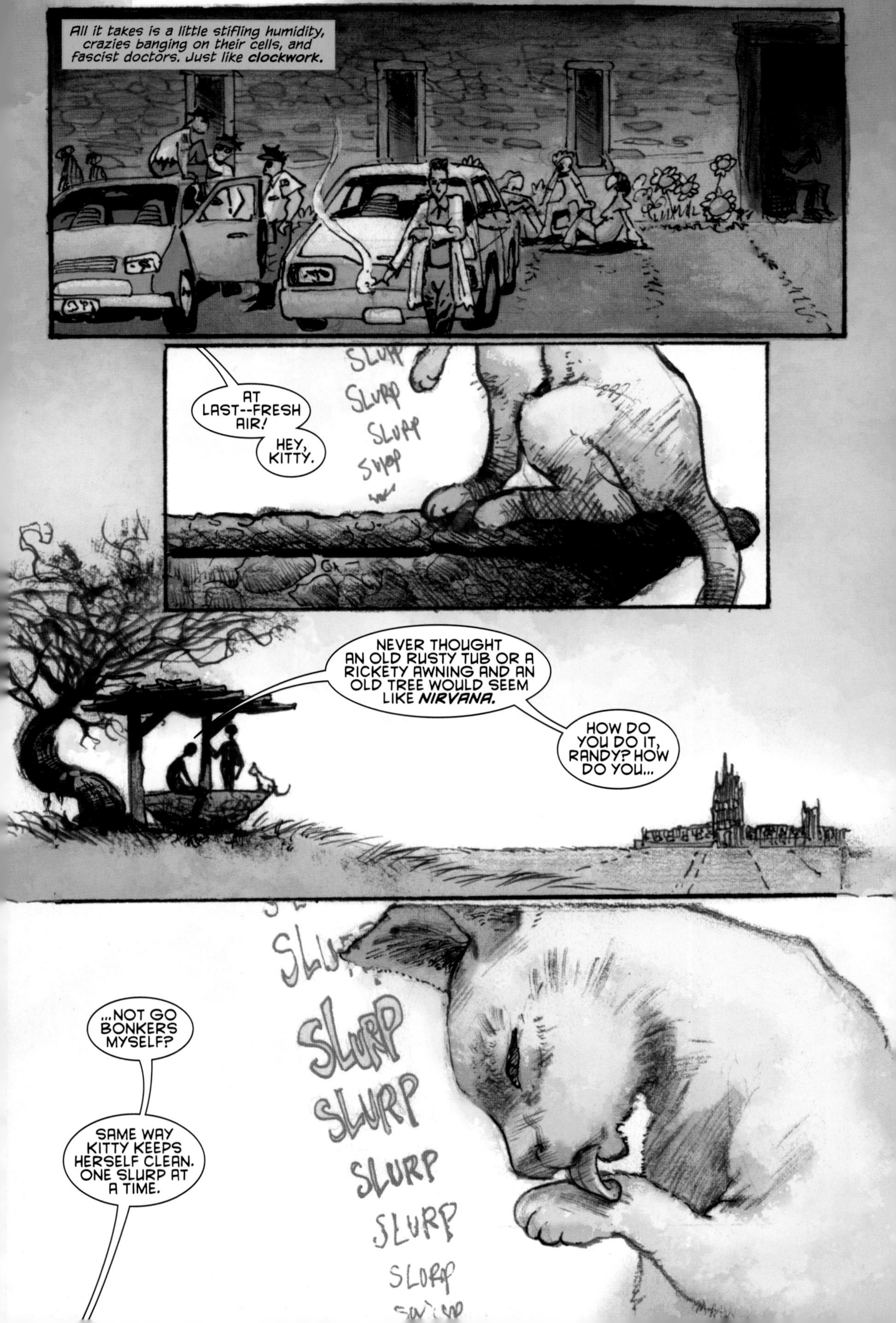
All it takes is a little stifling humidity, crazies banging on their cells, and fascist doctors. Just like clockwork.
AT LAST--FRESH AIR!
HEY, KITTY.
SLURP
SLURP
SLURP
NEVER THOUGHT AN OLD RUSTY TUB OR A RICKETY AWNING AND AN OLD TREE WOULD SEEM LIKE NIRVANA.
HOW DO YOU DO IT, RANDY? HOW DO YOU...
...NOT GO BONKERS MYSELF?
SAME WAY KITTY KEEPS HERSELF CLEAN. ONE SLURP AT A TIME.
SLURP
SLURP
SLURP
SLURP
SLURP

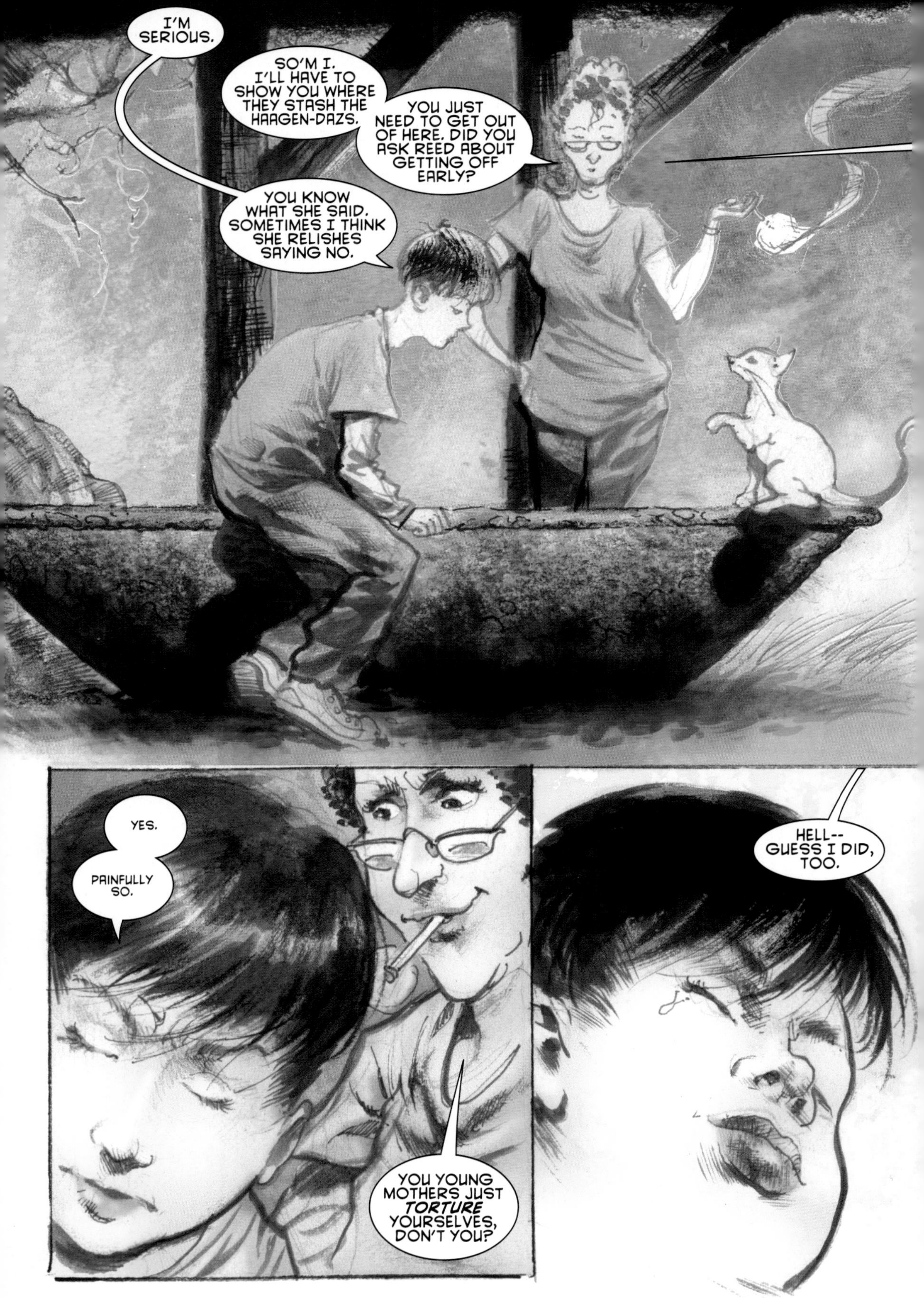
I'M SERIOUS.
SO'M I. I'LL HAVE TO SHOW YOU WHERE THEY STASH THE HAAGEN-DAZS.
YOU JUST NEED TO GET OUT OF HERE. DID YOU ASK REED ABOUT GETTING OFF EARLY?
YOU KNOW WHAT SHE SAID. SOMETIMES I THINK SHE RELISHES SAYING NO.
YES.
PAINFULLY SO.
YOU YOUNG MOTHERS JUST *TORTURE* YOURSELVES, DON'T YOU?
HELL-- GUESS I DID, TOO.

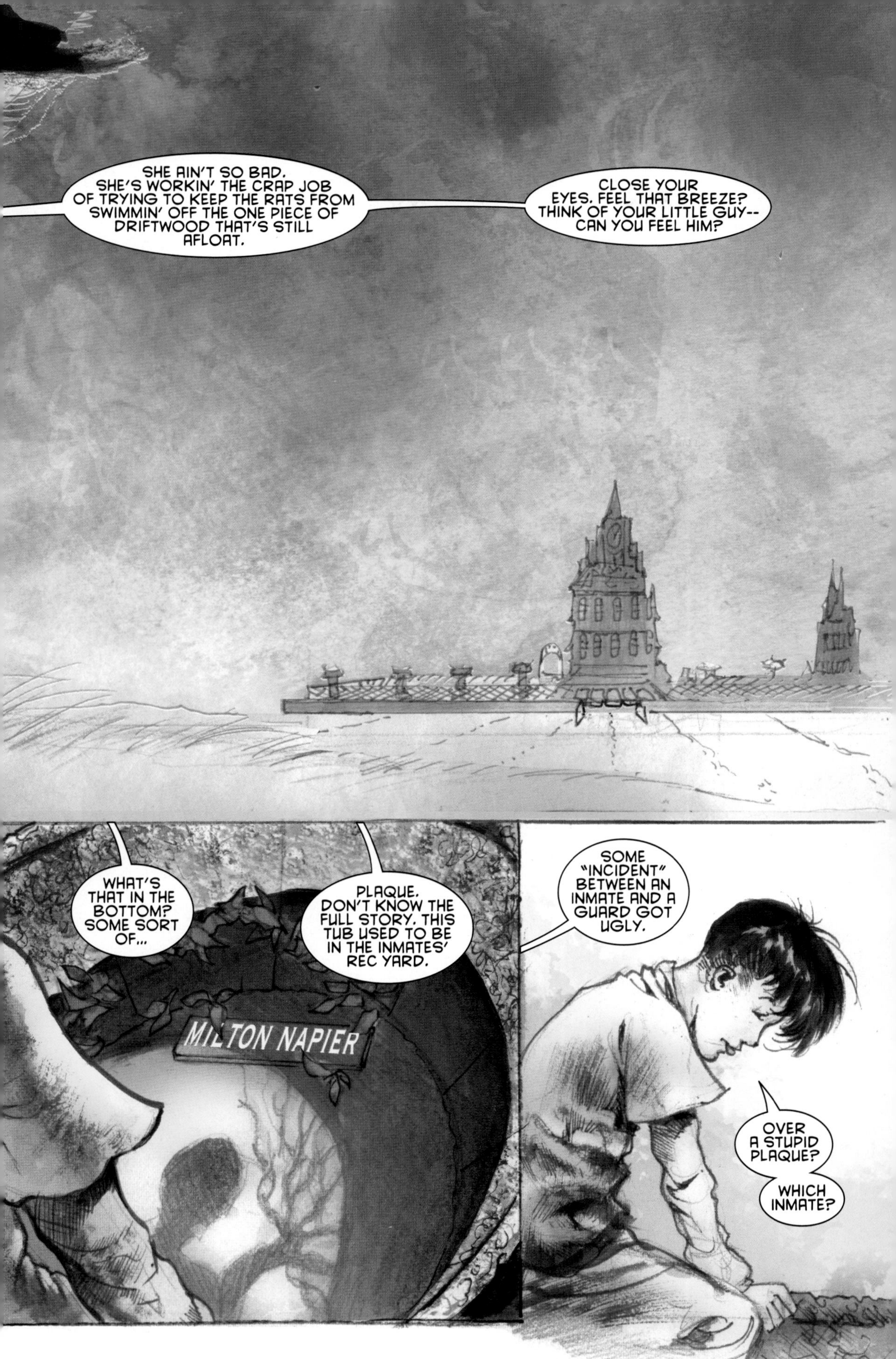
SHE AIN'T SO BAD. SHE'S WORKIN' THE CRAP JOB OF TRYING TO KEEP THE RATS FROM SWIMMIN' OFF THE ONE PIECE OF DRIFTWOOD THAT'S STILL AFLOAT.
CLOSE YOUR EYES. FEEL THAT BREEZE? THINK OF YOUR LITTLE GUY-- CAN YOU FEEL HIM?
WHAT'S THAT IN THE BOTTOM? SOME SORT OF...
PLAQUE. DON'T KNOW THE FULL STORY. THIS TUB USED TO BE IN THE INMATES' REC YARD.
MILTON NAPIER
SOME "INCIDENT" BETWEEN AN INMATE AND A GUARD GOT UGLY.
OVER A STUPID PLAQUE?
WHICH INMATE?

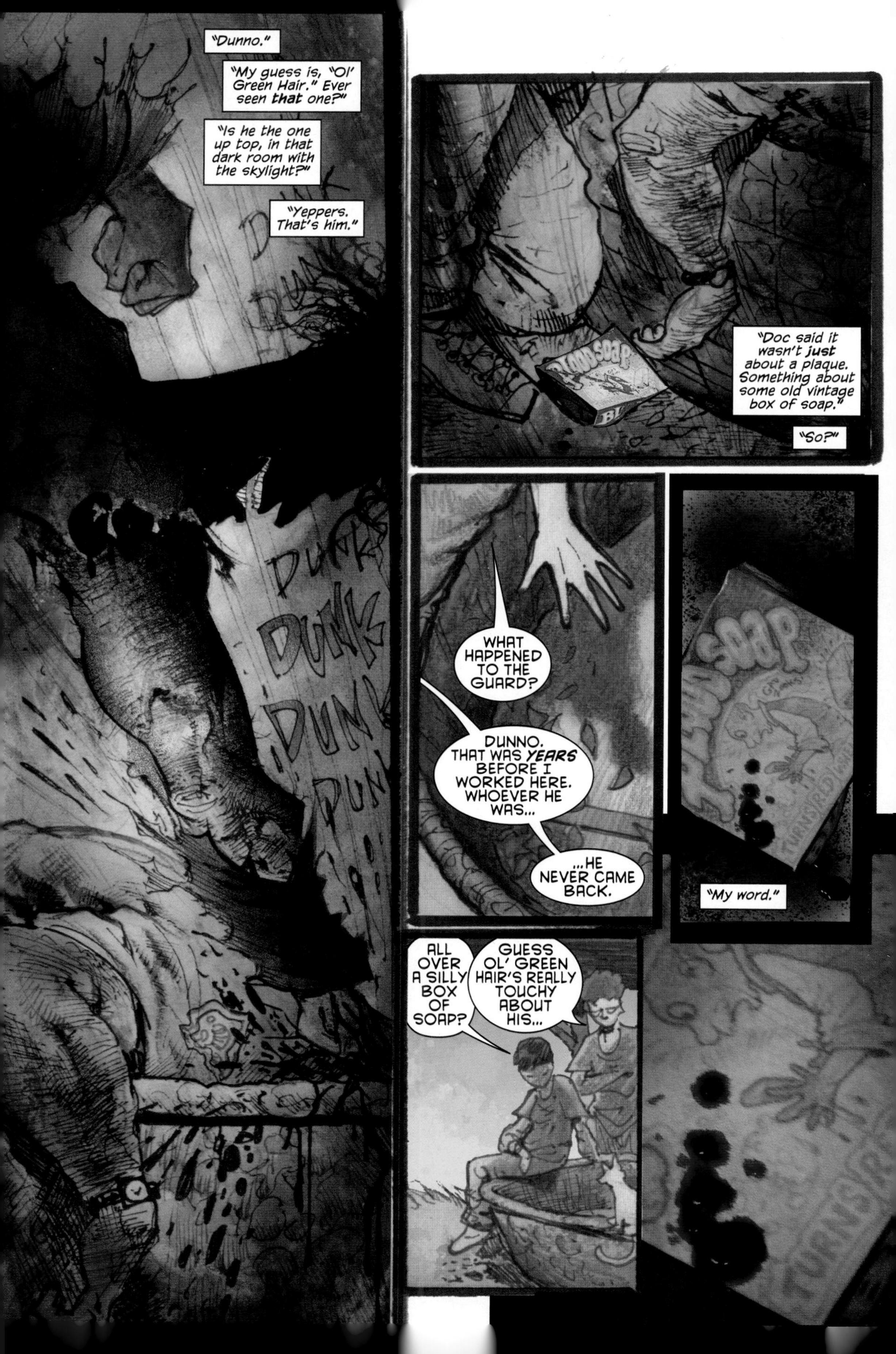
"Dunno."
"My guess is, "Ol' Green Hair." Ever seen that one?"
"Is he the one up top, in that dark room with the skylight?"
"Yeppers. That's him."
DUNK
DUNK
DUNK
DUN
"Doc said it wasn't just about a plaque. Something about some old vintage box of soap."
"So?"
WHAT HAPPENED TO THE GUARD?
DUNNO. THAT WAS YEARS BEFORE I WORKED HERE. WHOEVER HE WAS...
...HE NEVER CAME BACK.
"My word."
ALL OVER A SILLY BOX OF SOAP?
GUESS OL' GREEN HAIR'S REALLY TOUCHY ABOUT HIS...

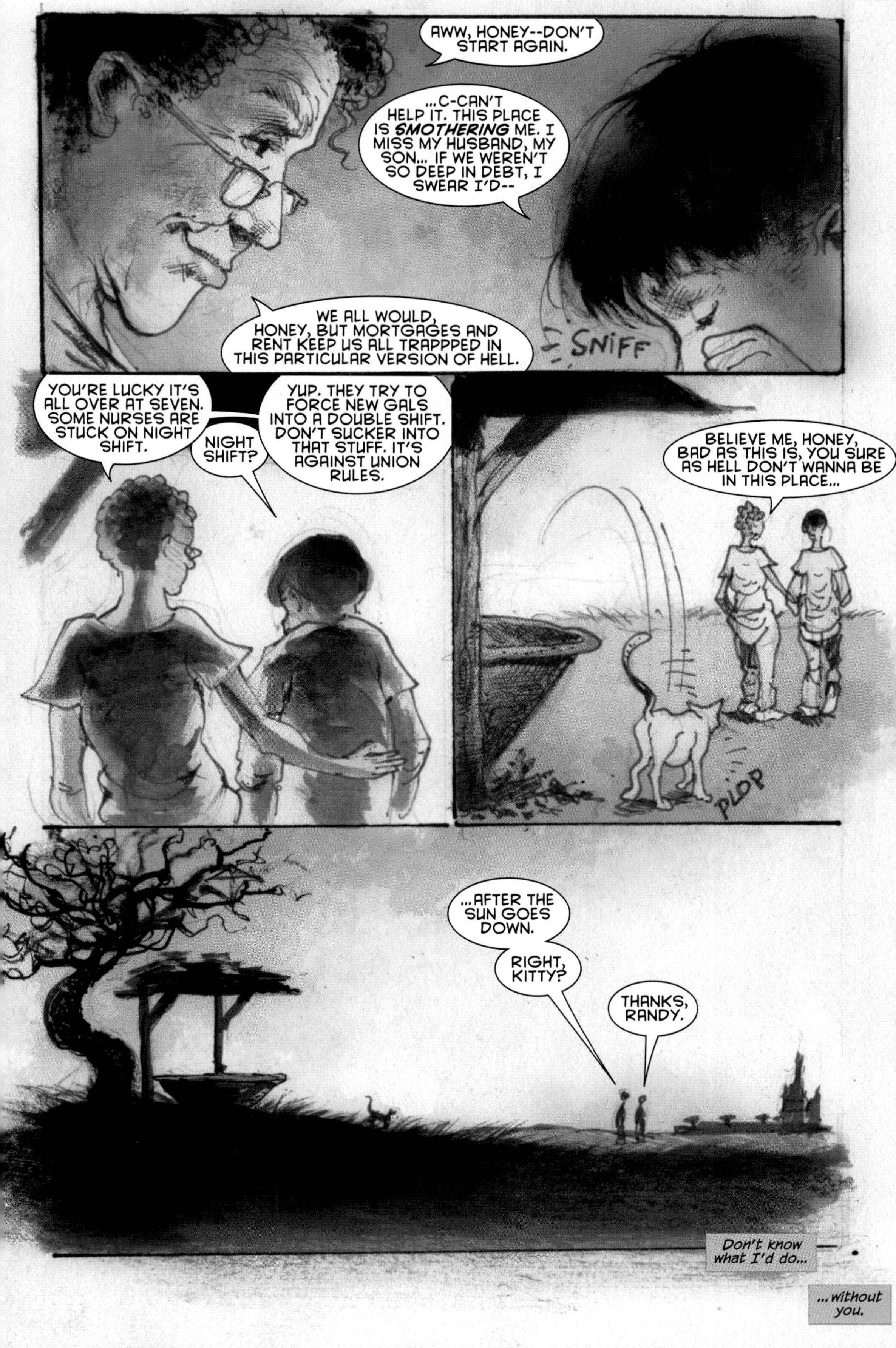
AWW, HONEY--DON'T START AGAIN.
...C-CAN'T HELP IT. THIS PLACE IS SMOTHERING ME. I MISS MY HUSBAND, MY SON... IF WE WEREN'T SO DEEP IN DEBT, I SWEAR I'D--
WE ALL WOULD, HONEY, BUT MORTGAGES AND RENT KEEP US ALL TRAPPPED IN THIS PARTICULAR VERSION OF HELL.
SNIFF
YOU'RE LUCKY IT'S ALL OVER AT SEVEN. SOME NURSES ARE STUCK ON NIGHT SHIFT.
NIGHT SHIFT?
YUP. THEY TRY TO FORCE NEW GALS INTO A DOUBLE SHIFT. DON'T SUCKER INTO THAT STUFF. IT'S AGAINST UNION RULES.
BELIEVE ME, HONEY, BAD AS THIS IS, YOU SURE AS HELL DON'T WANNA BE IN THIS PLACE...
PLOP
...AFTER THE SUN GOES DOWN.
RIGHT, KITTY?
THANKS, RANDY.
Don't know what I'd do...
...without you.

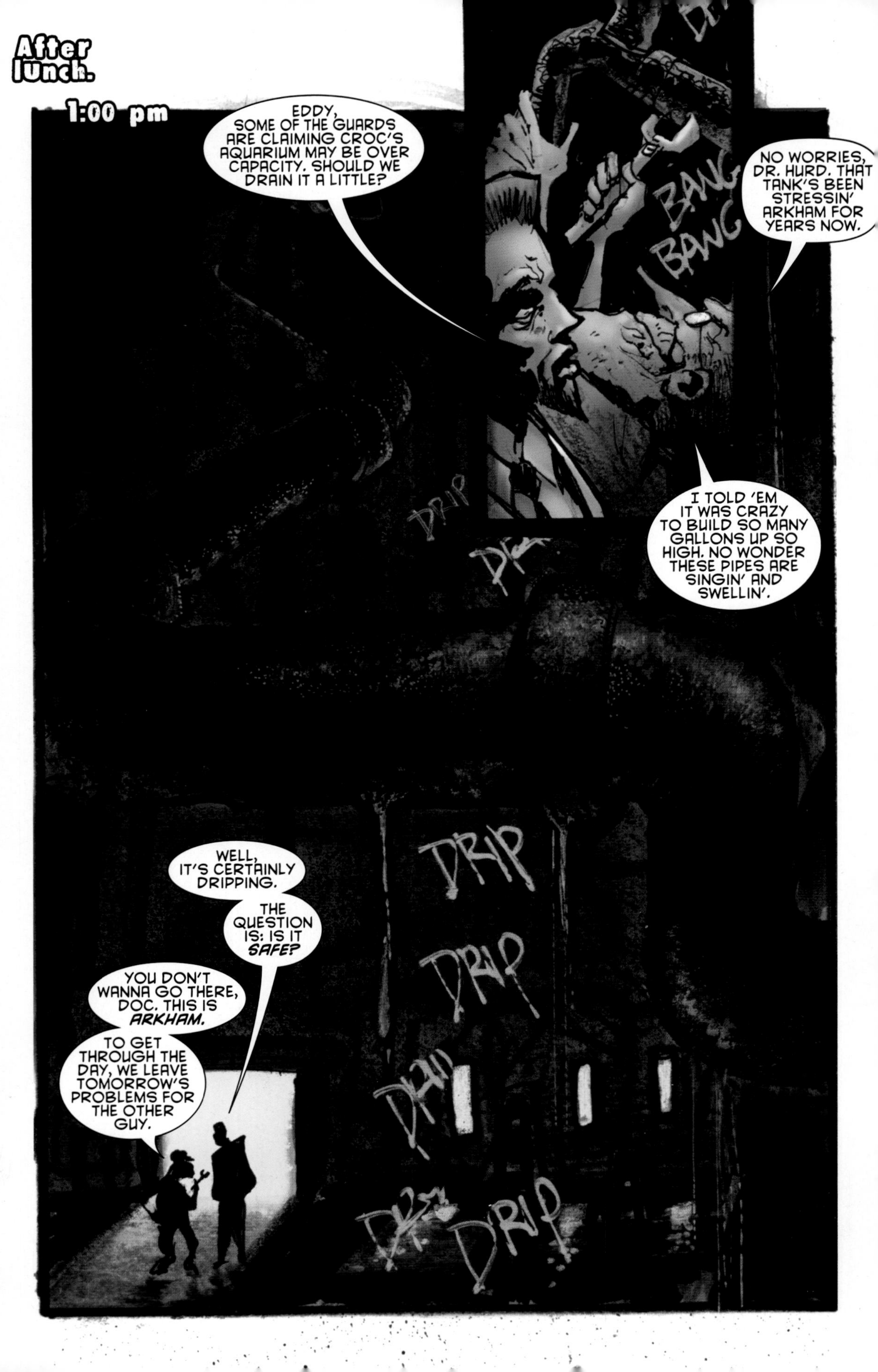
After lunch.
1:00 pm
EDDY, SOME OF THE GUARDS ARE CLAIMING CROC'S AQUARIUM MAY BE OVER CAPACITY. SHOULD WE DRAIN IT A LITTLE?
BANG BANG
NO WORRIES, DR. HURD. THAT TANK'S BEEN STRESSIN' ARKHAM FOR YEARS NOW.
I TOLD 'EM IT WAS CRAZY TO BUILD SO MANY GALLONS UP SO HIGH. NO WONDER THESE PIPES ARE SINGIN' AND SWELLIN'.
DRIP
WELL, IT'S CERTAINLY DRIPPING.
THE QUESTION IS: IS IT *SAFE?*
YOU DON'T WANNA GO THERE, DOC. THIS IS *ARKHAM.*
TO GET THROUGH THE DAY, WE LEAVE TOMORROW'S PROBLEMS FOR THE OTHER GUY.
DRIP
DRIP
DRIP

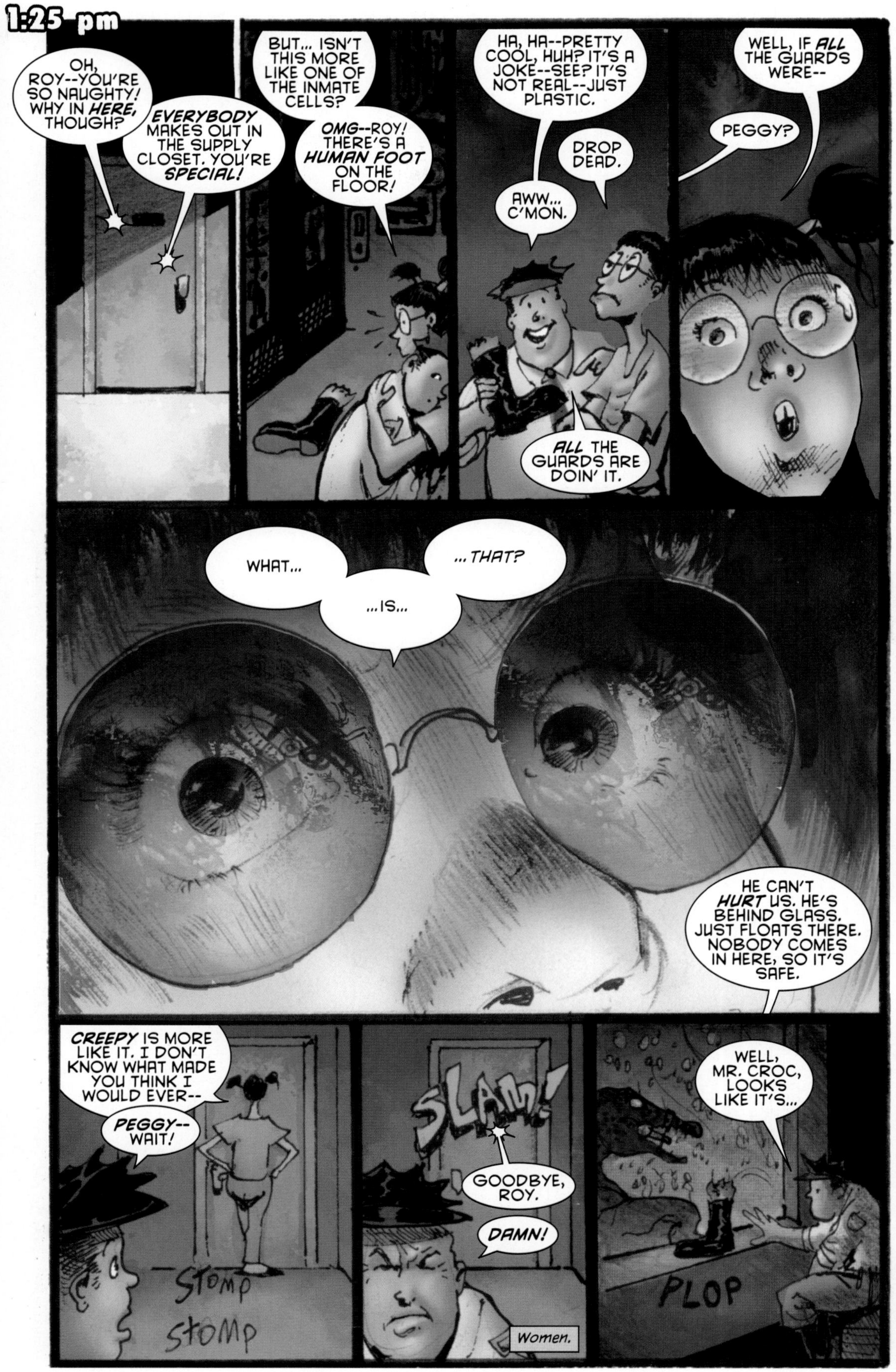
1:25 pm
OH, ROY--YOU'RE SO NAUGHTY! WHY IN HERE, THOUGH?
EVERYBODY MAKES OUT IN THE SUPPLY CLOSET. YOU'RE SPECIAL!
BUT... ISN'T THIS MORE LIKE ONE OF THE INMATE CELLS?
OMG--ROY! THERE'S A HUMAN FOOT ON THE FLOOR!
HA, HA--PRETTY COOL, HUH? IT'S A JOKE--SEE? IT'S NOT REAL--JUST PLASTIC.
DROP DEAD.
AWW... C'MON.
ALL THE GUARDS ARE DOIN' IT.
WELL, IF ALL THE GUARDS WERE--
PEGGY?
WHAT...
...IS...
...THAT?
HE CAN'T HURT US. HE'S BEHIND GLASS. JUST FLOATS THERE. NOBODY COMES IN HERE, SO IT'S SAFE.
CREEPY IS MORE LIKE IT. I DON'T KNOW WHAT MADE YOU THINK I WOULD EVER--
PEGGY--WAIT!
STOMP
STOMP
SLAM!
GOODBYE, ROY.
DAMN!
Women.
WELL, MR. CROC, LOOKS LIKE IT'S...
PLOP

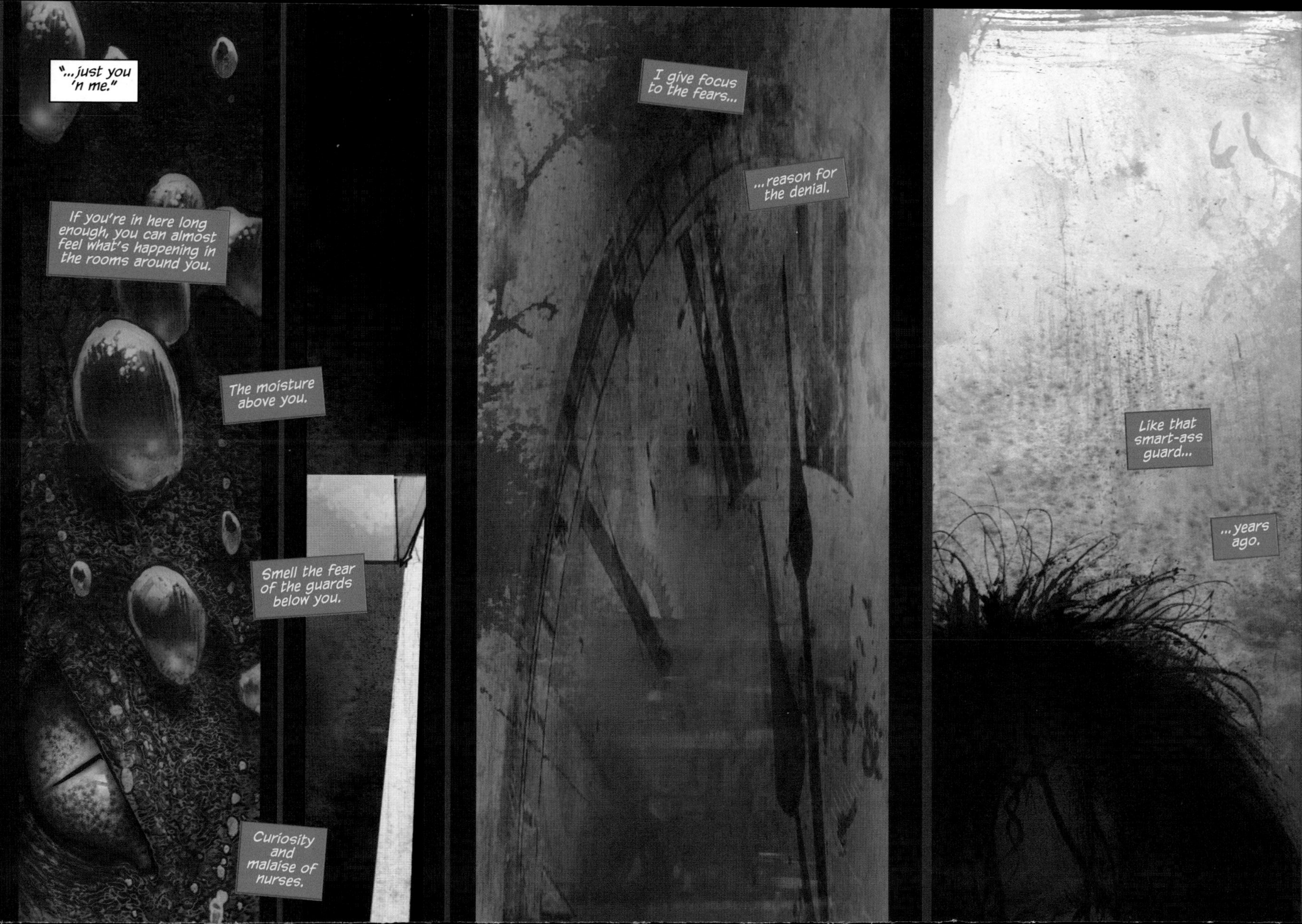
"...just you 'n me."
If you're in here long enough, you can almost feel what's happening in the rooms around you.
The moisture above you.
Smell the fear of the guards below you.
Curiosity and malaise of nurses.
I give focus to the fears...
...reason for the denial.
Like that smart-ass guard...
...years ago.

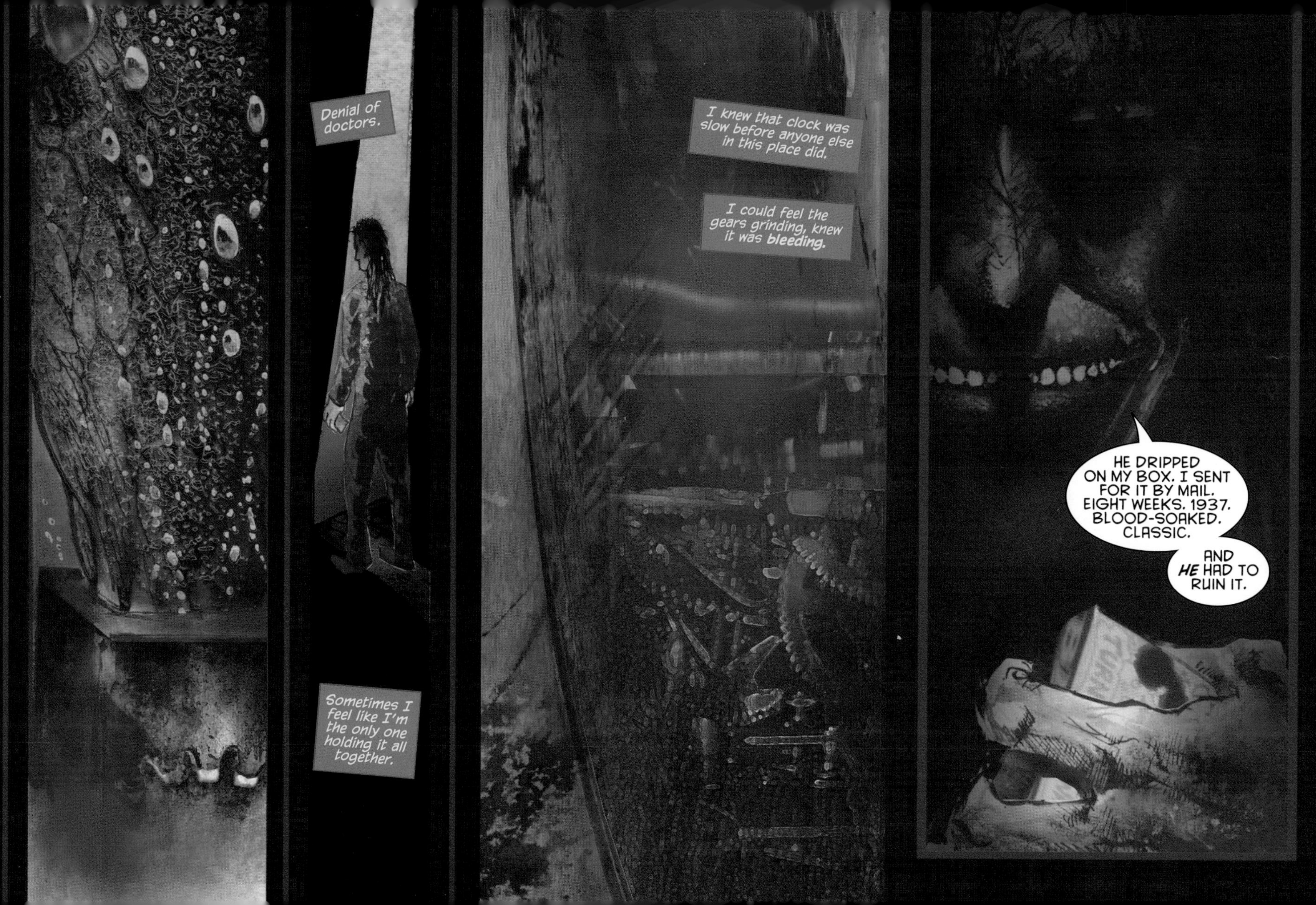
Denial of doctors.
Sometimes I feel like I'm the only one holding it all together.
I knew that clock was slow before anyone else in this place did.
I could feel the gears grinding, knew it was **bleeding.**
HE DRIPPED ON MY BOX. I SENT FOR IT BY MAIL. EIGHT WEEKS. 1937. BLOOD-SOAKED. CLASSIC.
AND ***HE*** HAD TO RUIN IT.

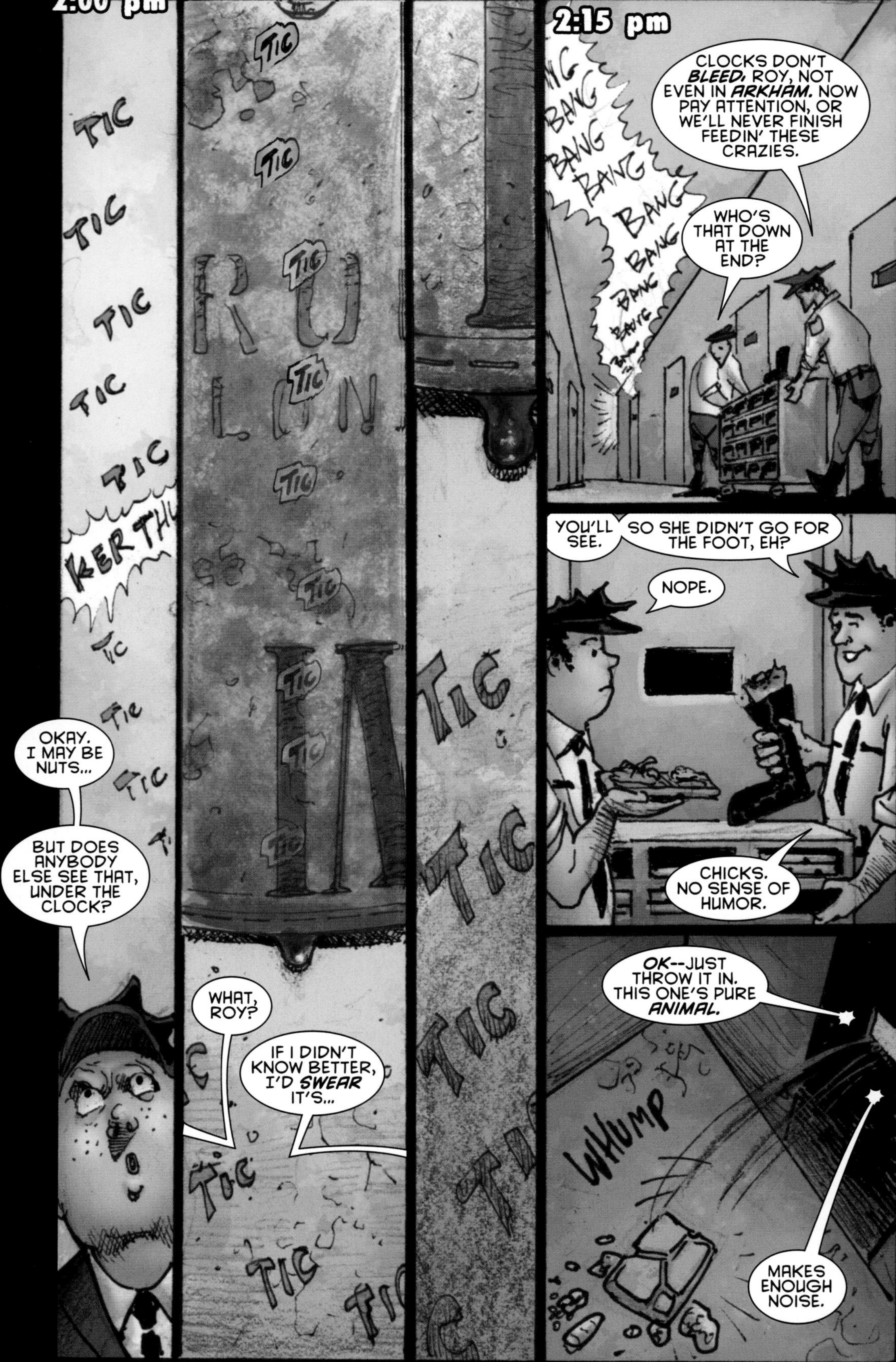
2:00 pm
TIC
TIC
TIC
TIC
TIC
KERTH
TIC
TIC
TIC
OKAY. I MAY BE NUTS...
BUT DOES ANYBODY ELSE SEE THAT, UNDER THE CLOCK?
WHAT, ROY?
IF I DIDN'T KNOW BETTER, I'D SWEAR IT'S...
TIC
TIC
2:15 pm
BANG BANG BANG BANG BANG BANG
CLOCKS DON'T BLEED, ROY, NOT EVEN IN ARKHAM. NOW PAY ATTENTION, OR WE'LL NEVER FINISH FEEDIN' THESE CRAZIES.
WHO'S THAT DOWN AT THE END?
YOU'LL SEE.
SO SHE DIDN'T GO FOR THE FOOT, EH?
NOPE.
CHICKS. NO SENSE OF HUMOR.
OK--JUST THROW IT IN. THIS ONE'S PURE ANIMAL.
WHUMP
MAKES ENOUGH NOISE.

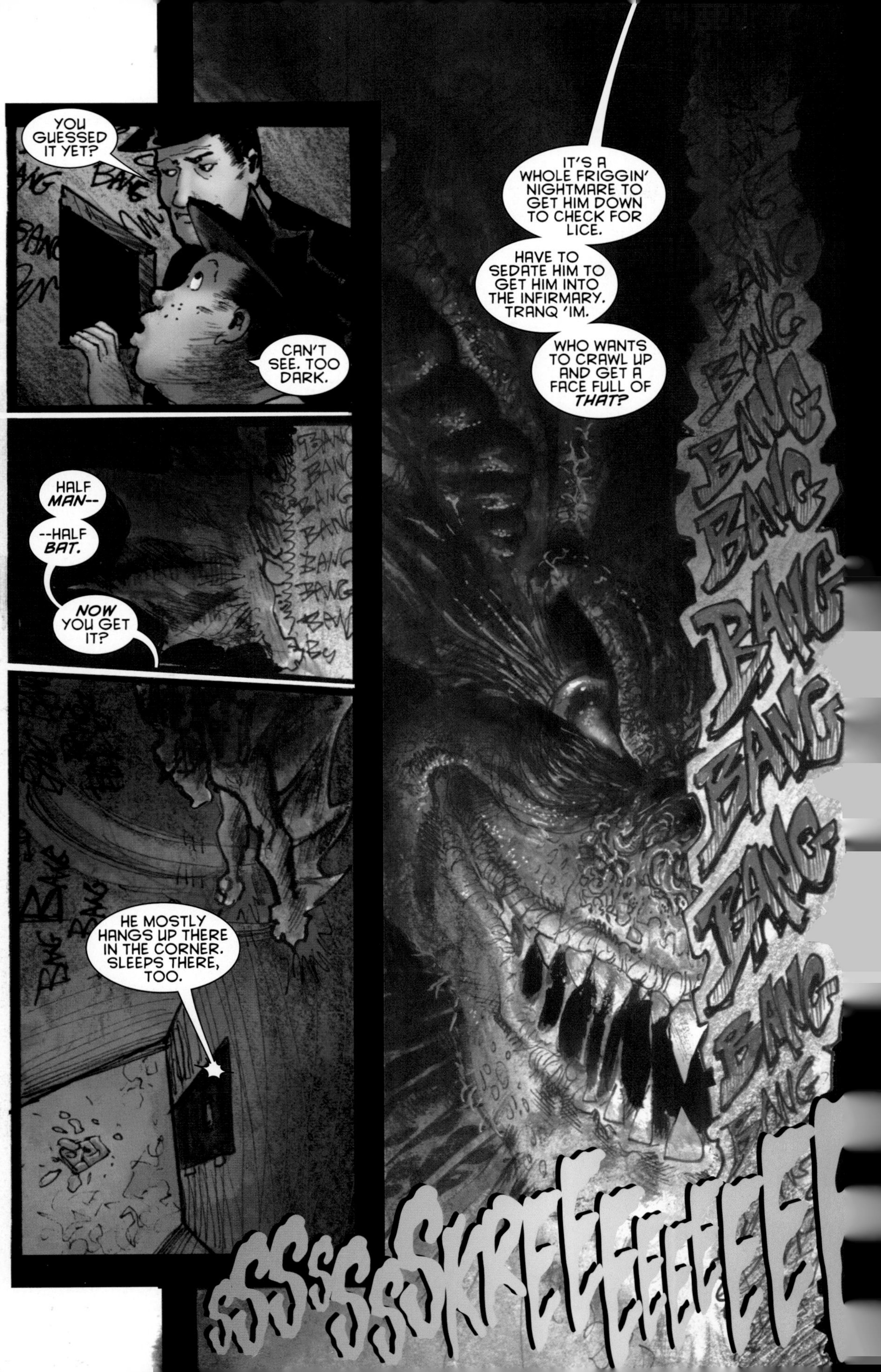

YOU GUESSED IT YET?
CAN'T SEE. TOO DARK.
IT'S A WHOLE FRIGGIN' NIGHTMARE TO GET HIM DOWN TO CHECK FOR LICE.
HAVE TO SEDATE HIM TO GET HIM INTO THE INFIRMARY. TRANQ 'IM.
WHO WANTS TO CRAWL UP AND GET A FACE FULL OF *THAT?*
HALF *MAN--*
--HALF *BAT.*
*NOW* YOU GET IT?
HE MOSTLY HANGS UP THERE IN THE CORNER. SLEEPS THERE, TOO.
BANG BANG BANG BANG BANG BANG BANG BANG BANG BANG BANG
SSSSSSSKREEEEEEE

2:45 pm

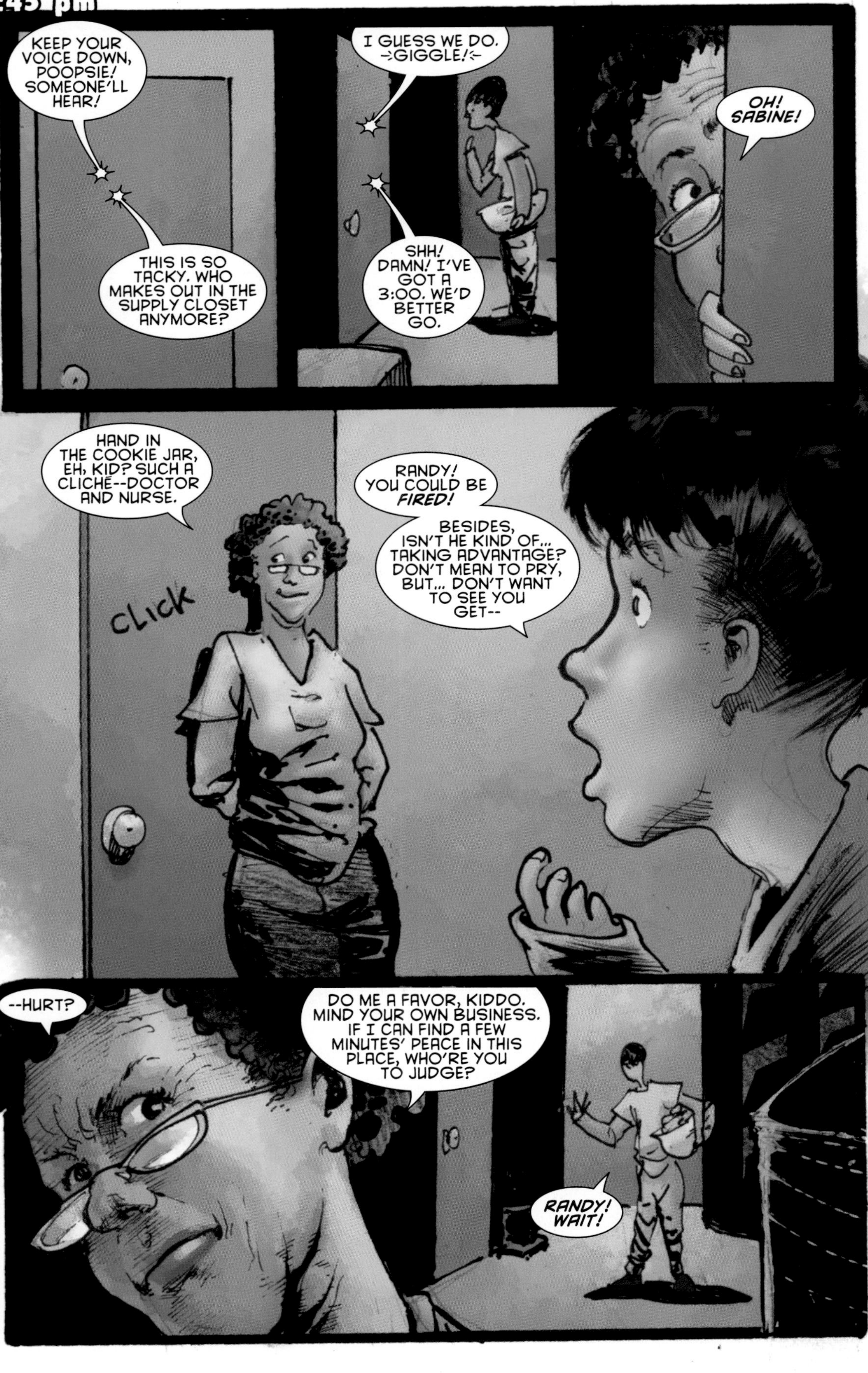
KEEP YOUR VOICE DOWN, POOPSIE! SOMEONE'LL HEAR!
THIS IS SO TACKY. WHO MAKES OUT IN THE SUPPLY CLOSET ANYMORE?
I GUESS WE DO. ->GIGGLE!<-
SHH! DAMN! I'VE GOT A 3:00. WE'D BETTER GO.
OH! SABINE!
HAND IN THE COOKIE JAR, EH, KID? SUCH A CLICHÉ--DOCTOR AND NURSE.
CLICK
RANDY! YOU COULD BE FIRED!
BESIDES, ISN'T HE KIND OF... TAKING ADVANTAGE? DON'T MEAN TO PRY, BUT... DON'T WANT TO SEE YOU GET--
--HURT?
DO ME A FAVOR, KIDDO. MIND YOUR OWN BUSINESS. IF I CAN FIND A FEW MINUTES' PEACE IN THIS PLACE, WHO'RE YOU TO JUDGE?
RANDY! WAIT!

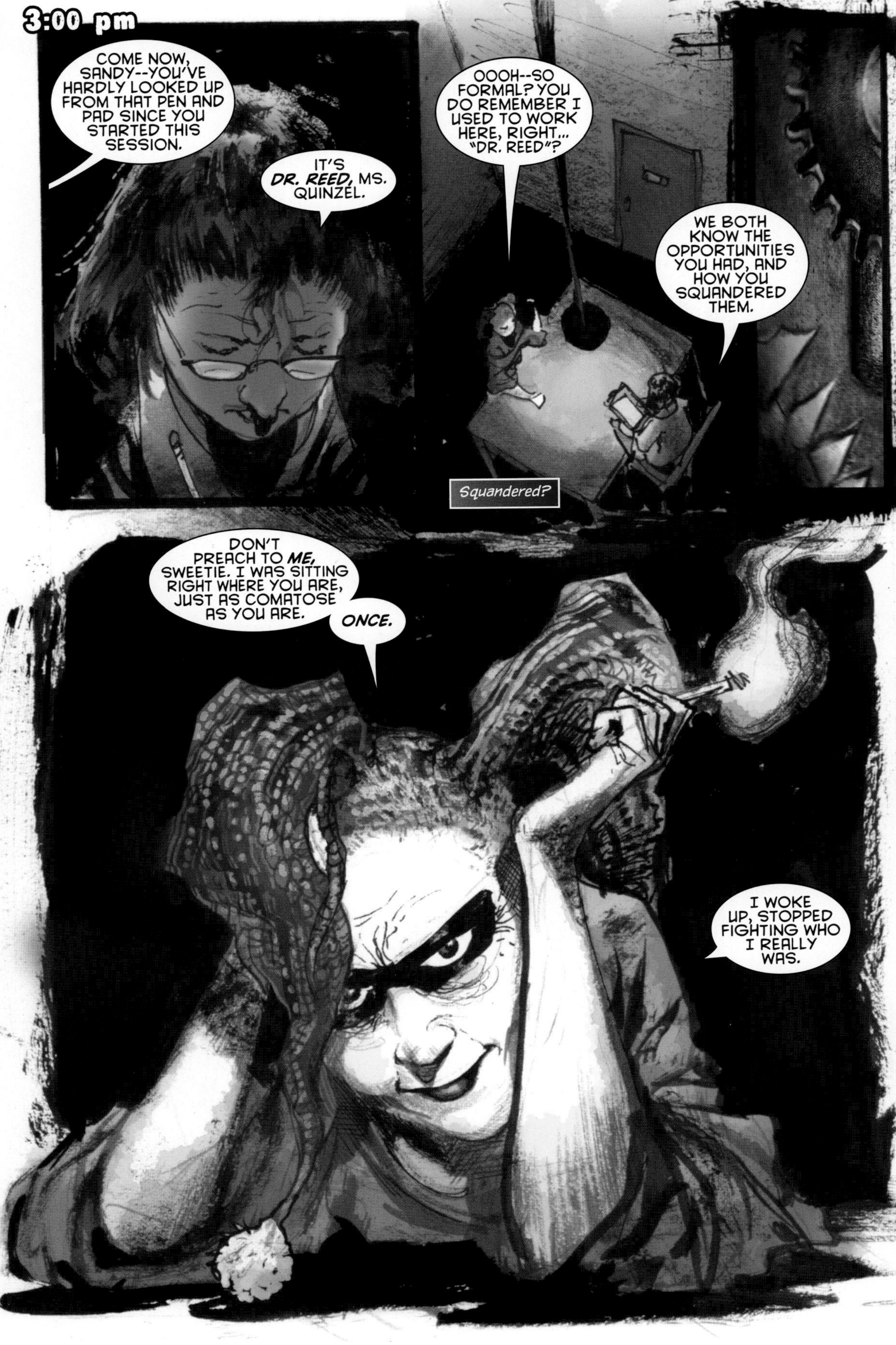
3:00 pm
COME NOW, SANDY--YOU'VE HARDLY LOOKED UP FROM THAT PEN AND PAD SINCE YOU STARTED THIS SESSION.
IT'S DR. REED, MS. QUINZEL.
OOOH--SO FORMAL? YOU DO REMEMBER I USED TO WORK HERE, RIGHT... "DR. REED"?
WE BOTH KNOW THE OPPORTUNITIES YOU HAD, AND HOW YOU SQUANDERED THEM.
Squandered?
DON'T PREACH TO ME, SWEETIE. I WAS SITTING RIGHT WHERE YOU ARE, JUST AS COMATOSE AS YOU ARE.
ONCE.
I WOKE UP, STOPPED FIGHTING WHO I REALLY WAS.

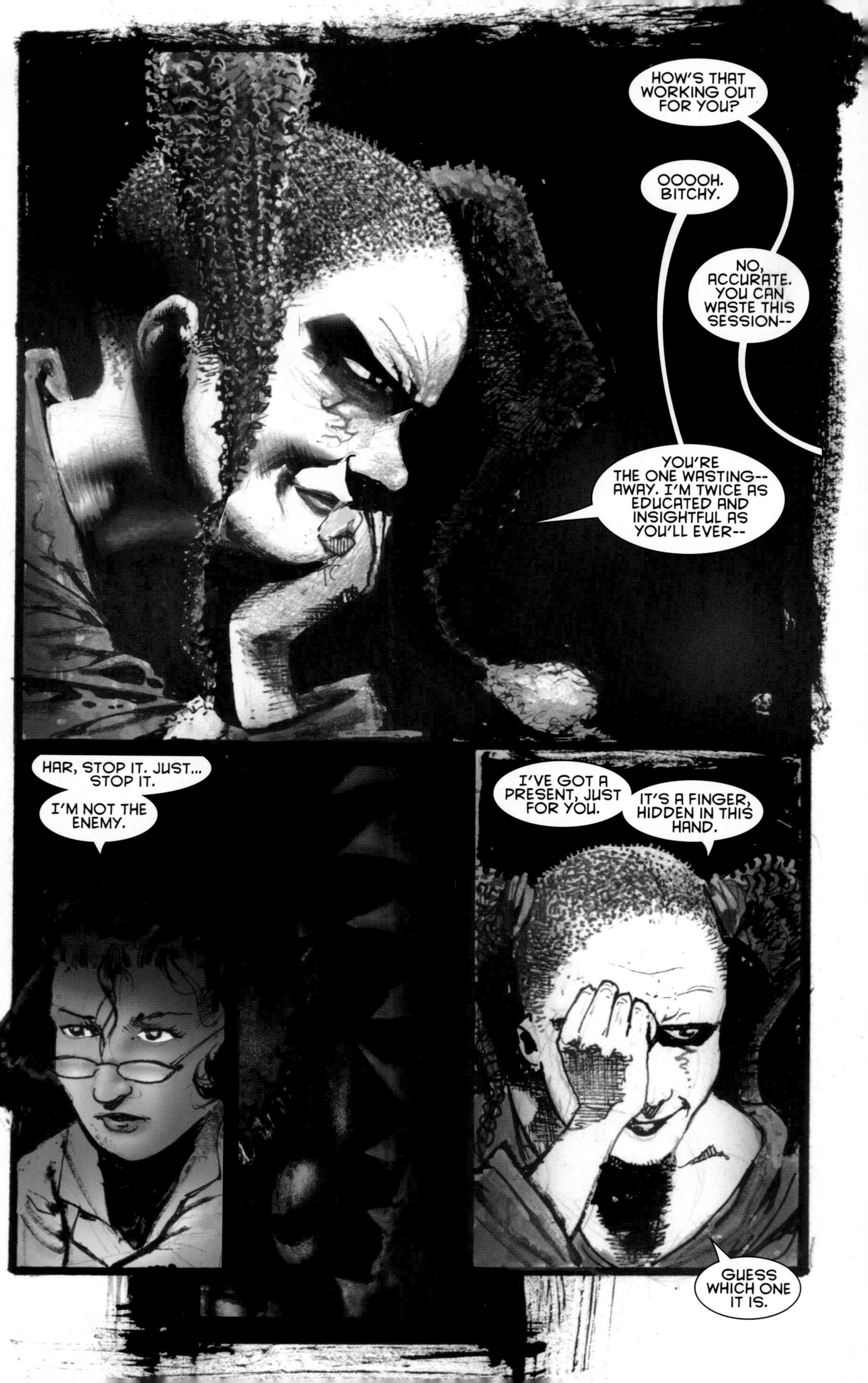
HOW'S THAT WORKING OUT FOR YOU?
OOOOH. BITCHY.
NO, ACCURATE. YOU CAN WASTE THIS SESSION--
YOU'RE THE ONE WASTING-- AWAY. I'M TWICE AS EDUCATED AND INSIGHTFUL AS YOU'LL EVER--
HAR, STOP IT. JUST... STOP IT.
I'M NOT THE ENEMY.
I'VE GOT A PRESENT, JUST FOR YOU.
IT'S A FINGER, HIDDEN IN THIS HAND.
GUESS WHICH ONE IT IS.

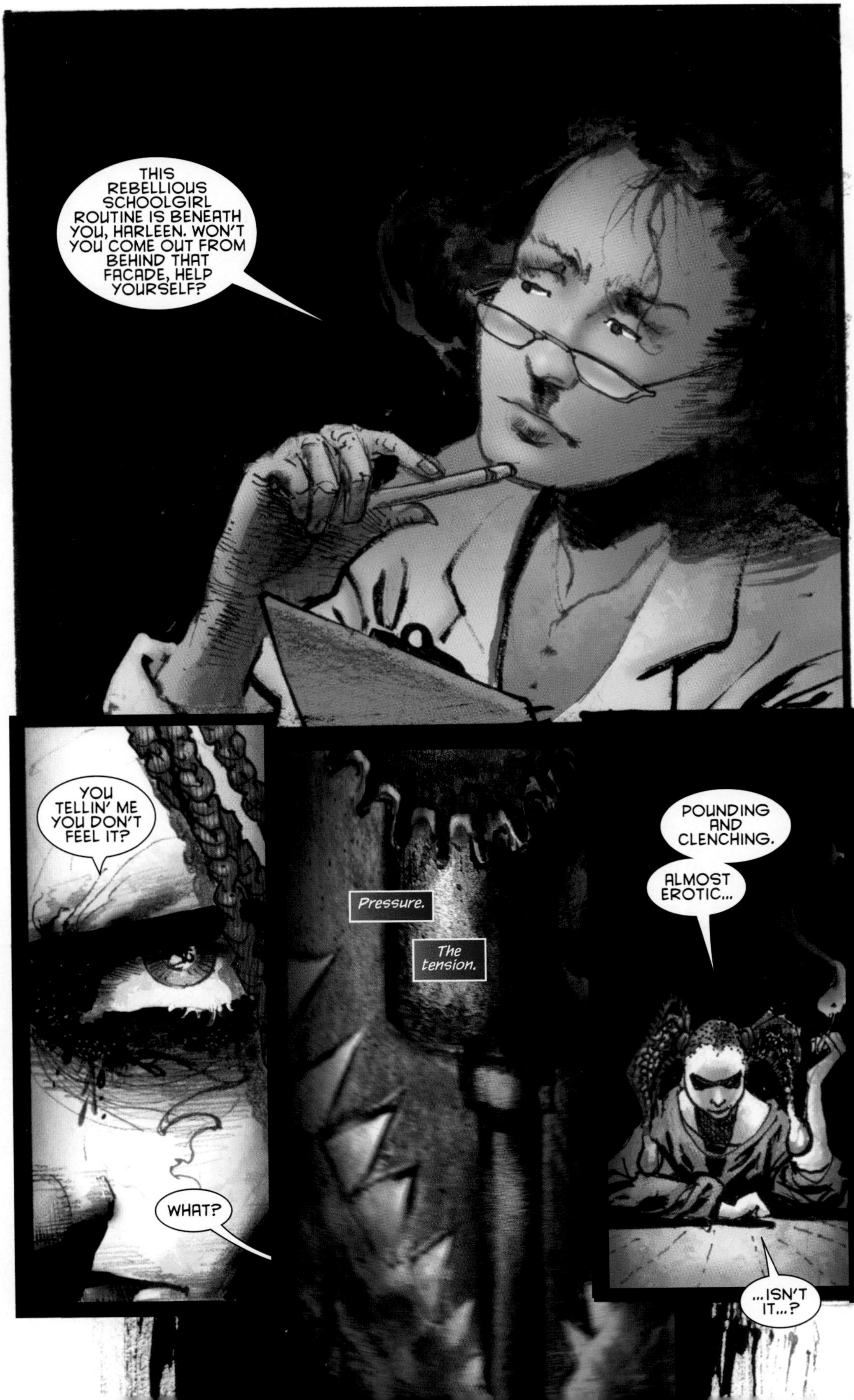
THIS REBELLIOUS SCHOOLGIRL ROUTINE IS BENEATH YOU, HARLEEN. WON'T YOU COME OUT FROM BEHIND THAT FACADE, HELP YOURSELF?
YOU TELLIN' ME YOU DON'T FEEL IT?
WHAT?
Pressure.
The tension.
POUNDING AND CLENCHING.
ALMOST EROTIC...
...ISN'T IT...?

3:30 pm

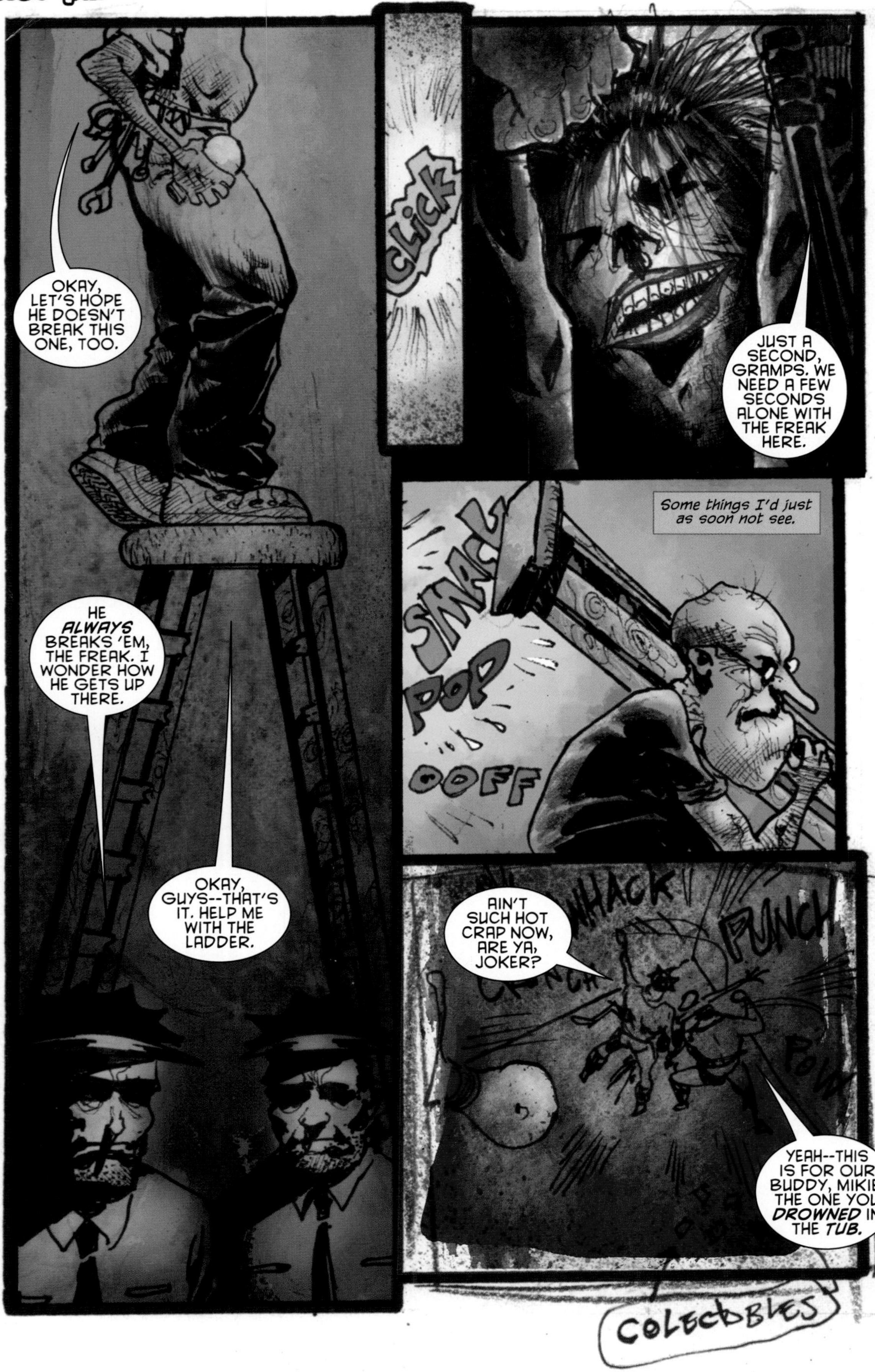

OKAY, LET'S HOPE HE DOESN'T BREAK THIS ONE, TOO.
HE *ALWAYS* BREAKS 'EM, THE FREAK. I WONDER HOW HE GETS UP THERE.
OKAY, GUYS--THAT'S IT. HELP ME WITH THE LADDER.
CLICK
JUST A SECOND, GRAMPS. WE NEED A FEW SECONDS ALONE WITH THE FREAK HERE.
Some things I'd just as soon not see.
SMACK
POP
OOFF
WHACK
PUNCH
CRUNCH
POW
AIN'T SUCH HOT CRAP NOW, ARE YA, JOKER?
YEAH--THIS IS FOR OUR BUDDY, MIKIE, THE ONE YOU *DROWNED* IN THE *TUB.*

**4:00 pm**

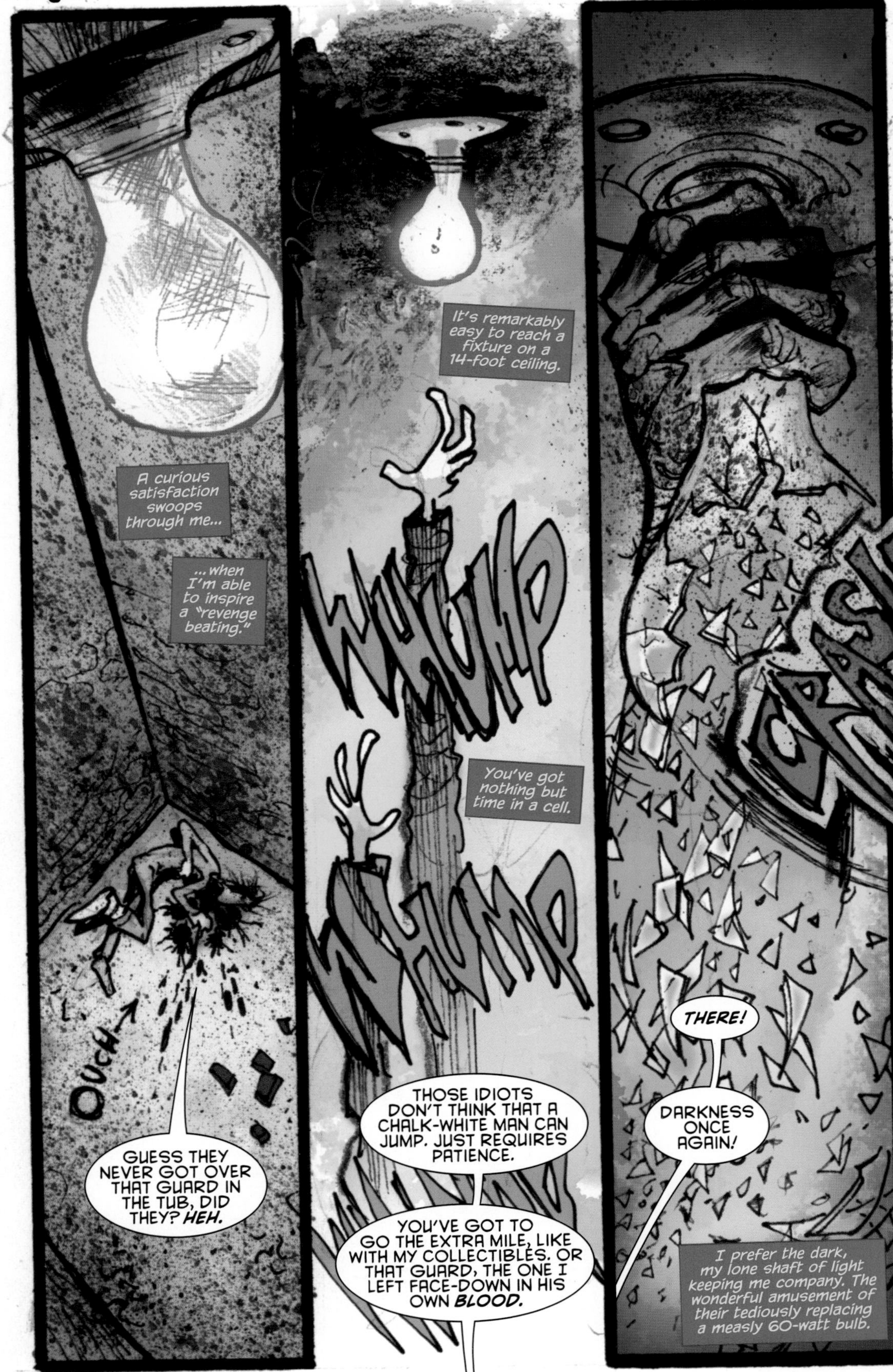
A curious satisfaction swoops through me...
...when I'm able to inspire a "revenge beating."
OUCH
GUESS THEY NEVER GOT OVER THAT GUARD IN THE TUB, DID THEY? *HEH.*
It's remarkably easy to reach a fixture on a 14-foot ceiling.
WHUMP
You've got nothing but time in a cell.
WHUMP
THOSE IDIOTS DON'T THINK THAT A CHALK-WHITE MAN CAN JUMP. JUST REQUIRES PATIENCE.
YOU'VE GOT TO GO THE EXTRA MILE, LIKE WITH MY COLLECTIBLES. OR THAT GUARD, THE ONE I LEFT FACE-DOWN IN HIS OWN *BLOOD.*
CRASH
*THERE!*
DARKNESS ONCE AGAIN!
I prefer the dark, my lone shaft of light keeping me company. The wonderful amusement of their tediously replacing a measly 60-watt bulb.

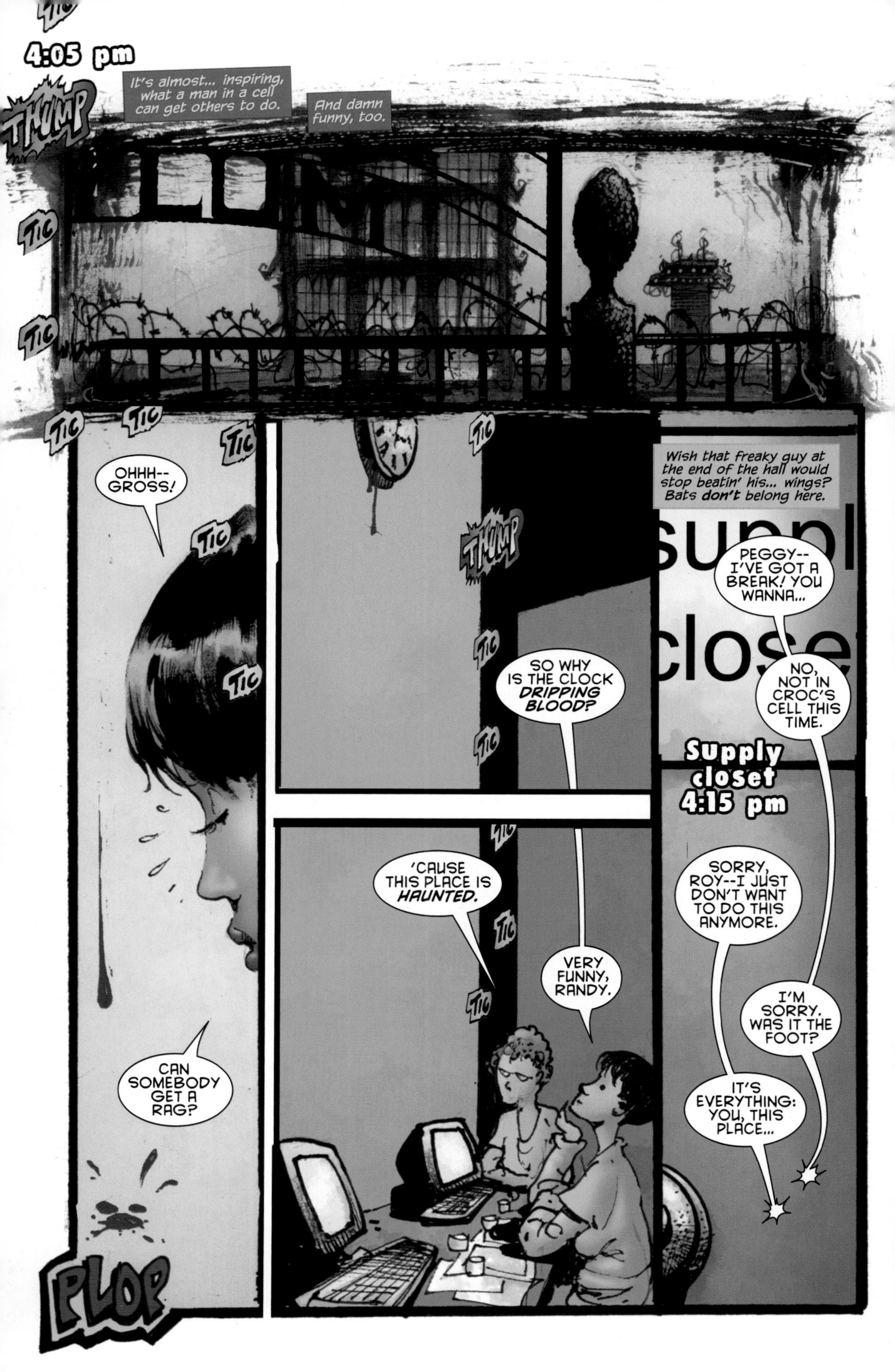
TIC
4:05 pm
It's almost... inspiring, what a man in a cell can get others to do.
And damn funny, too.
THUMP
TIC
TIC
TIC
TIC
TIC
OHHH-- GROSS!
TIC
TIC
TIC
CAN SOMEBODY GET A RAG?
PLOP
TIC
THUMP
TIC
SO WHY IS THE CLOCK *DRIPPING BLOOD?*
TIC
'CAUSE THIS PLACE IS *HAUNTED.*
TIC
VERY FUNNY, RANDY.
TIC
Wish that freaky guy at the end of the hall would stop beatin' his... wings? Bats **don't** belong here.
supply closet
PEGGY-- I'VE GOT A BREAK! YOU WANNA...
NO, NOT IN CROC'S CELL THIS TIME.
Supply closet 4:15 pm
SORRY, ROY--I JUST DON'T WANT TO DO THIS ANYMORE.
I'M SORRY. WAS IT THE FOOT?
IT'S EVERYTHING: YOU, THIS PLACE...

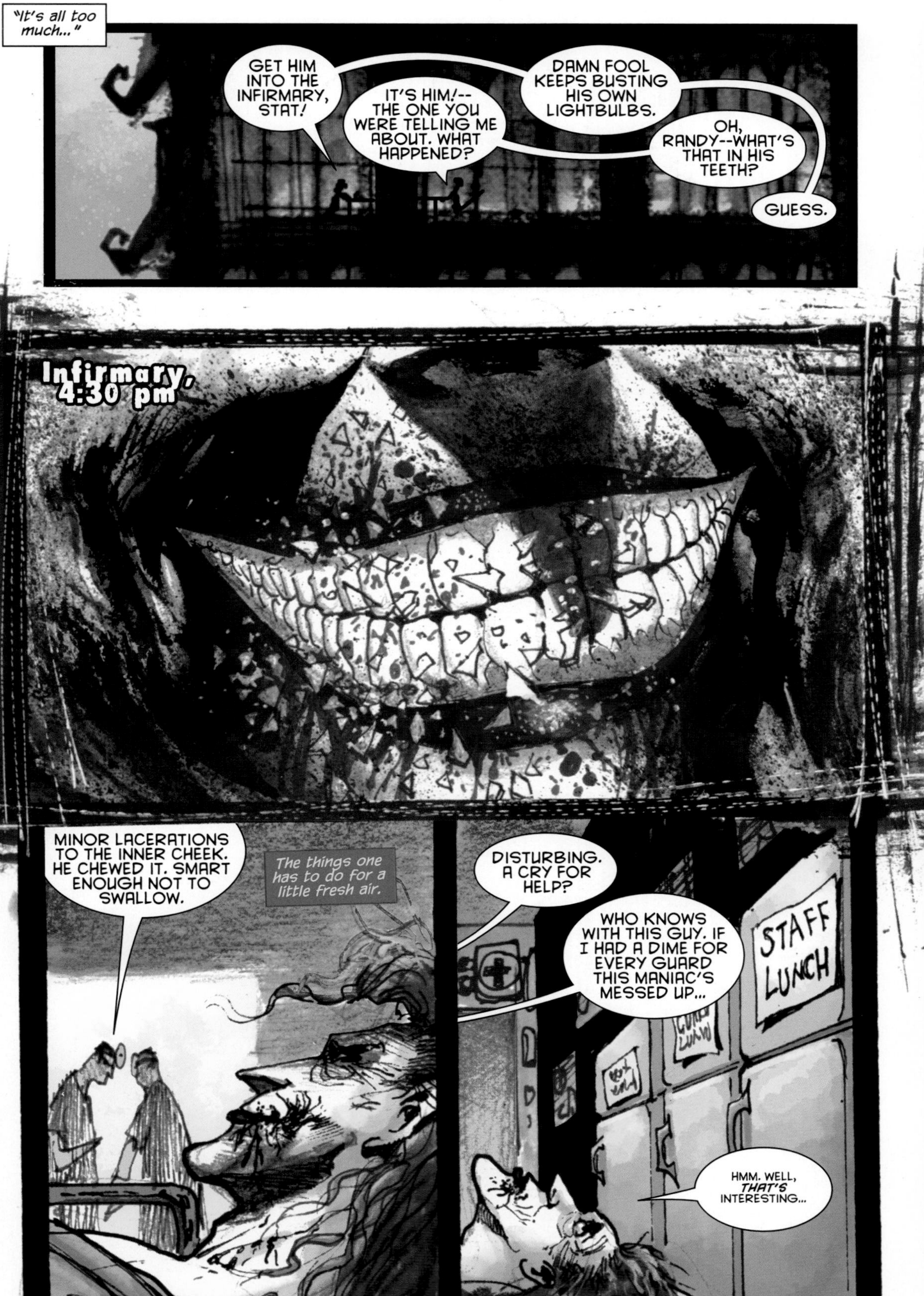
"It's all too much..."
GET HIM INTO THE INFIRMARY, STAT!
IT'S HIM!-- THE ONE YOU WERE TELLING ME ABOUT. WHAT HAPPENED?
DAMN FOOL KEEPS BUSTING HIS OWN LIGHTBULBS.
OH, RANDY--WHAT'S THAT IN HIS TEETH?
GUESS.
Infirmary, 4:30 pm
MINOR LACERATIONS TO THE INNER CHEEK. HE CHEWED IT. SMART ENOUGH NOT TO SWALLOW.
The things one has to do for a little fresh air.
DISTURBING. A CRY FOR HELP?
WHO KNOWS WITH THIS GUY. IF I HAD A DIME FOR EVERY GUARD THIS MANIAC'S MESSED UP...
STAFF LUNCH
HMM. WELL, *THAT'S* INTERESTING...

# 5:00 pm

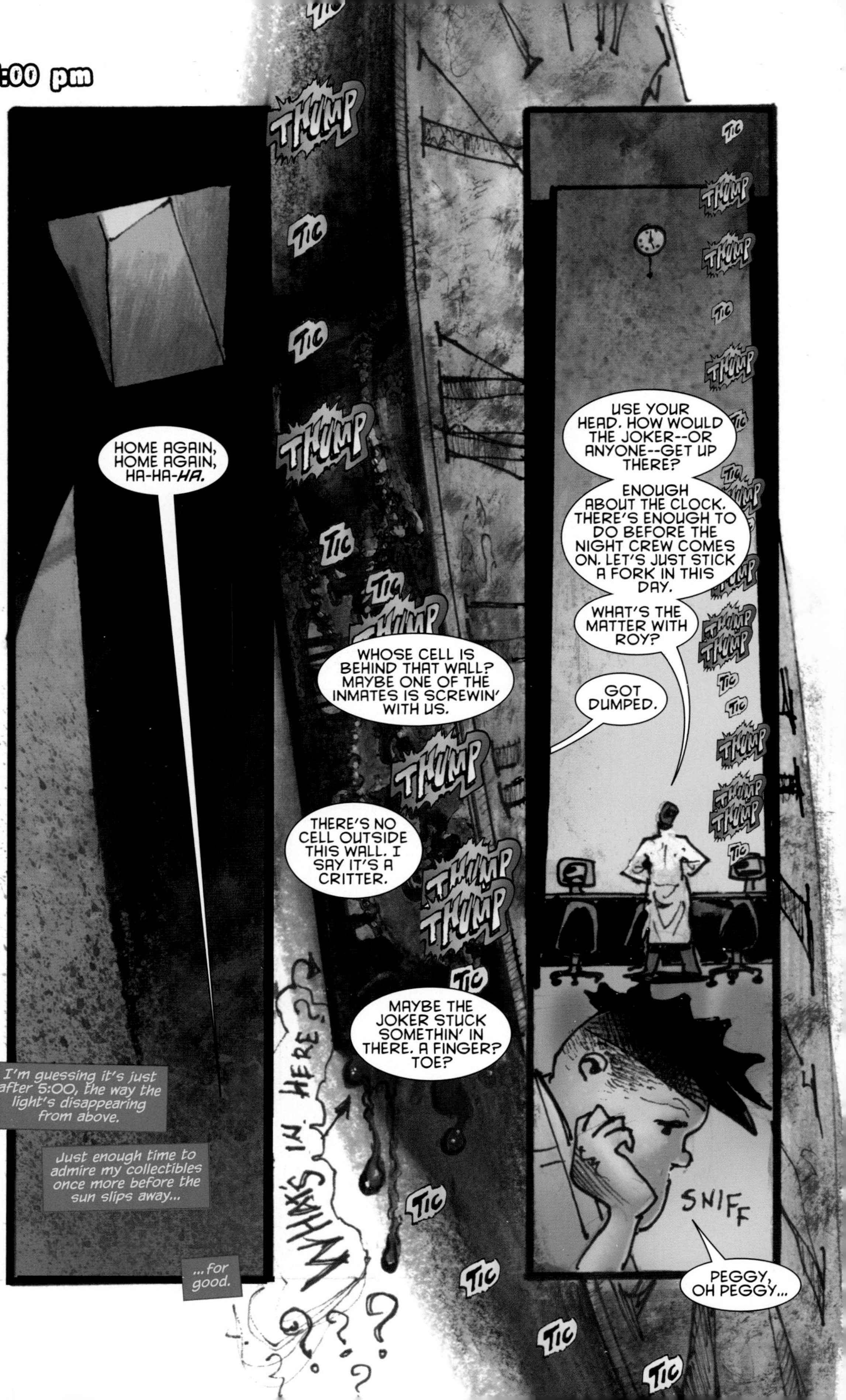

HOME AGAIN, HOME AGAIN, HA-HA-*HA.*
I'm guessing it's just after 5:00, the way the light's disappearing from above.
Just enough time to admire my collectibles once more before the sun slips away...
...for good.
THUMP
TIC
TIC
THUMP
TIC
TIC
THUMP
WHOSE CELL IS BEHIND THAT WALL? MAYBE ONE OF THE INMATES IS SCREWIN' WITH US.
THUMP
THERE'S NO CELL OUTSIDE THIS WALL. I SAY IT'S A CRITTER.
THUMP
THUMP
TIC
MAYBE THE JOKER STUCK SOMETHIN' IN THERE. A FINGER? TOE?
WHAT'S IN HERE?
TIC
TIC
TIC
THUMP
THUMP
TIC
THUMP
USE YOUR HEAD. HOW WOULD THE JOKER--OR ANYONE--GET UP THERE?
ENOUGH ABOUT THE CLOCK. THERE'S ENOUGH TO DO BEFORE THE NIGHT CREW COMES ON. LET'S JUST STICK A FORK IN THIS DAY.
WHAT'S THE MATTER WITH ROY?
GOT DUMPED.
THUMP
THUMP
TIC
TIC
THUMP
THUMP
THUMP
TIC
SNIFF
PEGGY, OH PEGGY...
TIC
TIC

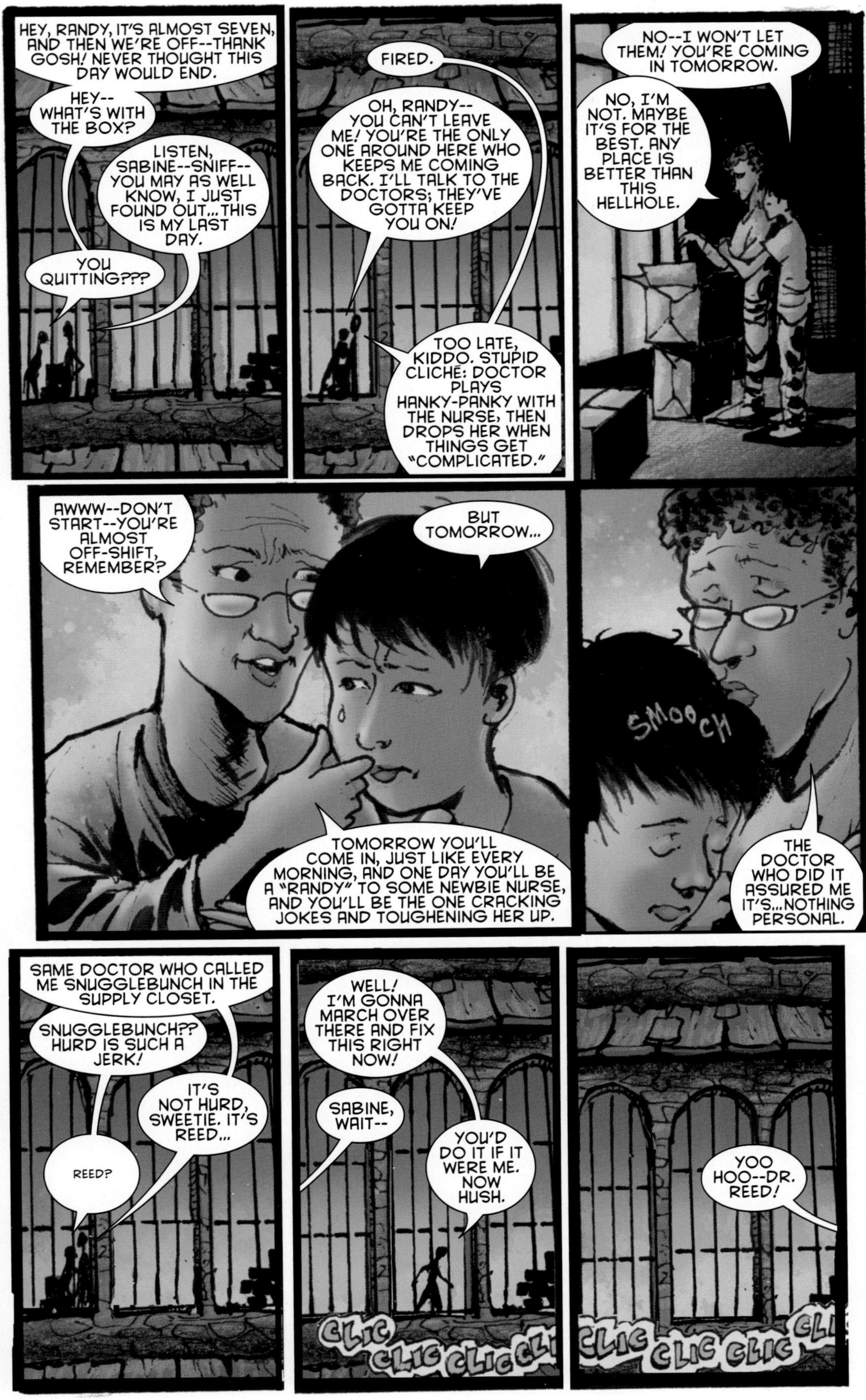
HEY, RANDY, IT'S ALMOST SEVEN, AND THEN WE'RE OFF--THANK GOSH! NEVER THOUGHT THIS DAY WOULD END.
HEY-- WHAT'S WITH THE BOX?
LISTEN, SABINE--SNIFF-- YOU MAY AS WELL KNOW, I JUST FOUND OUT...THIS IS MY LAST DAY.
YOU QUITTING???
FIRED.
OH, RANDY-- YOU CAN'T LEAVE ME! YOU'RE THE ONLY ONE AROUND HERE WHO KEEPS ME COMING BACK. I'LL TALK TO THE DOCTORS; THEY'VE GOTTA KEEP YOU ON!
TOO LATE, KIDDO. STUPID CLICHÉ: DOCTOR PLAYS HANKY-PANKY WITH THE NURSE, THEN DROPS HER WHEN THINGS GET "COMPLICATED."
NO--I WON'T LET THEM! YOU'RE COMING IN TOMORROW.
NO, I'M NOT. MAYBE IT'S FOR THE BEST. ANY PLACE IS BETTER THAN THIS HELLHOLE.
AWWW--DON'T START--YOU'RE ALMOST OFF-SHIFT, REMEMBER?
BUT TOMORROW...
TOMORROW YOU'LL COME IN, JUST LIKE EVERY MORNING, AND ONE DAY YOU'LL BE A "RANDY" TO SOME NEWBIE NURSE, AND YOU'LL BE THE ONE CRACKING JOKES AND TOUGHENING HER UP.
SMOOCH
THE DOCTOR WHO DID IT ASSURED ME IT'S...NOTHING PERSONAL.
SAME DOCTOR WHO CALLED ME SNUGGLEBUNCH IN THE SUPPLY CLOSET.
SNUGGLEBUNCH?? HURD IS SUCH A JERK!
IT'S NOT HURD, SWEETIE. IT'S REED...
REED?
WELL! I'M GONNA MARCH OVER THERE AND FIX THIS RIGHT NOW!
SABINE, WAIT--
YOU'D DO IT IF IT WERE ME. NOW HUSH.
CLIC CLIC CLIC CLIC
YOO HOO--DR. REED!
CLIC CLIC CLIC CLIC

SLAM

SABINE, I'M IN THE MIDDLE--

THIS STINKS!

WHAT?

DEFLOWERING YOUR NURSES... AND THEN *FIRING* THEM WHEN YOU'VE DECIDED TO MOVE ON. RANDY HAS A LIFE, BILLS, RENT. I'D'VE EXPECTED THIS FROM A *MALE*, LIKE DR. HURD--

RANDY WASN'T FIRED FOR... PERSONAL REASONS.

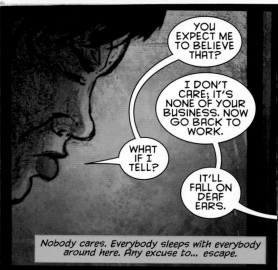

YOU EXPECT ME TO BELIEVE THAT?

I DON'T CARE; IT'S NONE OF YOUR BUSINESS. NOW GO BACK TO WORK.

WHAT IF I TELL?

IT'LL FALL ON DEAF EARS.

*Nobody cares. Everybody sleeps with everybody around here. Any excuse to... escape.*

SABINE, YOU CAN PAINT ME AS COLD-HEARTED AS YOU WANT, BUT RANDY'S A BIG GIRL. SHE DIDN'T WANT TO FACE THE FACT THAT SHE WASN'T CUTTING IT. SHE TRIED TO USE "US" TO HOLD ONTO A JOB SHE SHOULD'VE BEEN FIRED FROM YEARS AGO. HAS IT OCCURRED TO YOU THAT SHE USED ME?

UHH... RANDY WOULD NEVER...

BY THE WAY, NOW THAT SHE'S GONE, YOU HAVE TO WORK THE NIGHT SHIFT, TOO.

*WHAT??? NO* WAY!!

NO CHOICE. ONLY TWO NURSES COVERING FOUR POSTS TONIGHT. I'LL PAY YOU OVERTIME. IF YOU SAY NO, YOU'RE FIRED, TOO. AGREED?

YOU *KNOW* I HAVE NO CHOICE. I CAN'T MAKE IT WITHOUT THIS JOB.

I WON'T FORGET IT. SABINE--BELIEVE IT OR NOT, ASKING YOU TO DO THIS... WASN'T PERSONAL, EITHER.

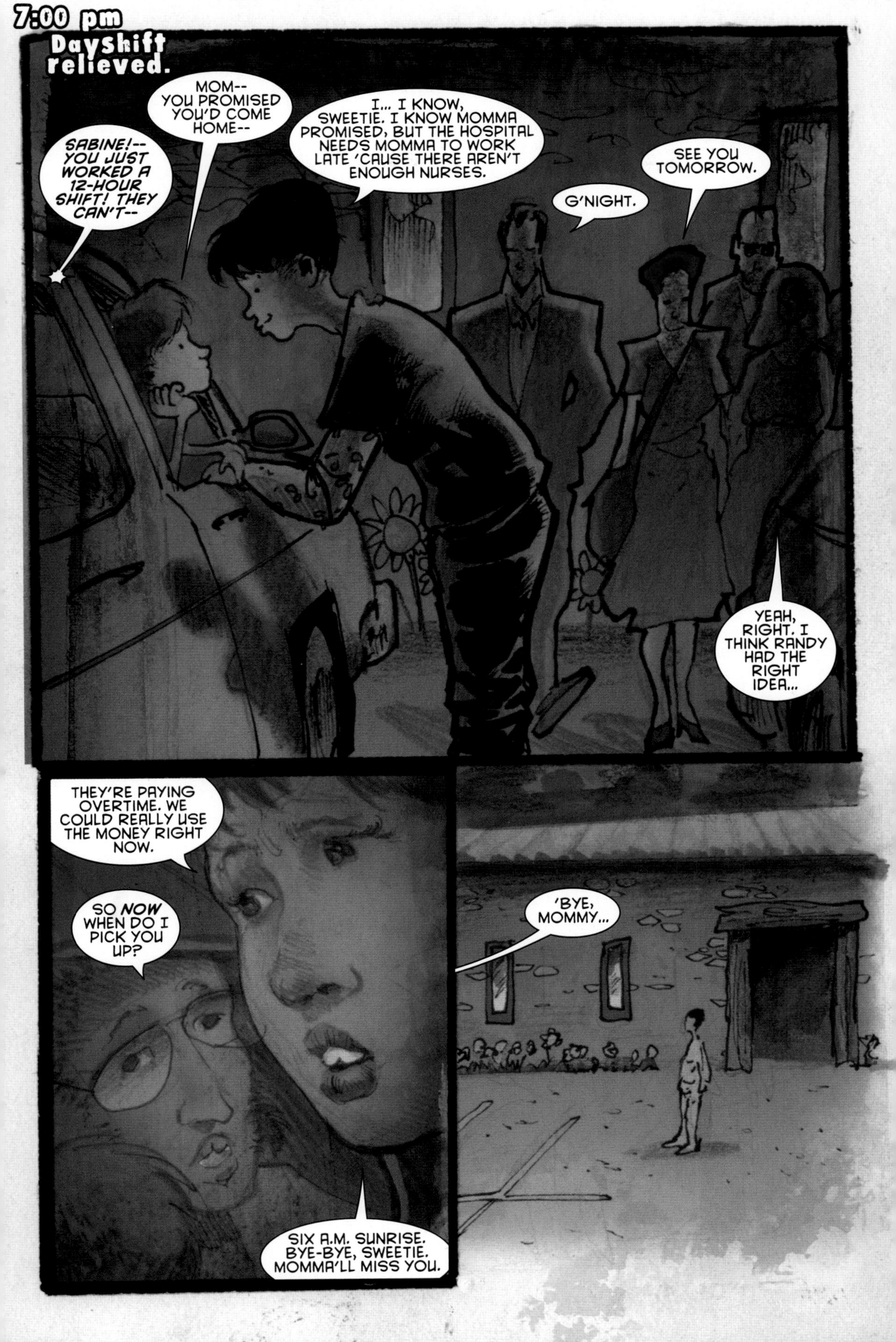
7:00 pm
Dayshift relieved.
SABINE!-- YOU JUST WORKED A 12-HOUR SHIFT! THEY CAN'T--
MOM-- YOU PROMISED YOU'D COME HOME--
I... I KNOW, SWEETIE. I KNOW MOMMA PROMISED, BUT THE HOSPITAL NEEDS MOMMA TO WORK LATE 'CAUSE THERE AREN'T ENOUGH NURSES.
G'NIGHT.
SEE YOU TOMORROW.
YEAH, RIGHT. I THINK RANDY HAD THE RIGHT IDEA...
THEY'RE PAYING OVERTIME. WE COULD REALLY USE THE MONEY RIGHT NOW.
SO NOW WHEN DO I PICK YOU UP?
'BYE, MOMMY...
SIX A.M. SUNRISE. BYE-BYE, SWEETIE. MOMMA'LL MISS YOU.

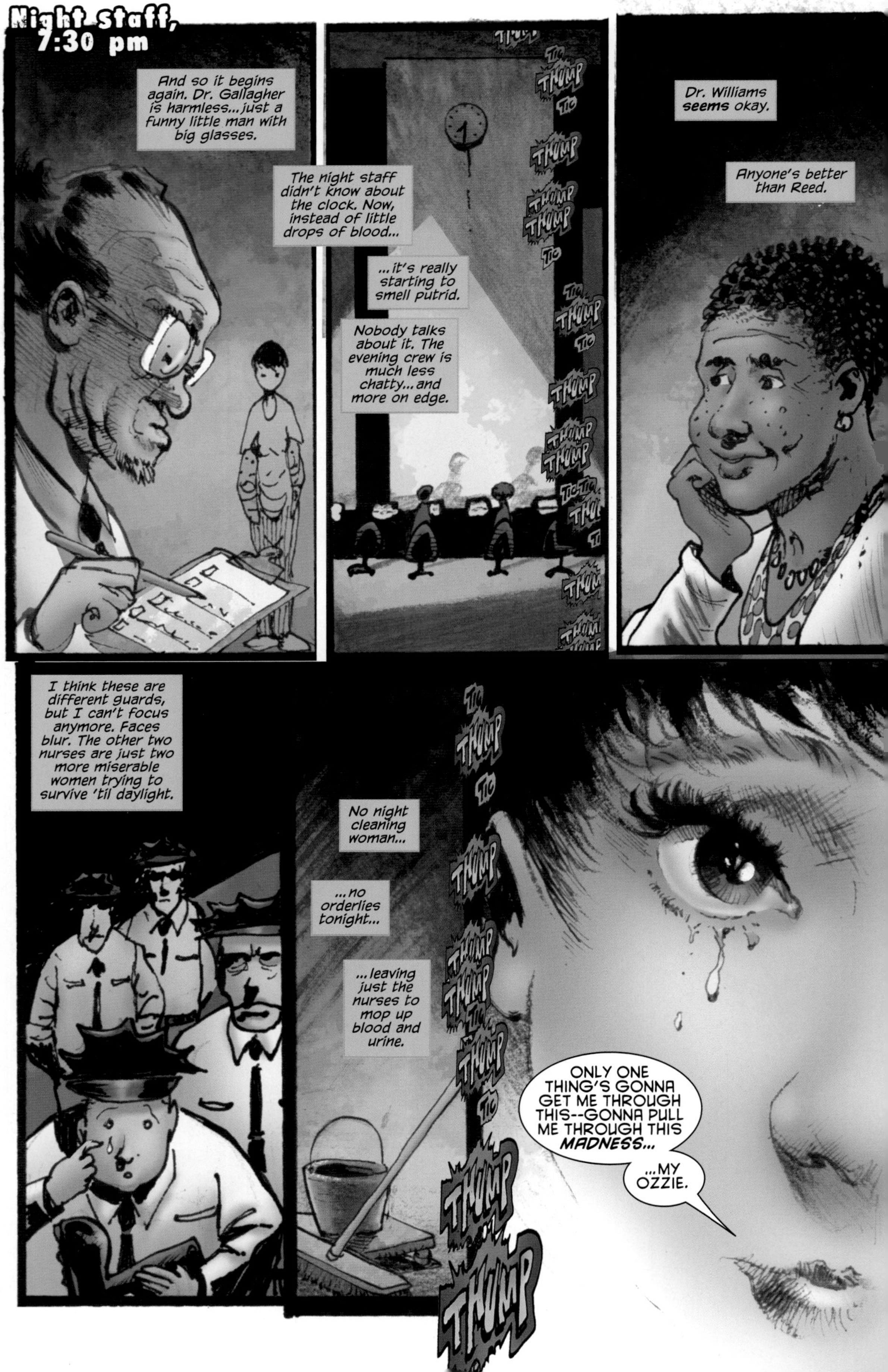
Night staff, 7:30 pm
And so it begins again. Dr. Gallagher is harmless...just a funny little man with big glasses.
The night staff didn't know about the clock. Now, instead of little drops of blood...
...it's really starting to smell putrid.
Nobody talks about it. The evening crew is much less chatty...and more on edge.
THUMP TIC THUMP THUMP THUMP TIC TIC THUMP TIC THUMP THUMP THUMP TIC TIC THUMP THUMP
Dr. Williams seems okay.
Anyone's better than Reed.
I think these are different guards, but I can't focus anymore. Faces blur. The other two nurses are just two more miserable women trying to survive 'til daylight.
No night cleaning woman...
...no orderlies tonight...
...leaving just the nurses to mop up blood and urine.
TIC THUMP TIC THUMP THUMP THUMP TIC THUMP TIC THUMP THUMP
ONLY ONE THING'S GONNA GET ME THROUGH THIS--GONNA PULL ME THROUGH THIS MADNESS...
...MY OZZIE.

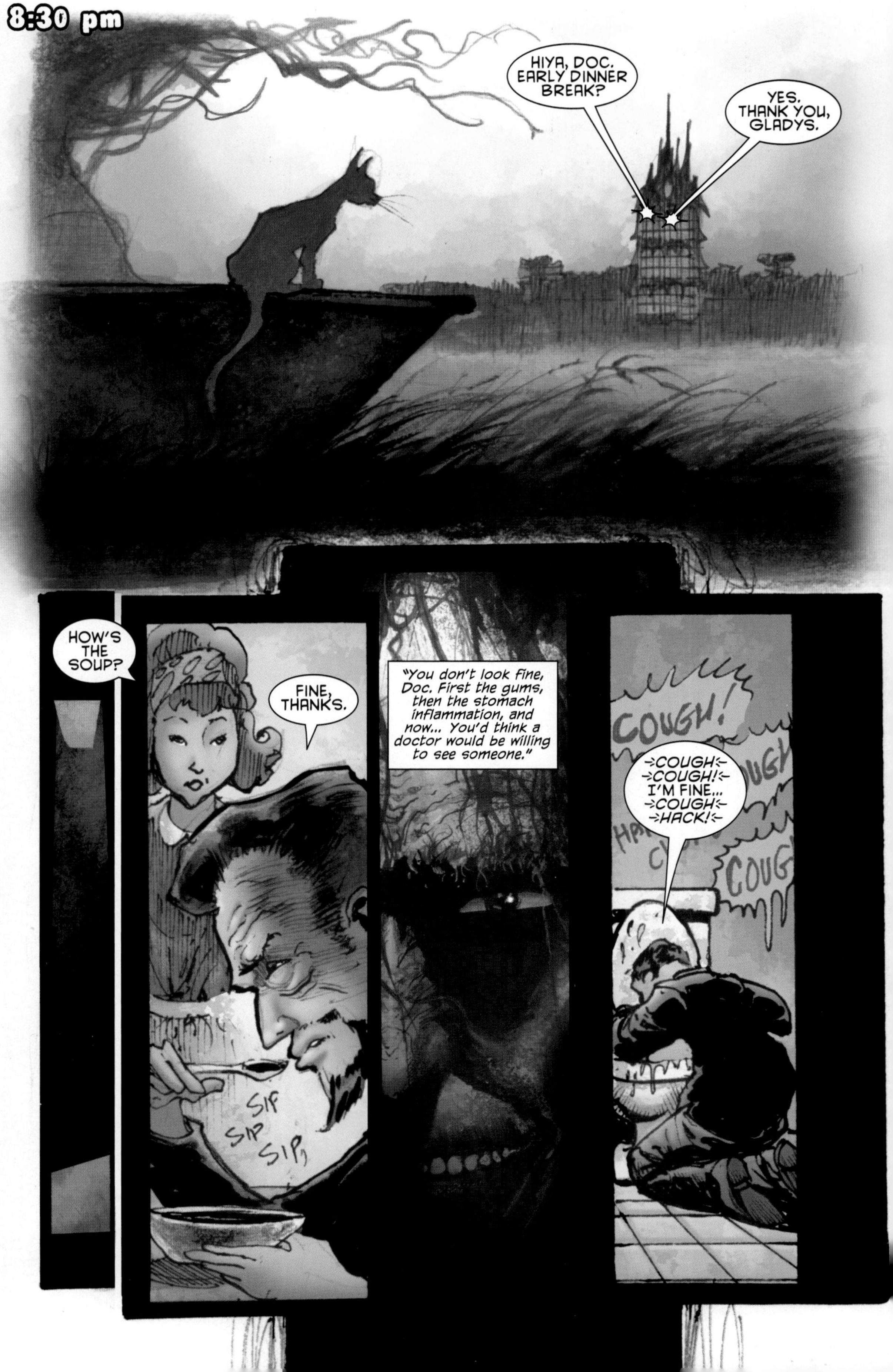
8:30 pm
HIYA, DOC. EARLY DINNER BREAK?
YES. THANK YOU, GLADYS.
HOW'S THE SOUP?
FINE, THANKS.
SIP SIP SIP
"You don't look fine, Doc. First the gums, then the stomach inflammation, and now... You'd think a doctor would be willing to see someone."
COUGH!
-COUGH- -COUGH!- I'M FINE... -COUGH- -HACK!-
COUGH

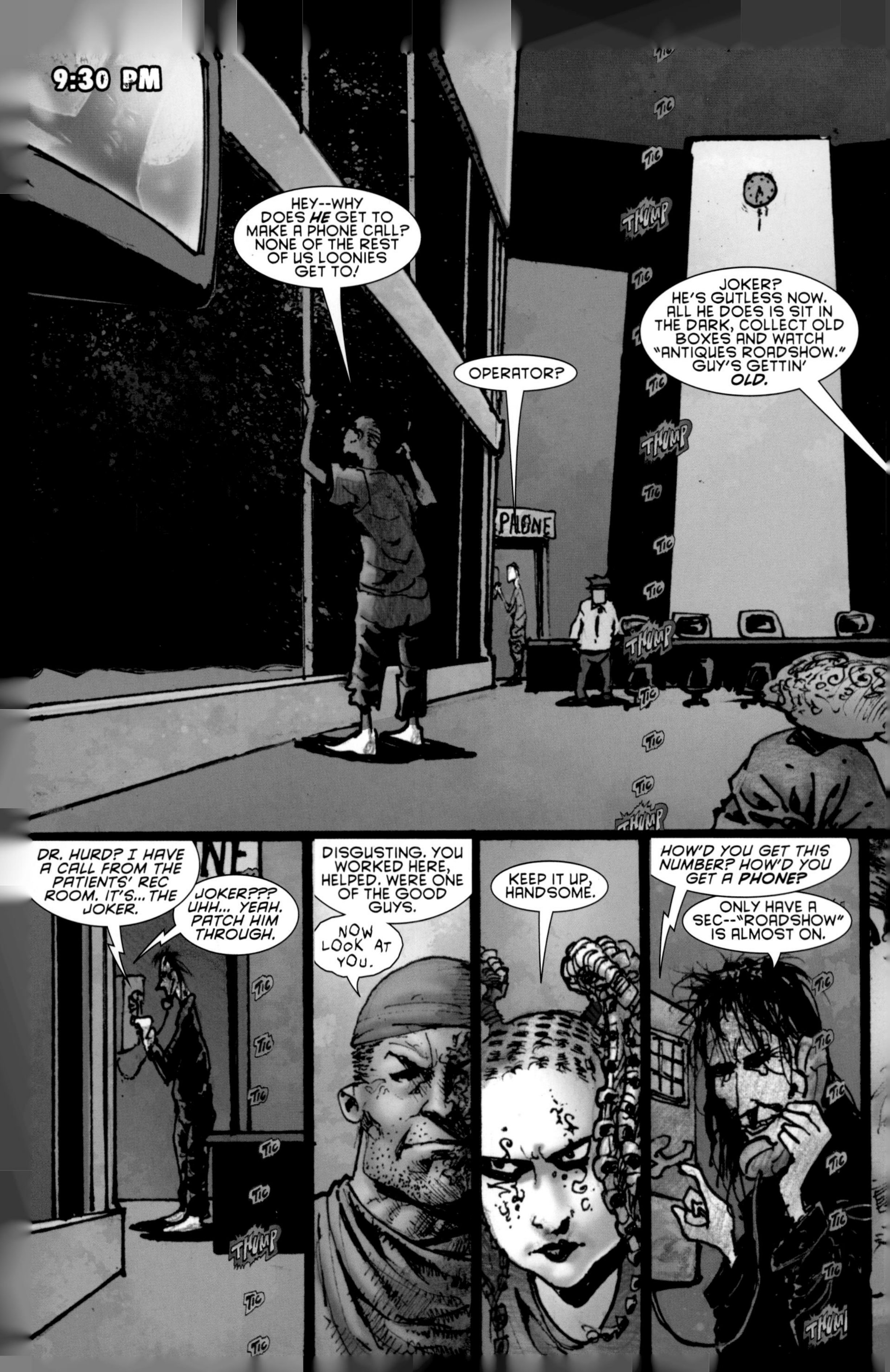
9:30 PM
HEY--WHY DOES HE GET TO MAKE A PHONE CALL? NONE OF THE REST OF US LOONIES GET TO!
OPERATOR?
JOKER? HE'S GUTLESS NOW. ALL HE DOES IS SIT IN THE DARK, COLLECT OLD BOXES AND WATCH "ANTIQUES ROADSHOW." GUY'S GETTIN' OLD.
PHONE
DR. HURD? I HAVE A CALL FROM THE PATIENTS' REC ROOM. IT'S... THE JOKER.
JOKER??? UHH... YEAH. PATCH HIM THROUGH.
DISGUSTING. YOU WORKED HERE, HELPED. WERE ONE OF THE GOOD GUYS.
NOW LOOK AT YOU.
KEEP IT UP, HANDSOME.
HOW'D YOU GET THIS NUMBER? HOW'D YOU GET A PHONE?
ONLY HAVE A SEC--"ROADSHOW" IS ALMOST ON.

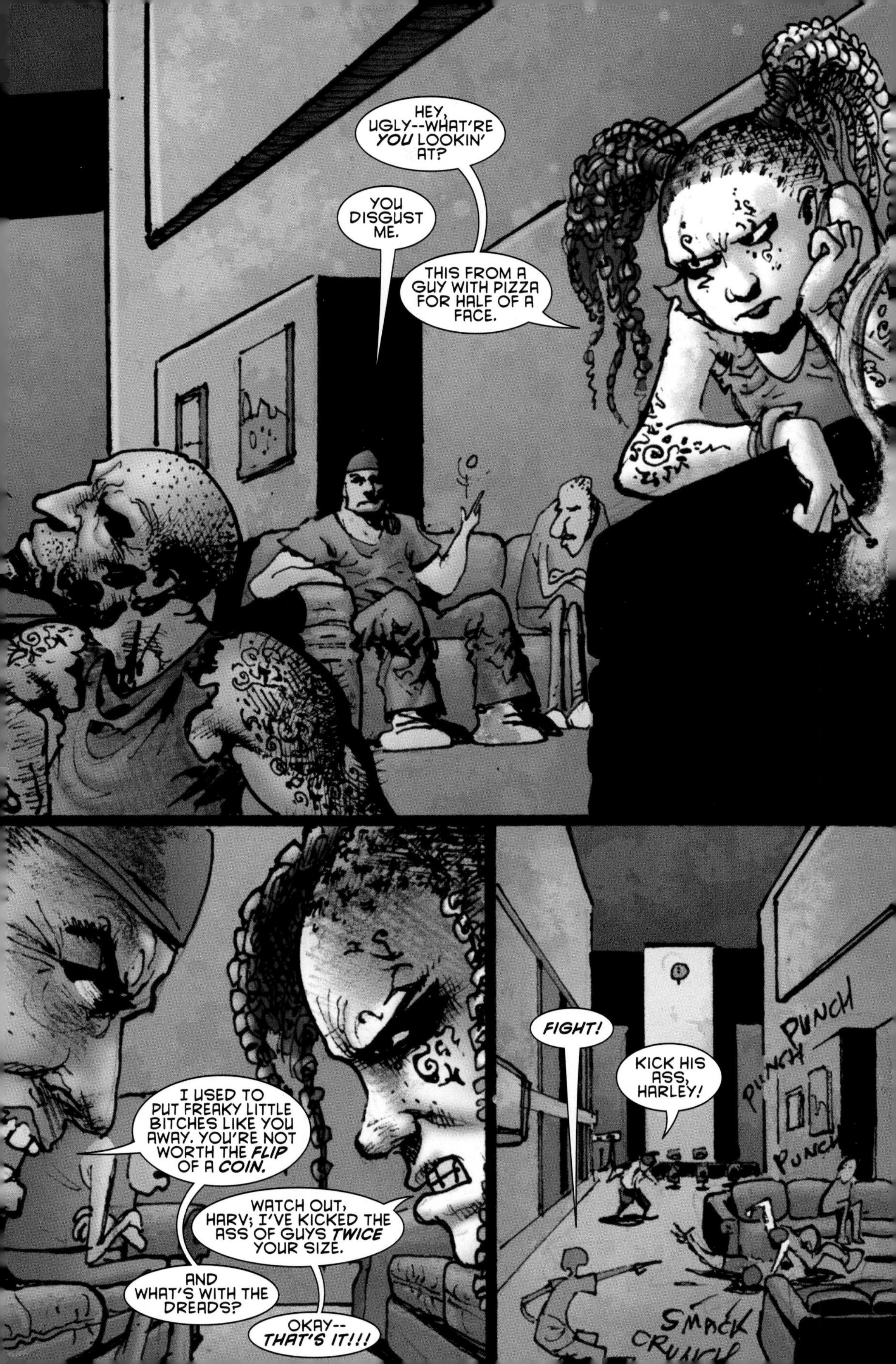
HEY, UGLY--WHAT'RE *YOU* LOOKIN' AT?
YOU DISGUST ME.
THIS FROM A GUY WITH PIZZA FOR HALF OF A FACE.
I USED TO PUT FREAKY LITTLE BITCHES LIKE YOU AWAY. YOU'RE NOT WORTH THE *FLIP* OF A *COIN.*
WATCH OUT, HARV; I'VE KICKED THE ASS OF GUYS *TWICE* YOUR SIZE.
AND WHAT'S WITH THE DREADS?
OKAY-- *THAT'S IT!!!*
*FIGHT!*
KICK HIS ASS, HARLEY!
PUNCH
PUNCH
PUNCH
PUNCH
SMACK
CRUNCH

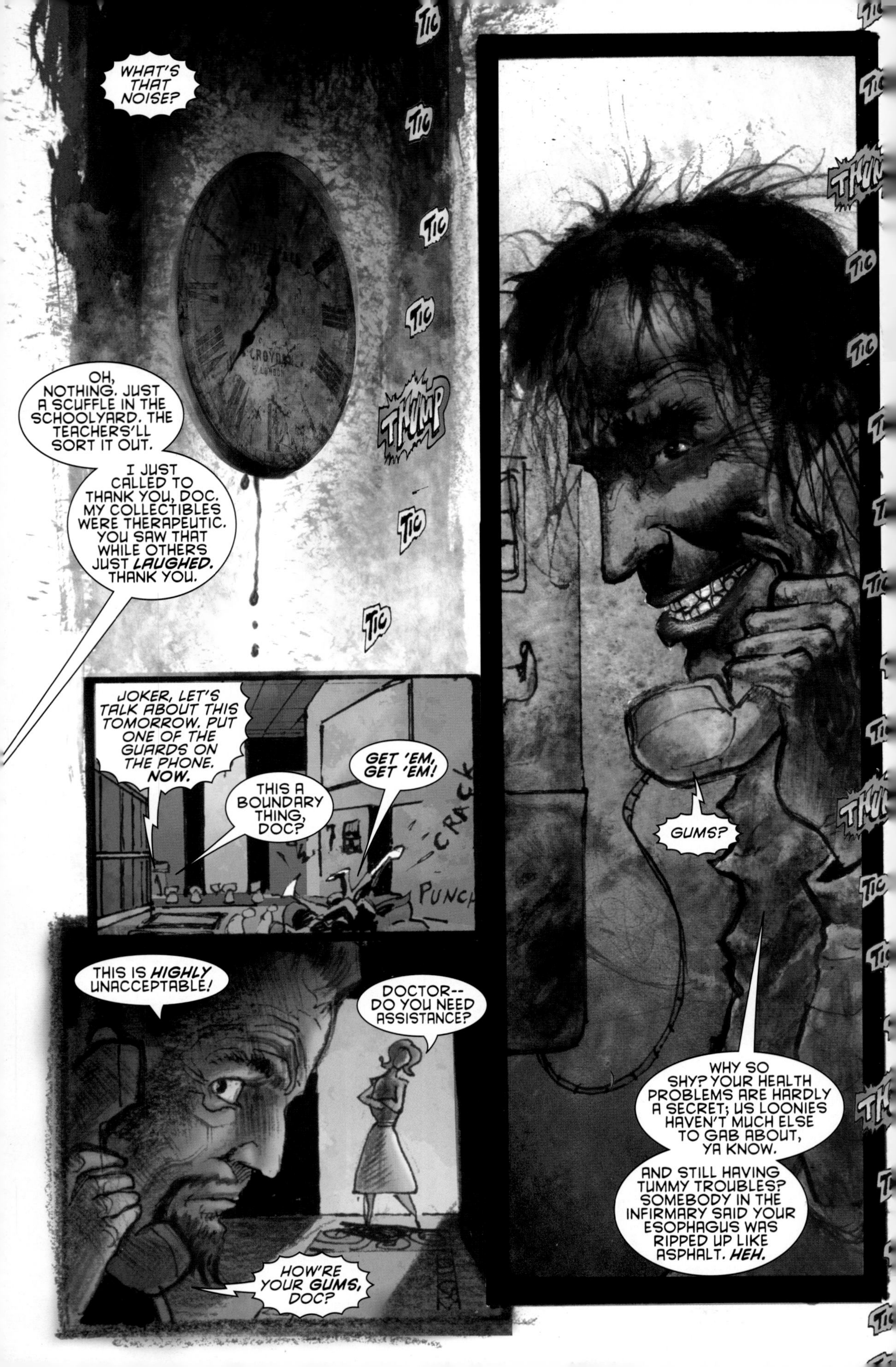
WHAT'S THAT NOISE?
TIC
TIC
TIC
TIC
THUMP
TIC
TIC
OH, NOTHING. JUST A SCUFFLE IN THE SCHOOLYARD. THE TEACHERS'LL SORT IT OUT.
I JUST CALLED TO THANK YOU, DOC. MY COLLECTIBLES WERE THERAPEUTIC. YOU SAW THAT WHILE OTHERS JUST LAUGHED. THANK YOU.
JOKER, LET'S TALK ABOUT THIS TOMORROW. PUT ONE OF THE GUARDS ON THE PHONE. NOW.
THIS A BOUNDARY THING, DOC?
GET 'EM, GET 'EM!
CRACK
PUNCH
THIS IS HIGHLY UNACCEPTABLE!
DOCTOR-- DO YOU NEED ASSISTANCE?
HOW'RE YOUR GUMS, DOC?
GUMS?
WHY SO SHY? YOUR HEALTH PROBLEMS ARE HARDLY A SECRET; US LOONIES HAVEN'T MUCH ELSE TO GAB ABOUT, YA KNOW.
AND STILL HAVING TUMMY TROUBLES? SOMEBODY IN THE INFIRMARY SAID YOUR ESOPHAGUS WAS RIPPED UP LIKE ASPHALT. HEH.

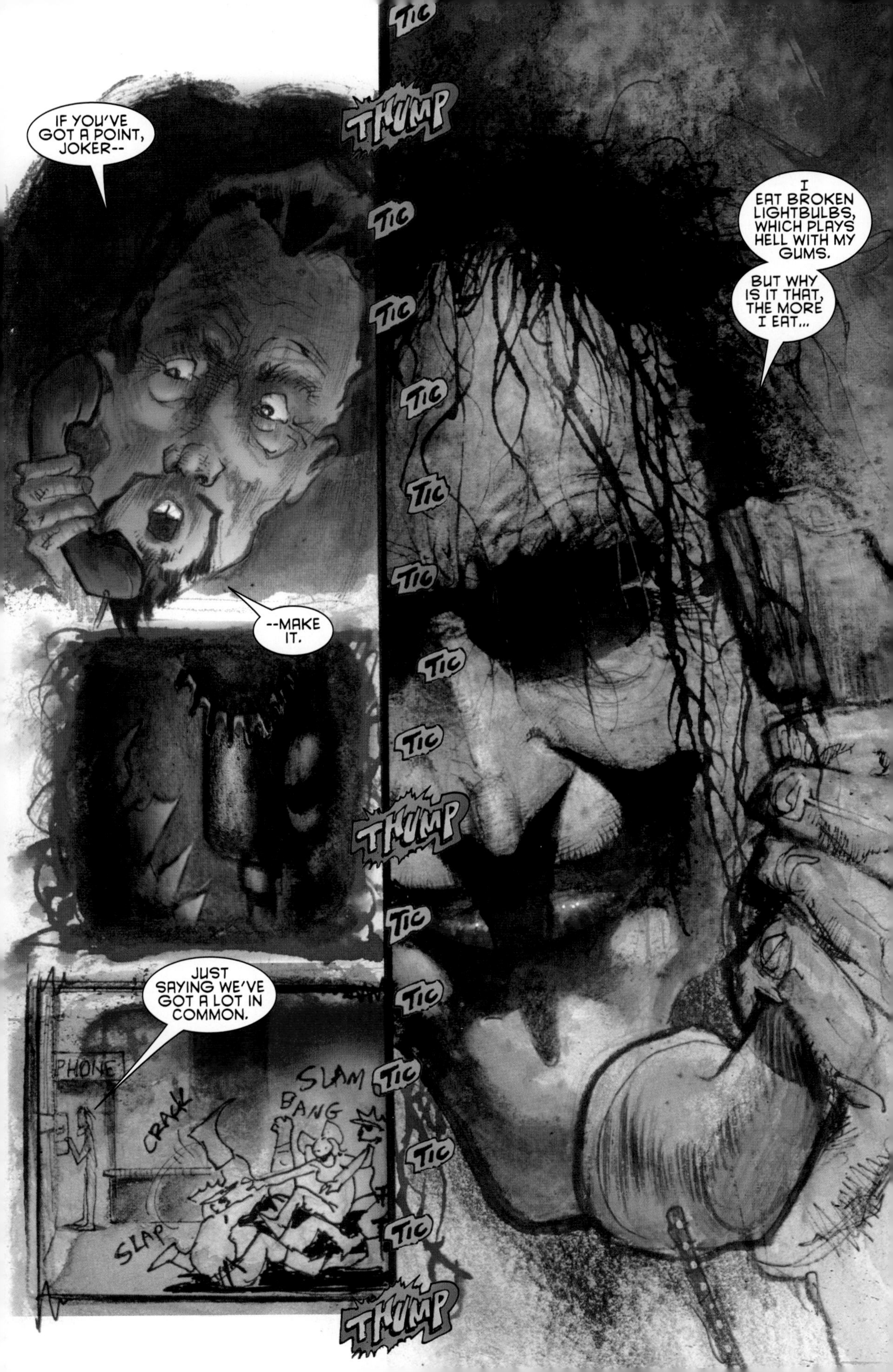
TIC
THUMP
IF YOU'VE GOT A POINT, JOKER--
TIC
I EAT BROKEN LIGHTBULBS, WHICH PLAYS HELL WITH MY GUMS.
BUT WHY IS IT THAT, THE MORE I EAT...
TIC
TIC
TIC
TIC
--MAKE IT.
TIC
TIC
THUMP
TIC
JUST SAYING WE'VE GOT A LOT IN COMMON.
TIC
PHONE
SLAM
BANG
CRACK
TIC
TIC
SLAP
TIC
THUMP

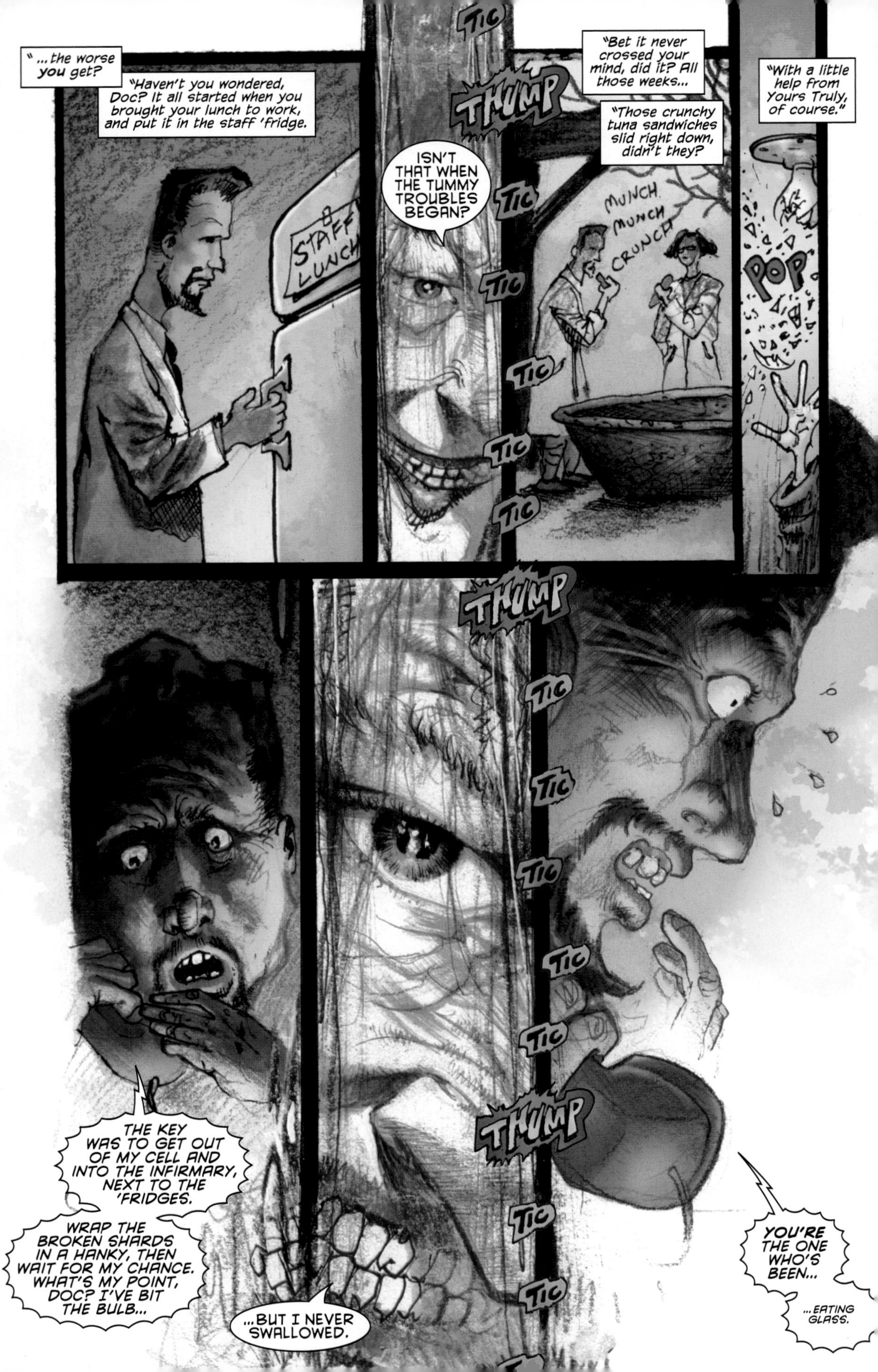
"...the worse you get?
"Haven't you wondered, Doc? It all started when you brought your lunch to work, and put it in the staff 'fridge.
STAFF LUNCH
TIC
THUMP
ISN'T THAT WHEN THE TUMMY TROUBLES BEGAN?
TIC
TIC
TIC
TIC
TIC
"Bet it never crossed your mind, did it? All those weeks...
"Those crunchy tuna sandwiches slid right down, didn't they?
MUNCH MUNCH CRUNCH
"With a little help from Yours Truly, of course."
POP
THUMP
TIC
TIC
TIC
TIC
TIC
THE KEY WAS TO GET OUT OF MY CELL AND INTO THE INFIRMARY, NEXT TO THE 'FRIDGES.
WRAP THE BROKEN SHARDS IN A HANKY, THEN WAIT FOR MY CHANCE. WHAT'S MY POINT, DOC? I'VE BIT THE BULB...
...BUT I NEVER SWALLOWED.
THUMP
TIC
TIC
YOU'RE THE ONE WHO'S BEEN...
...EATING GLASS.

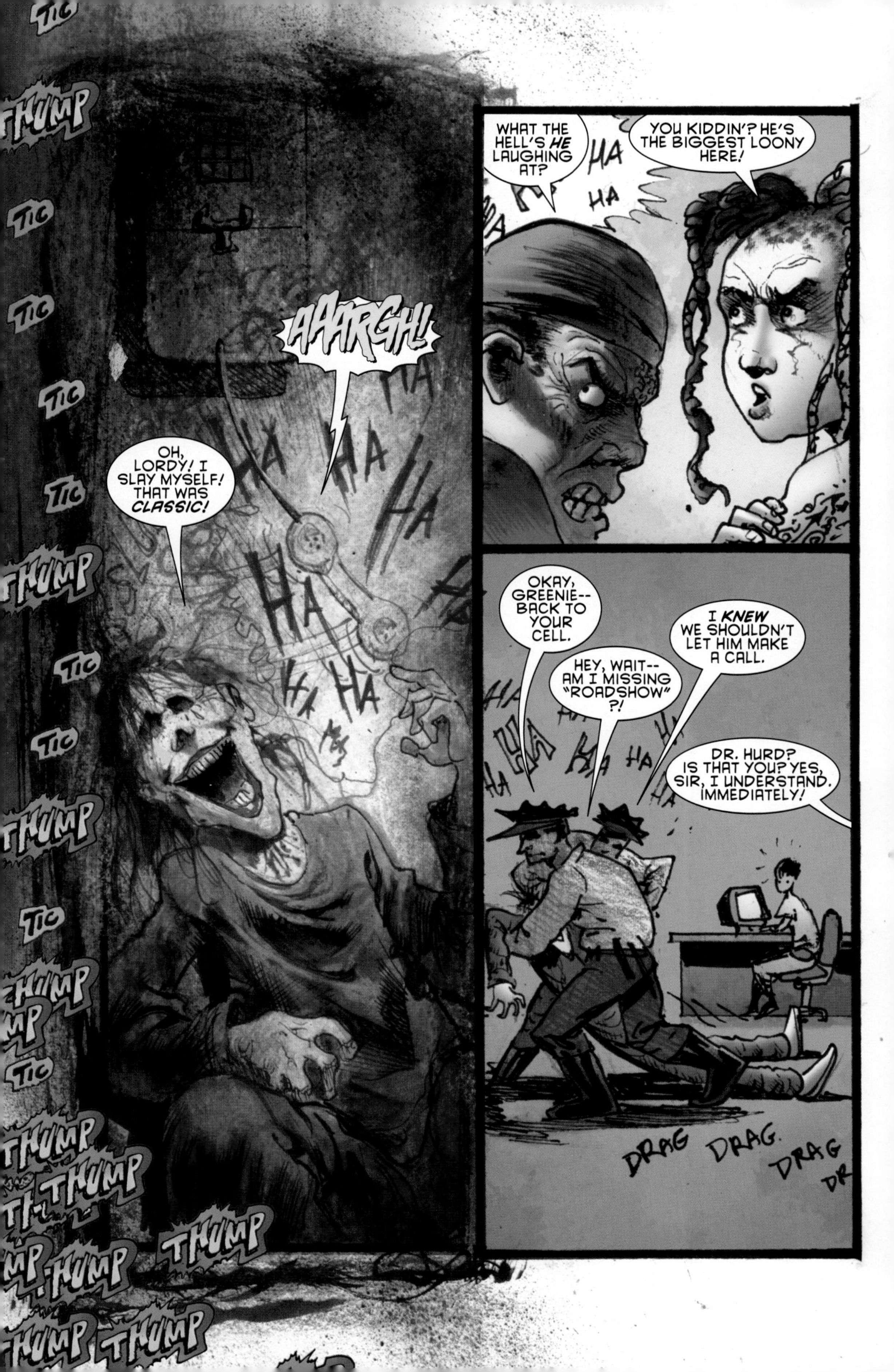

TIC
THUMP
TIC
TIC
TIC
TIC
AAARGH!
OH, LORDY! I SLAY MYSELF! THAT WAS CLASSIC!
HA HA HA HA HA HA HA HA
WHAT THE HELL'S HE LAUGHING AT?
YOU KIDDIN'? HE'S THE BIGGEST LOONY HERE!
HA HA
OKAY, GREENIE-- BACK TO YOUR CELL.
HEY, WAIT-- AM I MISSING "ROADSHOW"?!
I KNEW WE SHOULDN'T LET HIM MAKE A CALL.
DR. HURD? IS THAT YOU? YES, SIR, I UNDERSTAND. IMMEDIATELY!
DRAG DRAG DRAG DR
THUMP
THUMP
THUMP
THUMP

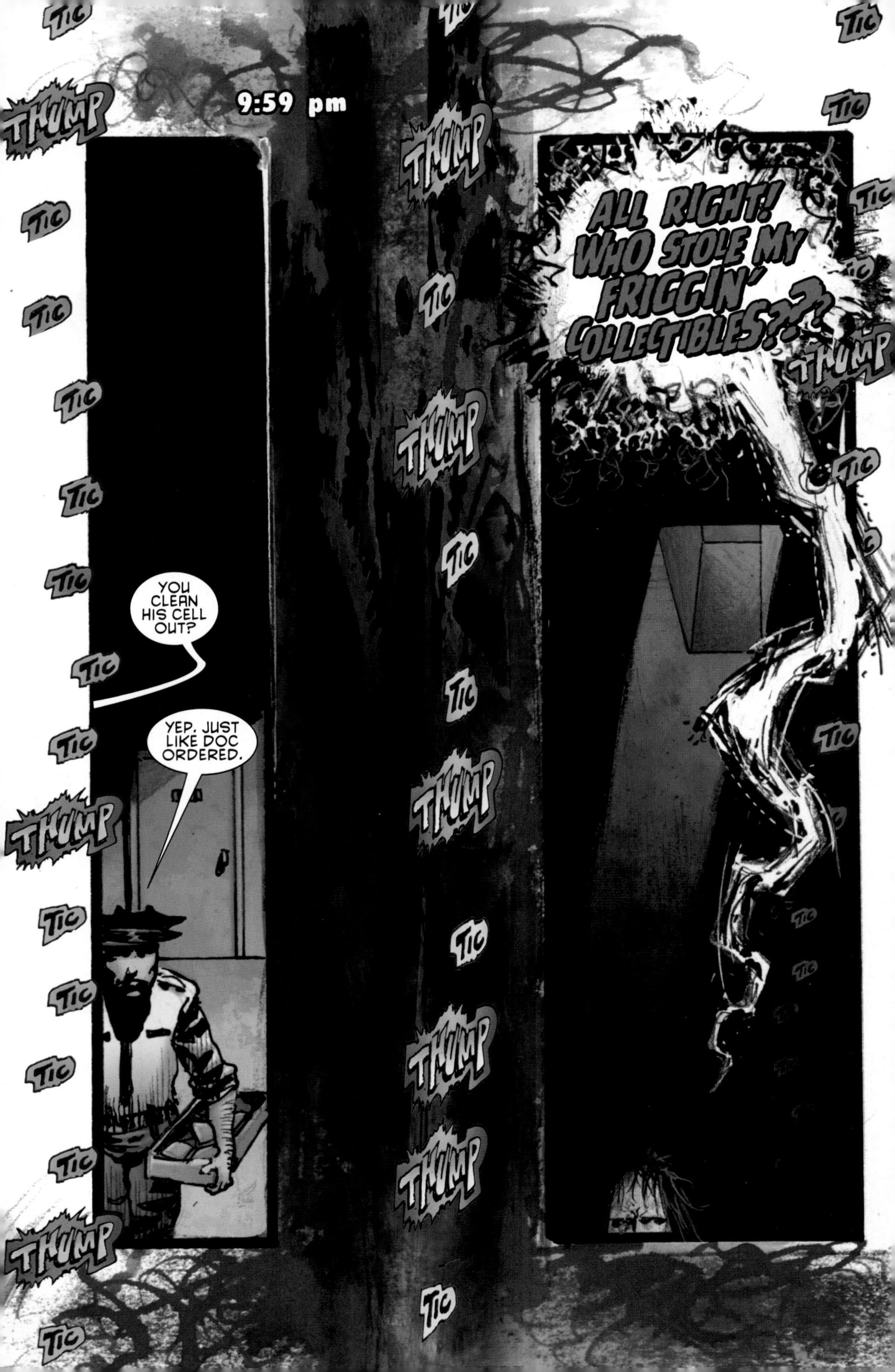
9:59 pm
YOU CLEAN HIS CELL OUT?
YEP. JUST LIKE DOC ORDERED.
ALL RIGHT! WHO STOLE MY FRIGGIN' COLLECTIBLES???
THUMP
TIC

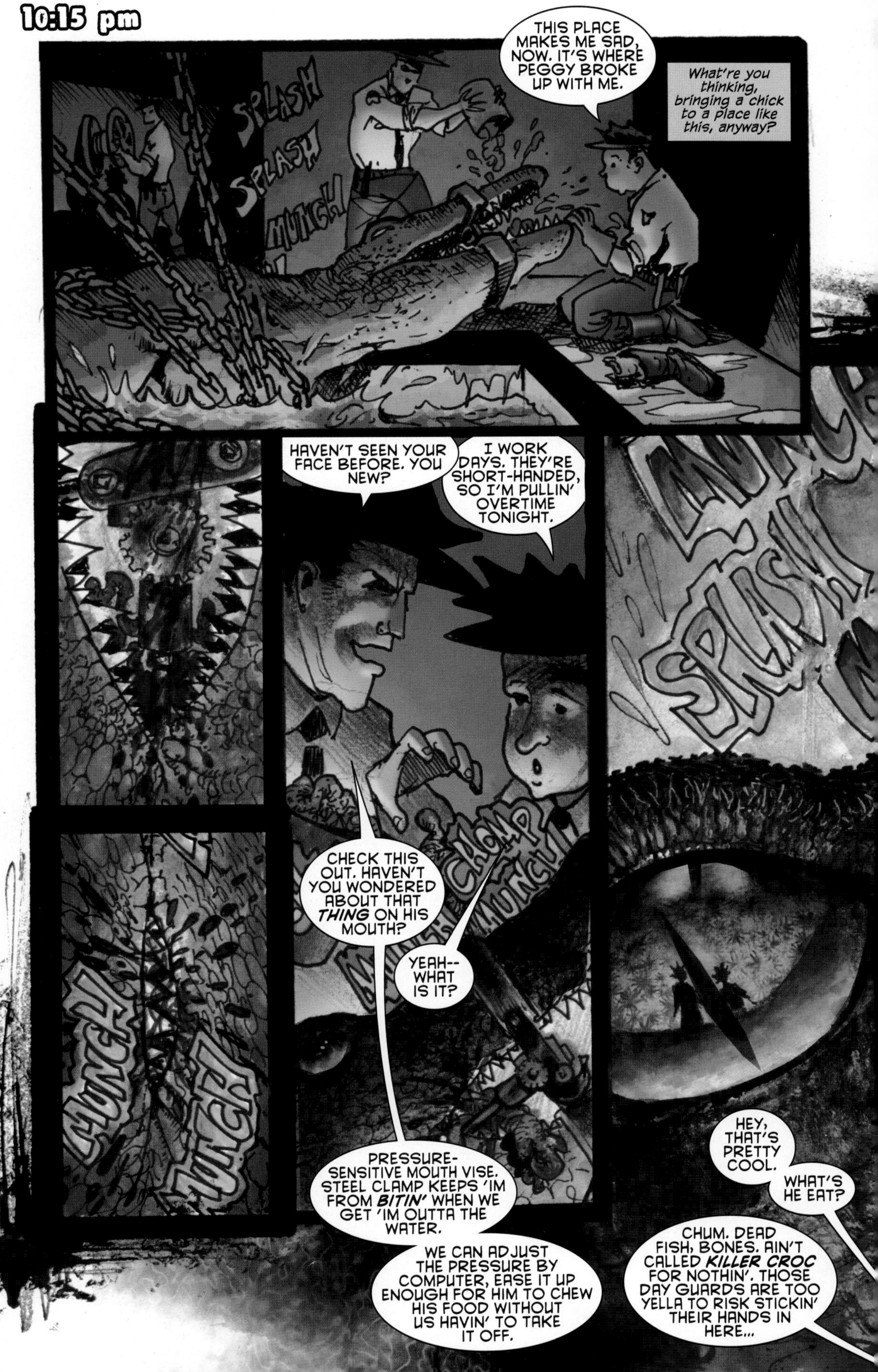
10:15 pm
THIS PLACE MAKES ME SAD, NOW. IT'S WHERE PEGGY BROKE UP WITH ME.
What're you thinking, bringing a chick to a place like this, anyway?
SPLASH
SPLASH
MUNCH
HAVEN'T SEEN YOUR FACE BEFORE. YOU NEW?
I WORK DAYS. THEY'RE SHORT-HANDED, SO I'M PULLIN' OVERTIME TONIGHT.
SPLASH
CHECK THIS OUT. HAVEN'T YOU WONDERED ABOUT THAT *THING* ON HIS MOUTH?
YEAH-- WHAT IS IT?
CLAMP
MUNCH
CHUNCH
PRESSURE-SENSITIVE MOUTH VISE. STEEL CLAMP KEEPS 'IM FROM *BITIN'* WHEN WE GET 'IM OUTTA THE WATER.
WE CAN ADJUST THE PRESSURE BY COMPUTER, EASE IT UP ENOUGH FOR HIM TO CHEW HIS FOOD WITHOUT US HAVIN' TO TAKE IT OFF.
HEY, THAT'S PRETTY COOL.
WHAT'S HE EAT?
CHUM. DEAD FISH, BONES. AIN'T CALLED *KILLER CROC* FOR NOTHIN'. THOSE DAY GUARDS ARE TOO YELLA TO RISK STICKIN' THEIR HANDS IN HERE...

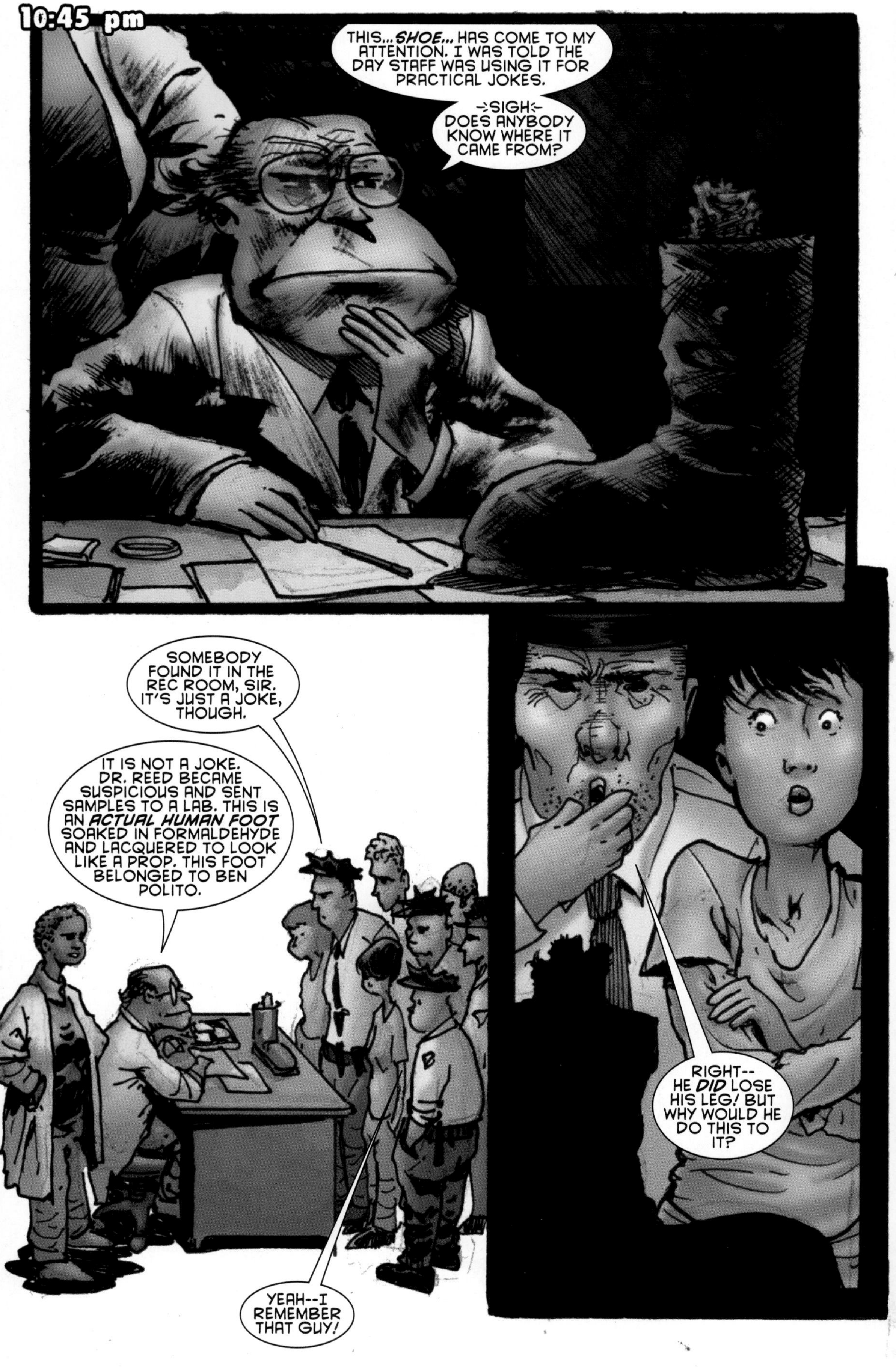

10:45 pm
THIS... SHOE... HAS COME TO MY ATTENTION. I WAS TOLD THE DAY STAFF WAS USING IT FOR PRACTICAL JOKES.
-SIGH- DOES ANYBODY KNOW WHERE IT CAME FROM?
SOMEBODY FOUND IT IN THE REC ROOM, SIR. IT'S JUST A JOKE, THOUGH.
IT IS NOT A JOKE. DR. REED BECAME SUSPICIOUS AND SENT SAMPLES TO A LAB. THIS IS AN ACTUAL HUMAN FOOT SOAKED IN FORMALDEHYDE AND LACQUERED TO LOOK LIKE A PROP. THIS FOOT BELONGED TO BEN POLITO.
YEAH--I REMEMBER THAT GUY!
RIGHT-- HE DID LOSE HIS LEG! BUT WHY WOULD HE DO THIS TO IT?

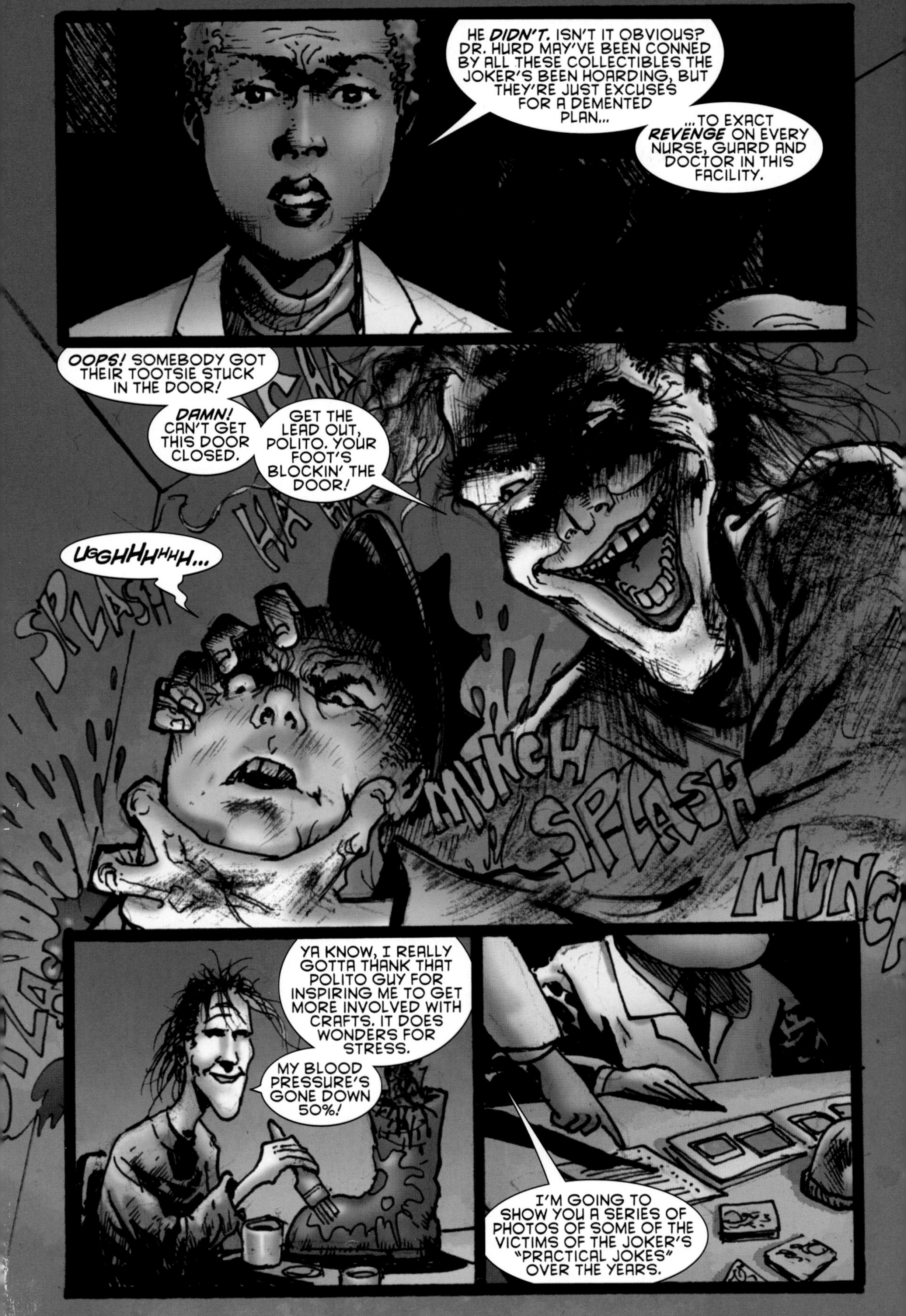
HE *DIDN'T*. ISN'T IT OBVIOUS? DR. HURD MAY'VE BEEN CONNED BY ALL THESE COLLECTIBLES THE JOKER'S BEEN HOARDING, BUT THEY'RE JUST EXCUSES FOR A DEMENTED PLAN...
...TO EXACT *REVENGE* ON EVERY NURSE, GUARD AND DOCTOR IN THIS FACILITY.
*OOPS!* SOMEBODY GOT THEIR TOOTSIE STUCK IN THE DOOR!
*DAMN!* CAN'T GET THIS DOOR CLOSED.
GET THE LEAD OUT, POLITO. YOUR FOOT'S BLOCKIN' THE DOOR!
UGHHHHHH...
SPLASH
MUNCH
SPLASH
MUNCH
YA KNOW, I REALLY GOTTA THANK THAT POLITO GUY FOR INSPIRING ME TO GET MORE INVOLVED WITH CRAFTS. IT DOES WONDERS FOR STRESS.
MY BLOOD PRESSURE'S GONE DOWN 50%!
I'M GOING TO SHOW YOU A SERIES OF PHOTOS OF SOME OF THE VICTIMS OF THE JOKER'S "PRACTICAL JOKES" OVER THE YEARS.

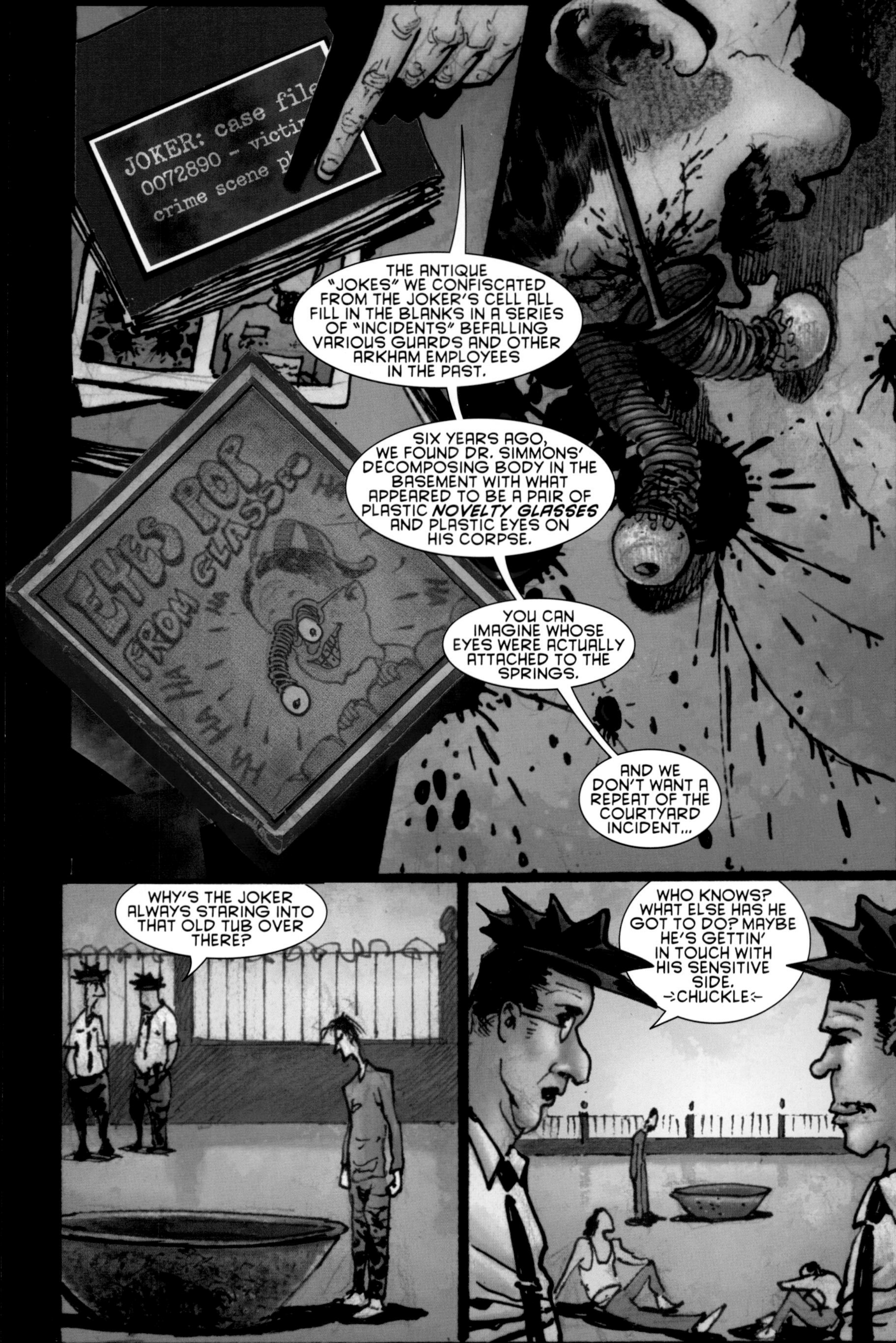
JOKER: case fil
0072890 - victi
crime scene ph
THE ANTIQUE "JOKES" WE CONFISCATED FROM THE JOKER'S CELL ALL FILL IN THE BLANKS IN A SERIES OF "INCIDENTS" BEFALLING VARIOUS GUARDS AND OTHER ARKHAM EMPLOYEES IN THE PAST.
EYES POP FROM GLASSES
SIX YEARS AGO, WE FOUND DR. SIMMONS' DECOMPOSING BODY IN THE BASEMENT WITH WHAT APPEARED TO BE A PAIR OF PLASTIC ***NOVELTY GLASSES*** AND PLASTIC EYES ON HIS CORPSE.
YOU CAN IMAGINE WHOSE EYES WERE ACTUALLY ATTACHED TO THE SPRINGS.
AND WE DON'T WANT A REPEAT OF THE COURTYARD INCIDENT...
WHY'S THE JOKER ALWAYS STARING INTO THAT OLD TUB OVER THERE?
WHO KNOWS? WHAT ELSE HAS HE GOT TO DO? MAYBE HE'S GETTIN' IN TOUCH WITH HIS SENSITIVE SIDE. -CHUCKLE-

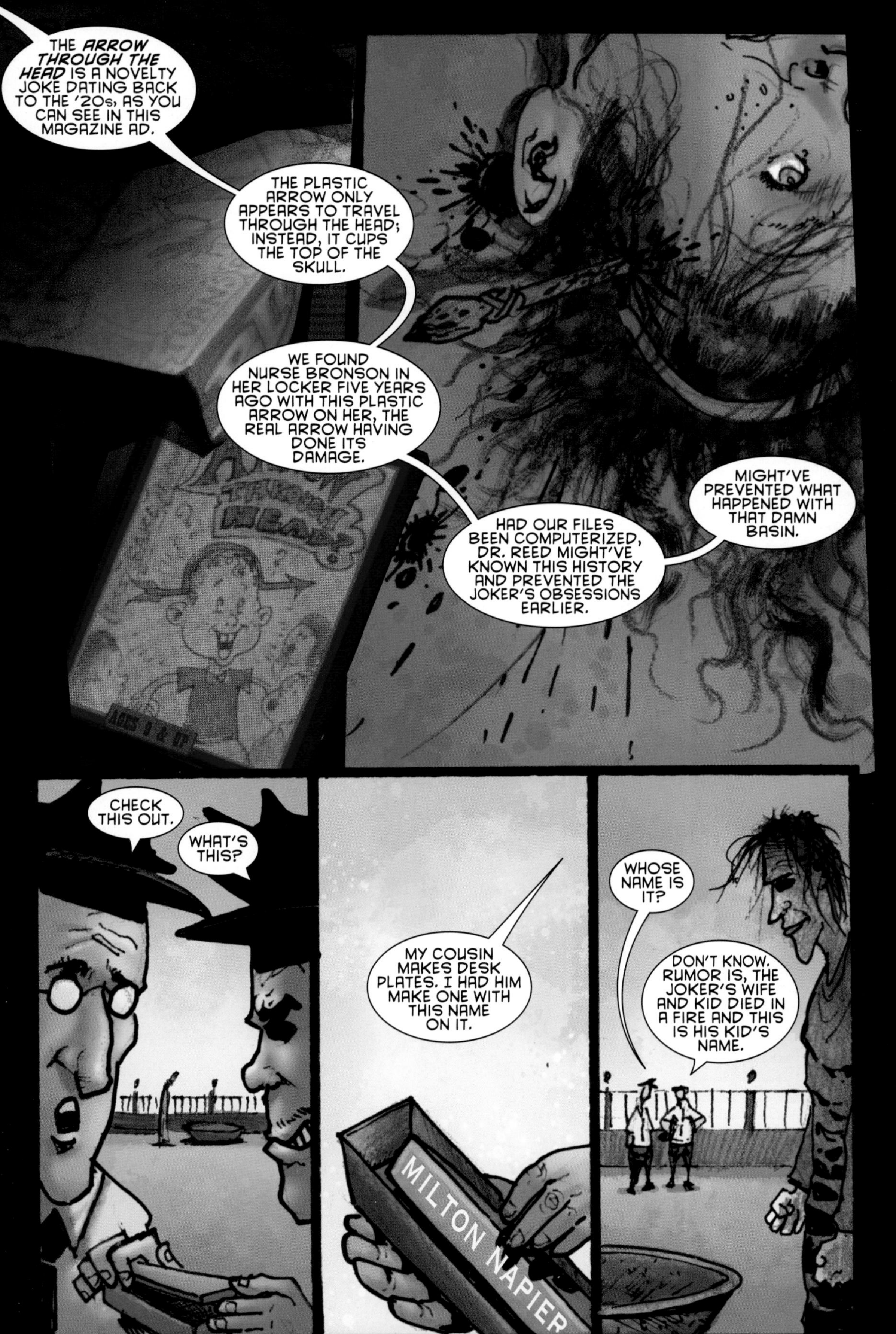
THE ARROW THROUGH THE HEAD IS A NOVELTY JOKE DATING BACK TO THE '20s, AS YOU CAN SEE IN THIS MAGAZINE AD.
THE PLASTIC ARROW ONLY APPEARS TO TRAVEL THROUGH THE HEAD; INSTEAD, IT CUPS THE TOP OF THE SKULL.
WE FOUND NURSE BRONSON IN HER LOCKER FIVE YEARS AGO WITH THIS PLASTIC ARROW ON HER, THE REAL ARROW HAVING DONE ITS DAMAGE.
HAD OUR FILES BEEN COMPUTERIZED, DR. REED MIGHT'VE KNOWN THIS HISTORY AND PREVENTED THE JOKER'S OBSESSIONS EARLIER.
MIGHT'VE PREVENTED WHAT HAPPENED WITH THAT DAMN BASIN.
AGES 8 & UP
CHECK THIS OUT.
WHAT'S THIS?
MY COUSIN MAKES DESK PLATES. I HAD HIM MAKE ONE WITH THIS NAME ON IT.
MILTON NAPIER
WHOSE NAME IS IT?
DON'T KNOW. RUMOR IS, THE JOKER'S WIFE AND KID DIED IN A FIRE AND THIS IS HIS KID'S NAME.

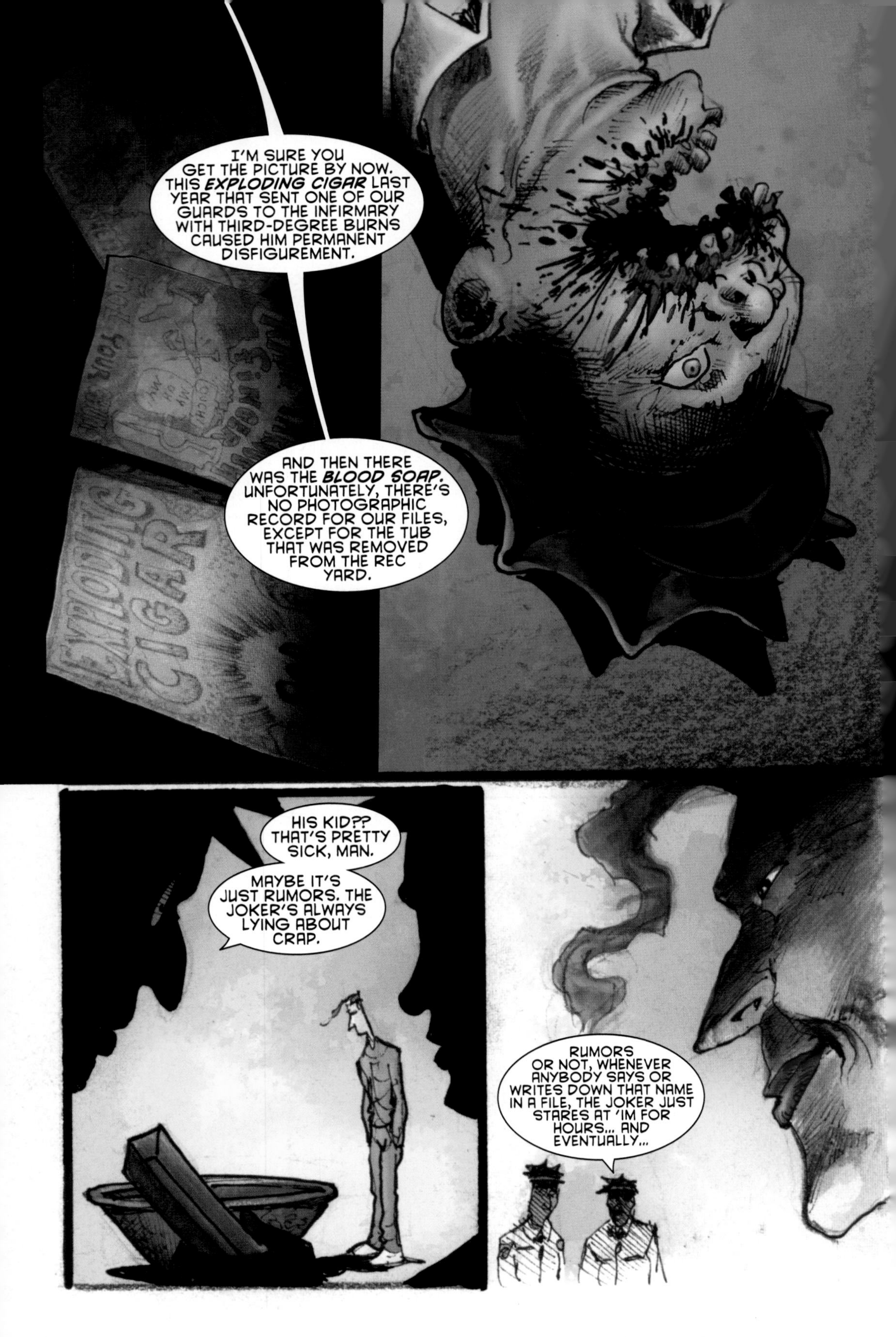

I'M SURE YOU GET THE PICTURE BY NOW. THIS *EXPLODING CIGAR* LAST YEAR THAT SENT ONE OF OUR GUARDS TO THE INFIRMARY WITH THIRD-DEGREE BURNS CAUSED HIM PERMANENT DISFIGUREMENT.
EXPLODING CIGAR
AND THEN THERE WAS THE *BLOOD SOAP.* UNFORTUNATELY, THERE'S NO PHOTOGRAPHIC RECORD FOR OUR FILES, EXCEPT FOR THE TUB THAT WAS REMOVED FROM THE REC YARD.
HIS KID?? THAT'S PRETTY SICK, MAN.
MAYBE IT'S JUST RUMORS. THE JOKER'S ALWAYS LYING ABOUT CRAP.
RUMORS OR NOT, WHENEVER ANYBODY SAYS OR WRITES DOWN THAT NAME IN A FILE, THE JOKER JUST STARES AT 'IM FOR HOURS... AND EVENTUALLY...

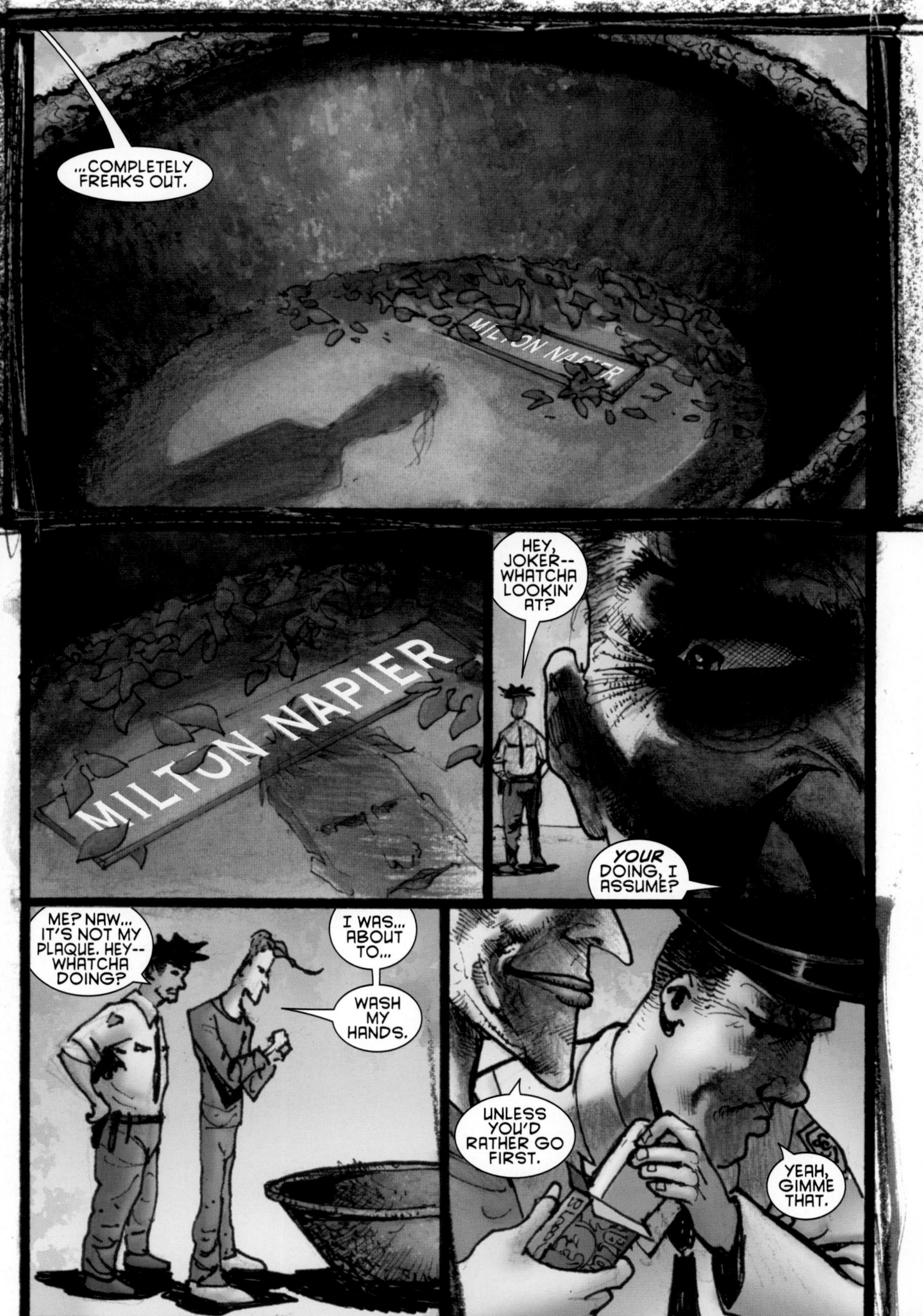
...COMPLETELY FREAKS OUT.
MILTON NAPIER
MILTON NAPIER
HEY, JOKER-- WHATCHA LOOKIN' AT?
YOUR DOING, I ASSUME?
ME? NAW... IT'S NOT MY PLAQUE. HEY-- WHATCHA DOING?
I WAS... ABOUT TO...
WASH MY HANDS.
UNLESS YOU'D RATHER GO FIRST.
YEAH, GIMME THAT.

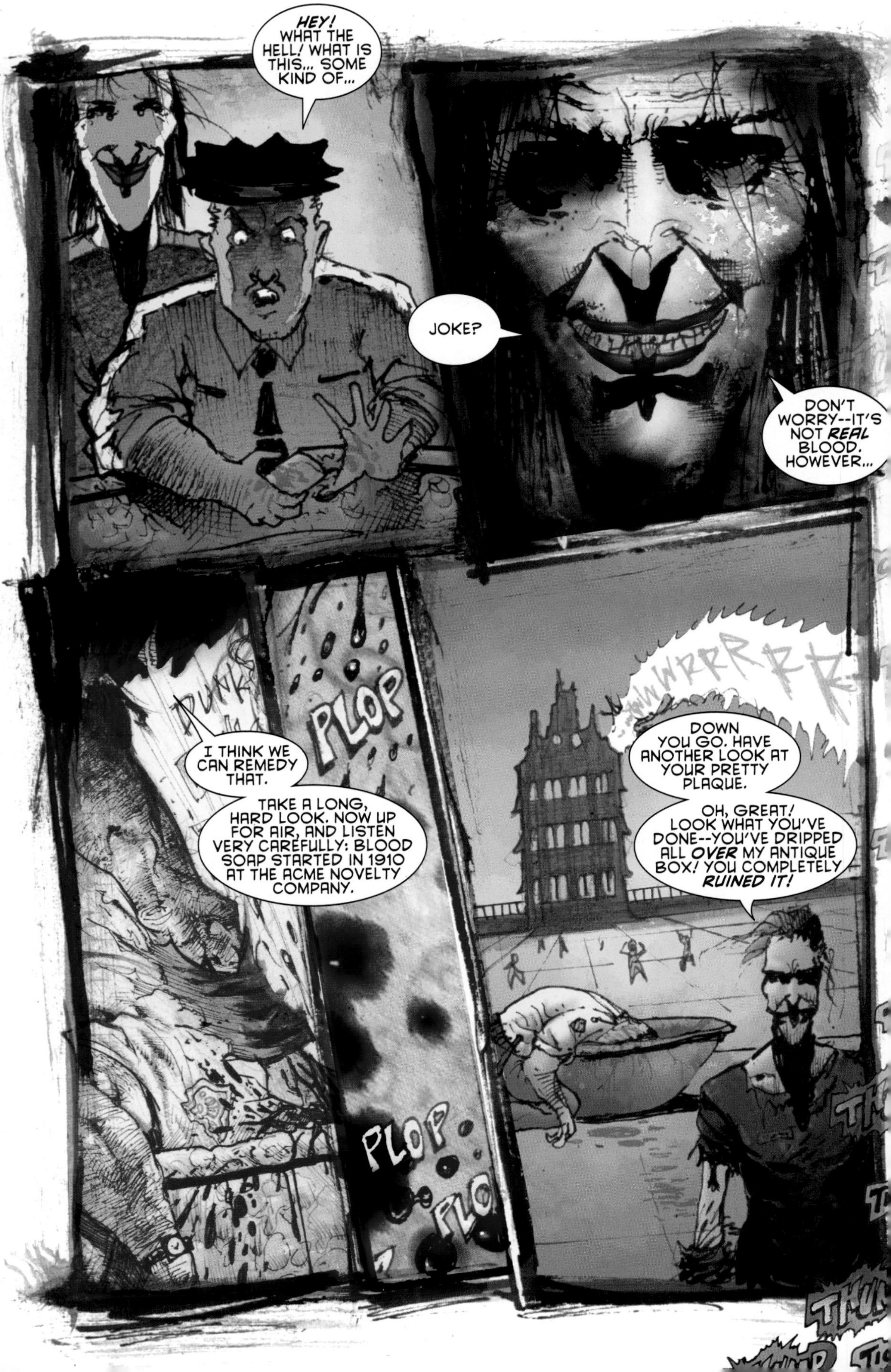
HEY! WHAT THE HELL! WHAT IS THIS... SOME KIND OF...
JOKE?
DON'T WORRY--IT'S NOT REAL BLOOD. HOWEVER...
I THINK WE CAN REMEDY THAT.
TAKE A LONG, HARD LOOK. NOW UP FOR AIR, AND LISTEN VERY CAREFULLY: BLOOD SOAP STARTED IN 1910 AT THE ACME NOVELTY COMPANY.
PLOP
PLOP
WRRRRR
DOWN YOU GO. HAVE ANOTHER LOOK AT YOUR PRETTY PLAQUE.
OH, GREAT! LOOK WHAT YOU'VE DONE--YOU'VE DRIPPED ALL OVER MY ANTIQUE BOX! YOU COMPLETELY RUINED IT!

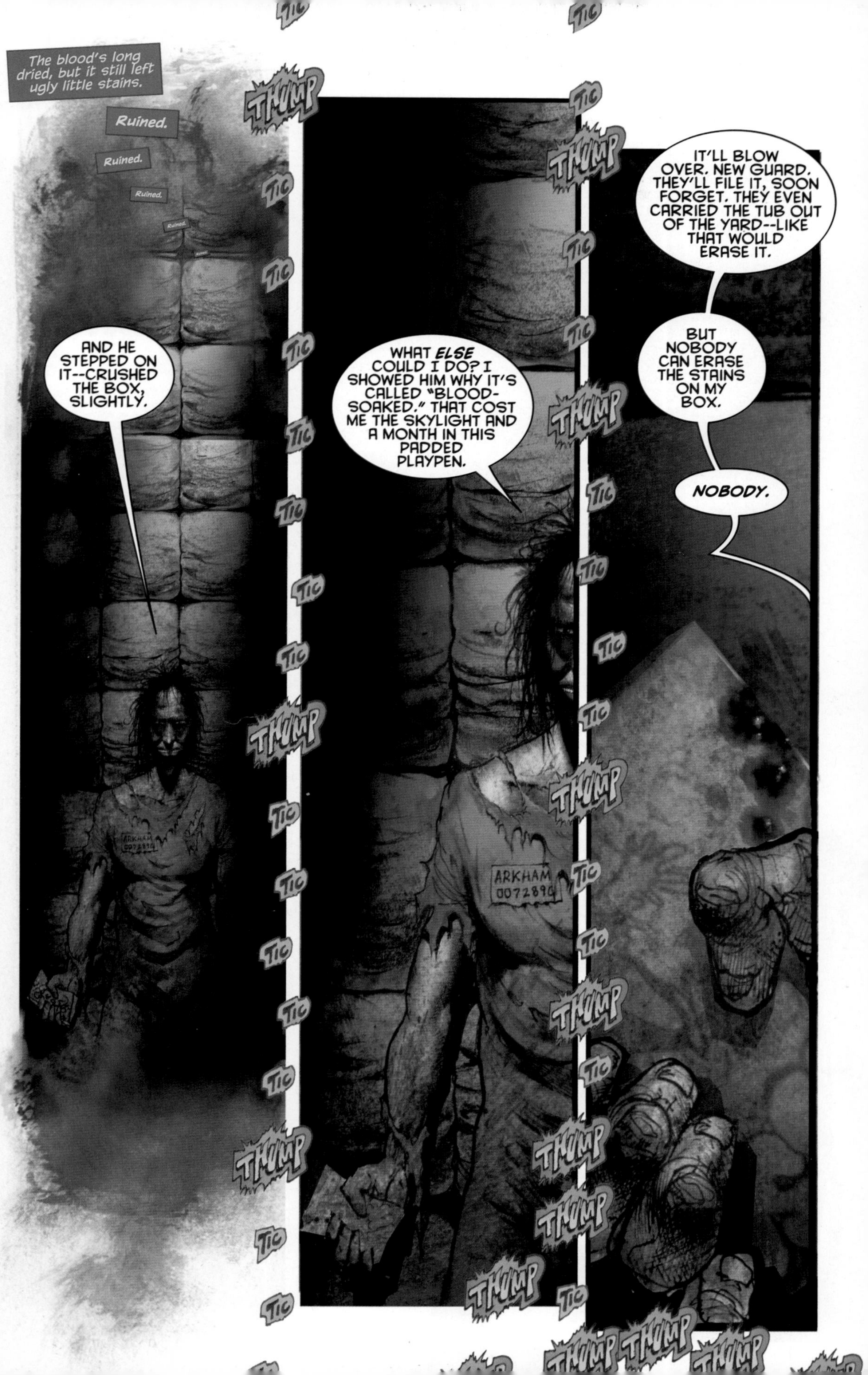
The blood's long dried, but it still left ugly little stains.
Ruined.
Ruined.
Ruined.
Ruined.
THUMP
TIC
AND HE STEPPED ON IT--CRUSHED THE BOX, SLIGHTLY.
WHAT ELSE COULD I DO? I SHOWED HIM WHY IT'S CALLED "BLOOD-SOAKED." THAT COST ME THE SKYLIGHT AND A MONTH IN THIS PADDED PLAYPEN.
THUMP
TIC
IT'LL BLOW OVER. NEW GUARD. THEY'LL FILE IT, SOON FORGET. THEY EVEN CARRIED THE TUB OUT OF THE YARD--LIKE THAT WOULD ERASE IT.
BUT NOBODY CAN ERASE THE STAINS ON MY BOX.
NOBODY.
THUMP
TIC
THUMP THUMP THUMP

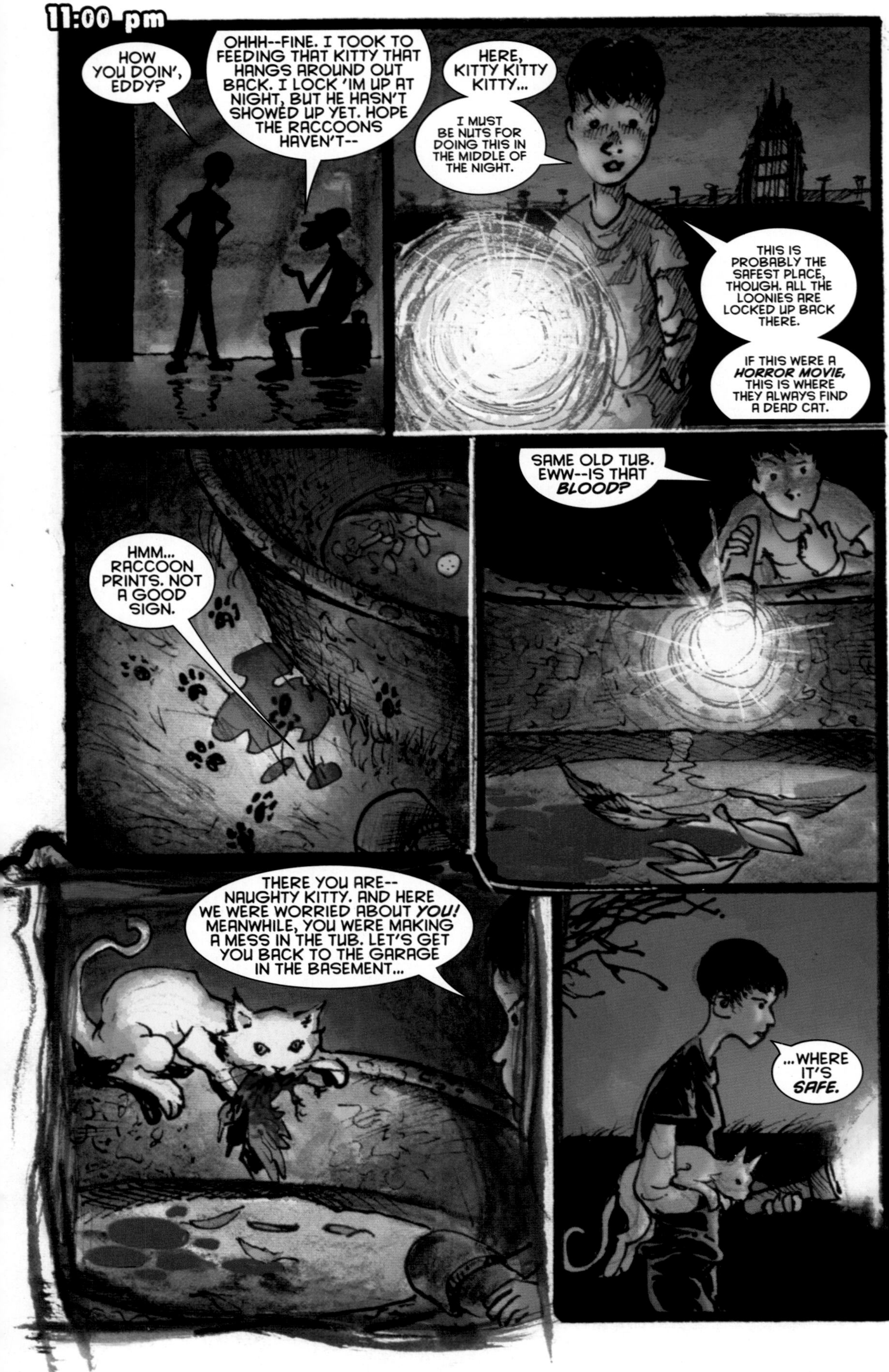
11:00 pm
HOW YOU DOIN', EDDY?
OHHH--FINE. I TOOK TO FEEDING THAT KITTY THAT HANGS AROUND OUT BACK. I LOCK 'IM UP AT NIGHT, BUT HE HASN'T SHOWED UP YET. HOPE THE RACCOONS HAVEN'T--
HERE, KITTY KITTY KITTY...
I MUST BE NUTS FOR DOING THIS IN THE MIDDLE OF THE NIGHT.
THIS IS PROBABLY THE SAFEST PLACE, THOUGH. ALL THE LOONIES ARE LOCKED UP BACK THERE.
IF THIS WERE A HORROR MOVIE, THIS IS WHERE THEY ALWAYS FIND A DEAD CAT.
HMM... RACCOON PRINTS. NOT A GOOD SIGN.
SAME OLD TUB. EWW--IS THAT BLOOD?
THERE YOU ARE--NAUGHTY KITTY. AND HERE WE WERE WORRIED ABOUT YOU! MEANWHILE, YOU WERE MAKING A MESS IN THE TUB. LET'S GET YOU BACK TO THE GARAGE IN THE BASEMENT...
...WHERE IT'S SAFE.

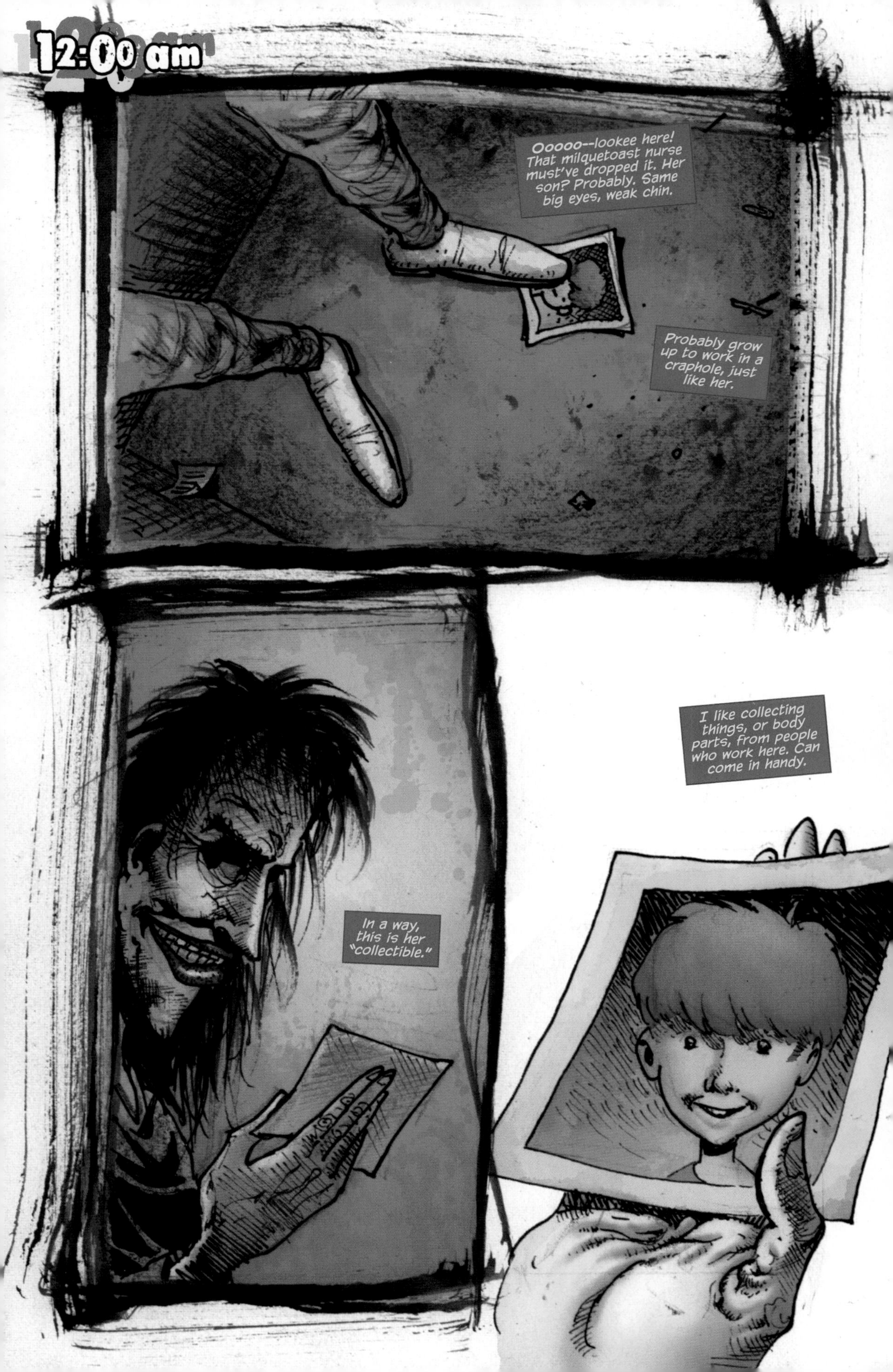
12:00 am
Ooooo--lookee here! That milquetoast nurse must've dropped it. Her son? Probably. Same big eyes, weak chin.
Probably grow up to work in a craphole, just like her.
I like collecting things, or body parts, from people who work here. Can come in handy.
In a way, this is her "collectible."

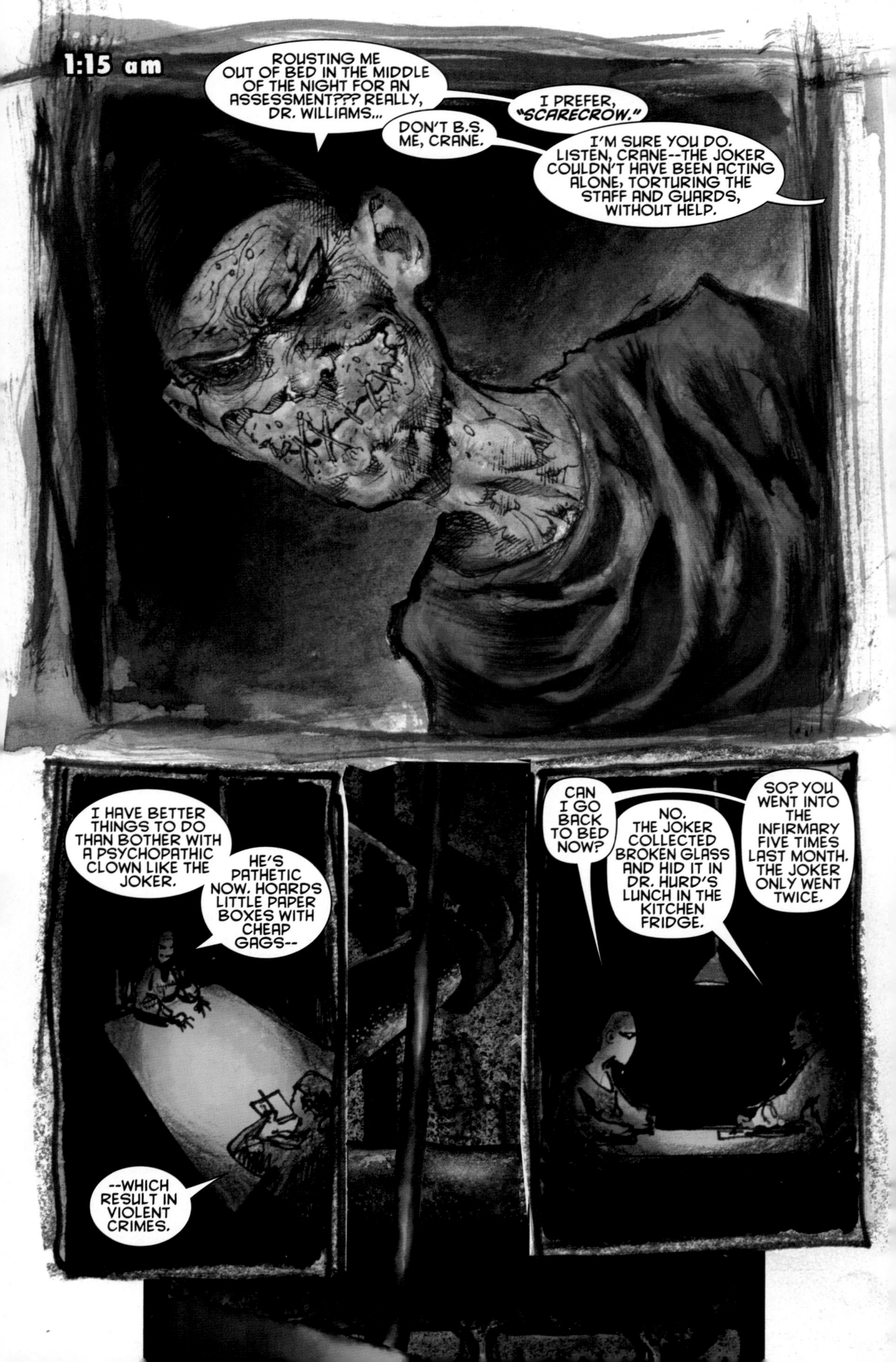
1:15 am
ROUSTING ME OUT OF BED IN THE MIDDLE OF THE NIGHT FOR AN ASSESSMENT??? REALLY, DR. WILLIAMS...
I PREFER, "SCARECROW."
DON'T B.S. ME, CRANE.
I'M SURE YOU DO. LISTEN, CRANE--THE JOKER COULDN'T HAVE BEEN ACTING ALONE, TORTURING THE STAFF AND GUARDS, WITHOUT HELP.
I HAVE BETTER THINGS TO DO THAN BOTHER WITH A PSYCHOPATHIC CLOWN LIKE THE JOKER.
HE'S PATHETIC NOW. HOARDS LITTLE PAPER BOXES WITH CHEAP GAGS--
--WHICH RESULT IN VIOLENT CRIMES.
CAN I GO BACK TO BED NOW?
NO. THE JOKER COLLECTED BROKEN GLASS AND HID IT IN DR. HURD'S LUNCH IN THE KITCHEN FRIDGE.
SO? YOU WENT INTO THE INFIRMARY FIVE TIMES LAST MONTH. THE JOKER ONLY WENT TWICE.

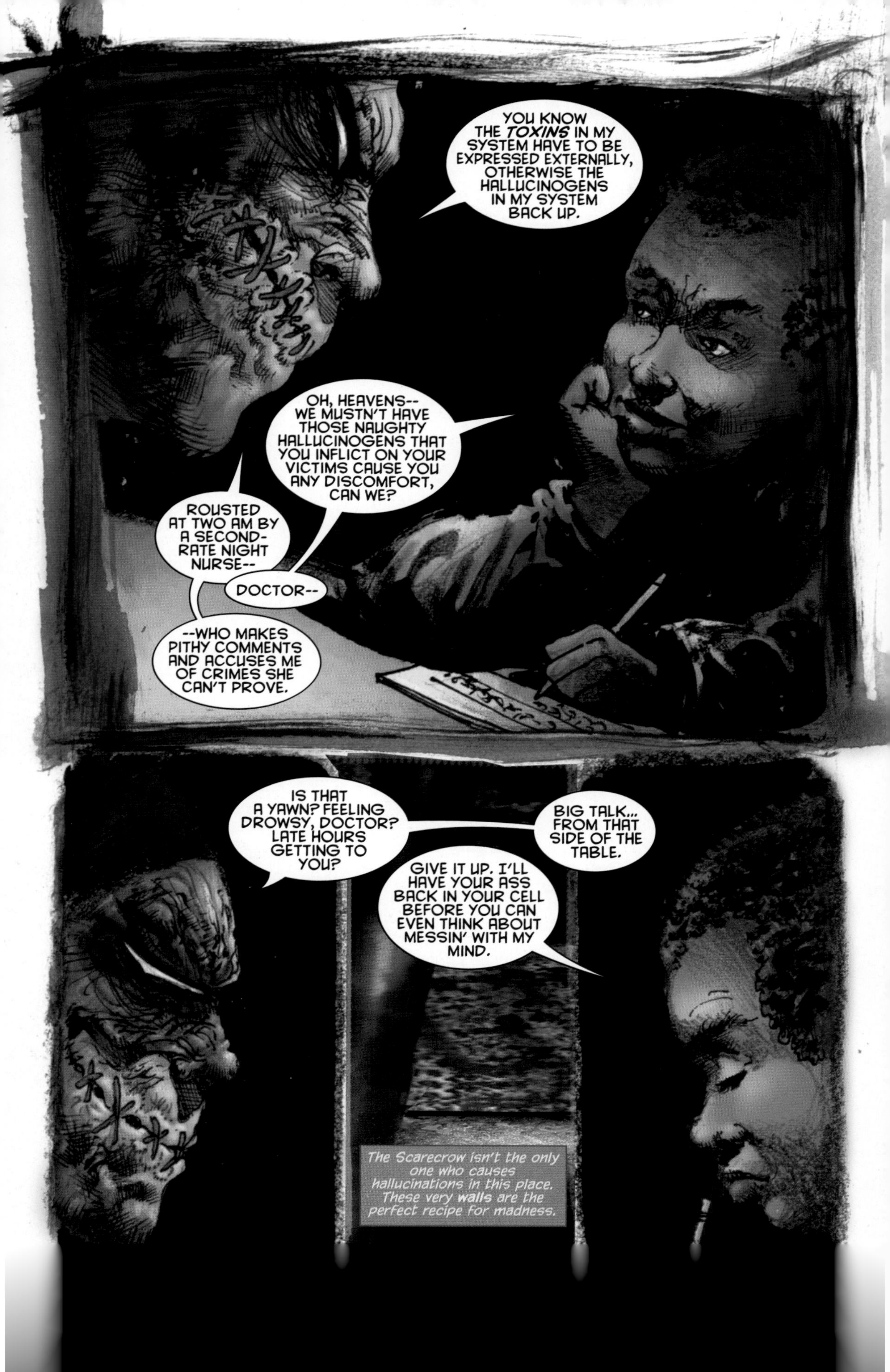
YOU KNOW THE *TOXINS* IN MY SYSTEM HAVE TO BE EXPRESSED EXTERNALLY, OTHERWISE THE HALLUCINOGENS IN MY SYSTEM BACK UP.
OH, HEAVENS-- WE MUSTN'T HAVE THOSE NAUGHTY HALLUCINOGENS THAT YOU INFLICT ON YOUR VICTIMS CAUSE YOU ANY DISCOMFORT, CAN WE?
ROUSTED AT TWO AM BY A SECOND-RATE NIGHT NURSE--
DOCTOR--
--WHO MAKES PITHY COMMENTS AND ACCUSES ME OF CRIMES SHE CAN'T PROVE.
IS THAT A YAWN? FEELING DROWSY, DOCTOR? LATE HOURS GETTING TO YOU?
BIG TALK... FROM THAT SIDE OF THE TABLE.
GIVE IT UP. I'LL HAVE YOUR ASS BACK IN YOUR CELL BEFORE YOU CAN EVEN THINK ABOUT MESSIN' WITH MY MIND.
The Scarecrow isn't the only one who causes hallucinations in this place. These very **walls** are the perfect recipe for madness.

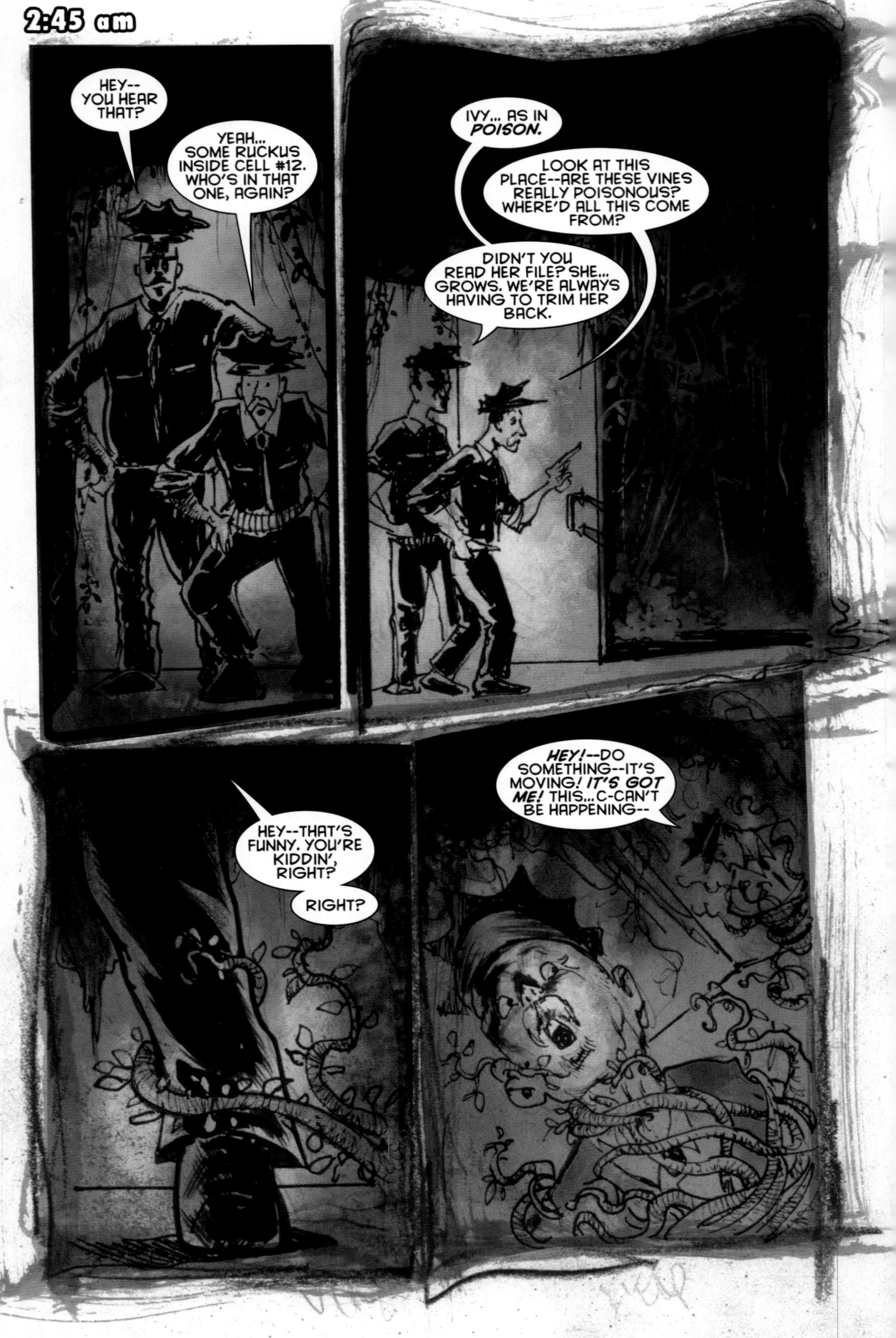
2:45 am
HEY-- YOU HEAR THAT?
YEAH... SOME RUCKUS INSIDE CELL #12. WHO'S IN THAT ONE, AGAIN?
IVY... AS IN *POISON.*
LOOK AT THIS PLACE--ARE THESE VINES REALLY POISONOUS? WHERE'D ALL THIS COME FROM?
DIDN'T YOU READ HER FILE? SHE... GROWS. WE'RE ALWAYS HAVING TO TRIM HER BACK.
HEY--THAT'S FUNNY. YOU'RE KIDDIN', RIGHT?
RIGHT?
*HEY!*--DO SOMETHING--IT'S MOVING! *IT'S GOT ME!* THIS...C-CAN'T BE HAPPENING--

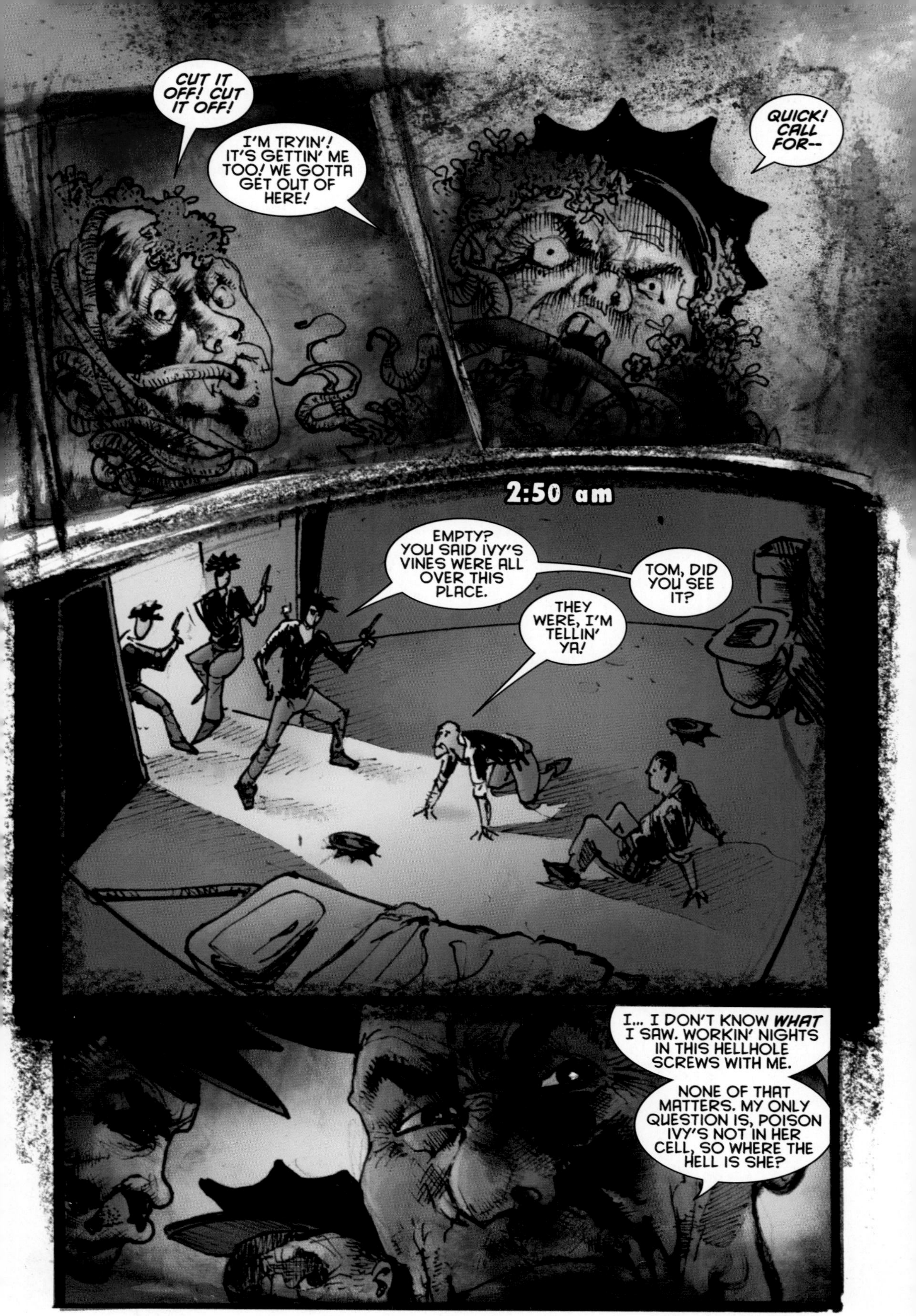

CUT IT OFF! CUT IT OFF!
I'M TRYIN'! IT'S GETTIN' ME TOO! WE GOTTA GET OUT OF HERE!
QUICK! CALL FOR--
2:50 am
EMPTY? YOU SAID IVY'S VINES WERE ALL OVER THIS PLACE.
TOM, DID YOU SEE IT?
THEY WERE, I'M TELLIN' YA!
I... I DON'T KNOW WHAT I SAW. WORKIN' NIGHTS IN THIS HELLHOLE SCREWS WITH ME.
NONE OF THAT MATTERS. MY ONLY QUESTION IS, POISON IVY'S NOT IN HER CELL, SO WHERE THE HELL IS SHE?

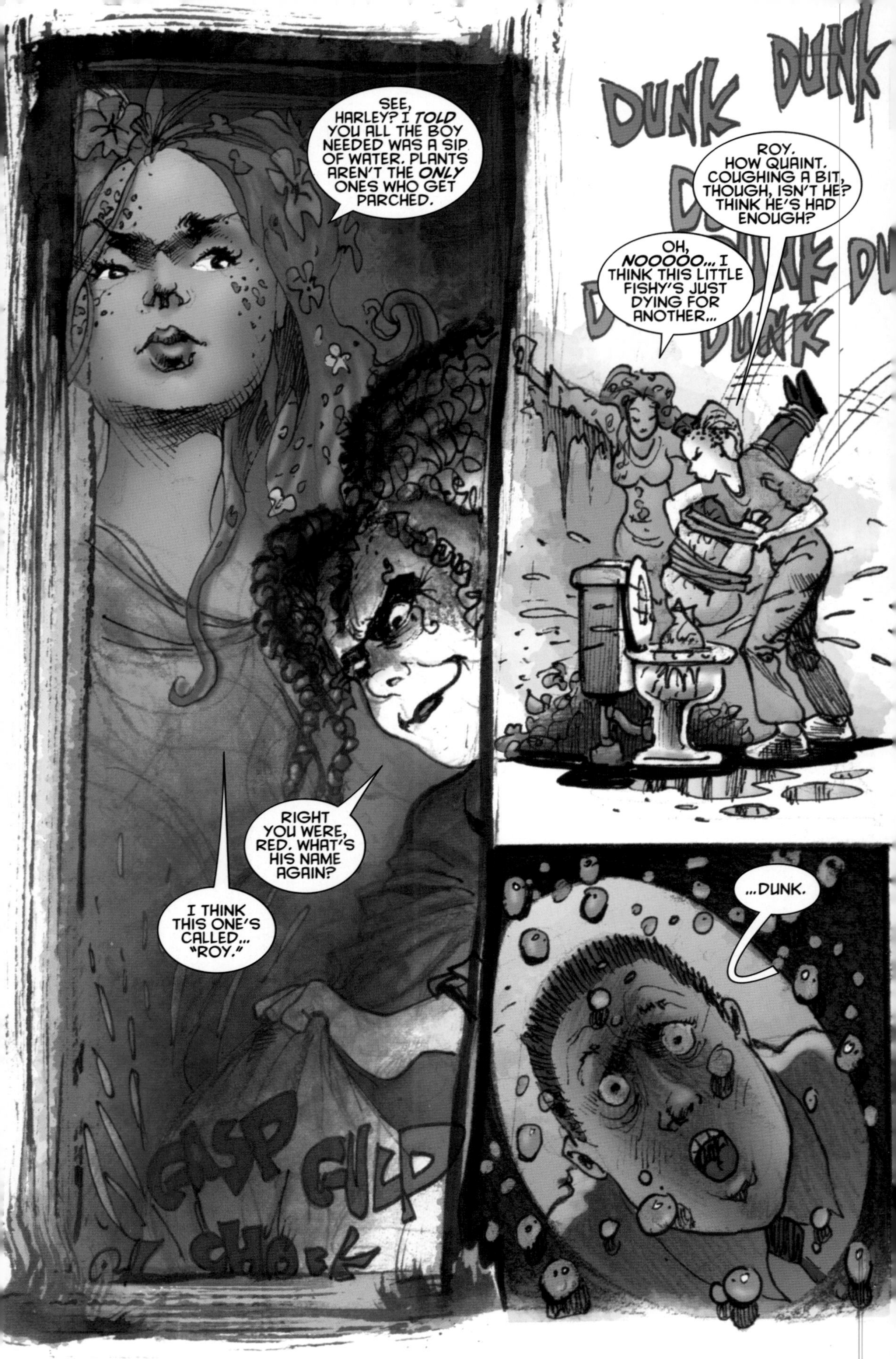
SEE, HARLEY? I TOLD YOU ALL THE BOY NEEDED WAS A SIP OF WATER. PLANTS AREN'T THE ONLY ONES WHO GET PARCHED.
RIGHT YOU WERE, RED. WHAT'S HIS NAME AGAIN?
I THINK THIS ONE'S CALLED... "ROY."
GASP GULP
CHOKE
DUNK DUNK
DUNK
DUNK
ROY. HOW QUAINT. COUGHING A BIT, THOUGH, ISN'T HE? THINK HE'S HAD ENOUGH?
OH, NOOOOO... I THINK THIS LITTLE FISHY'S JUST DYING FOR ANOTHER...
...DUNK.

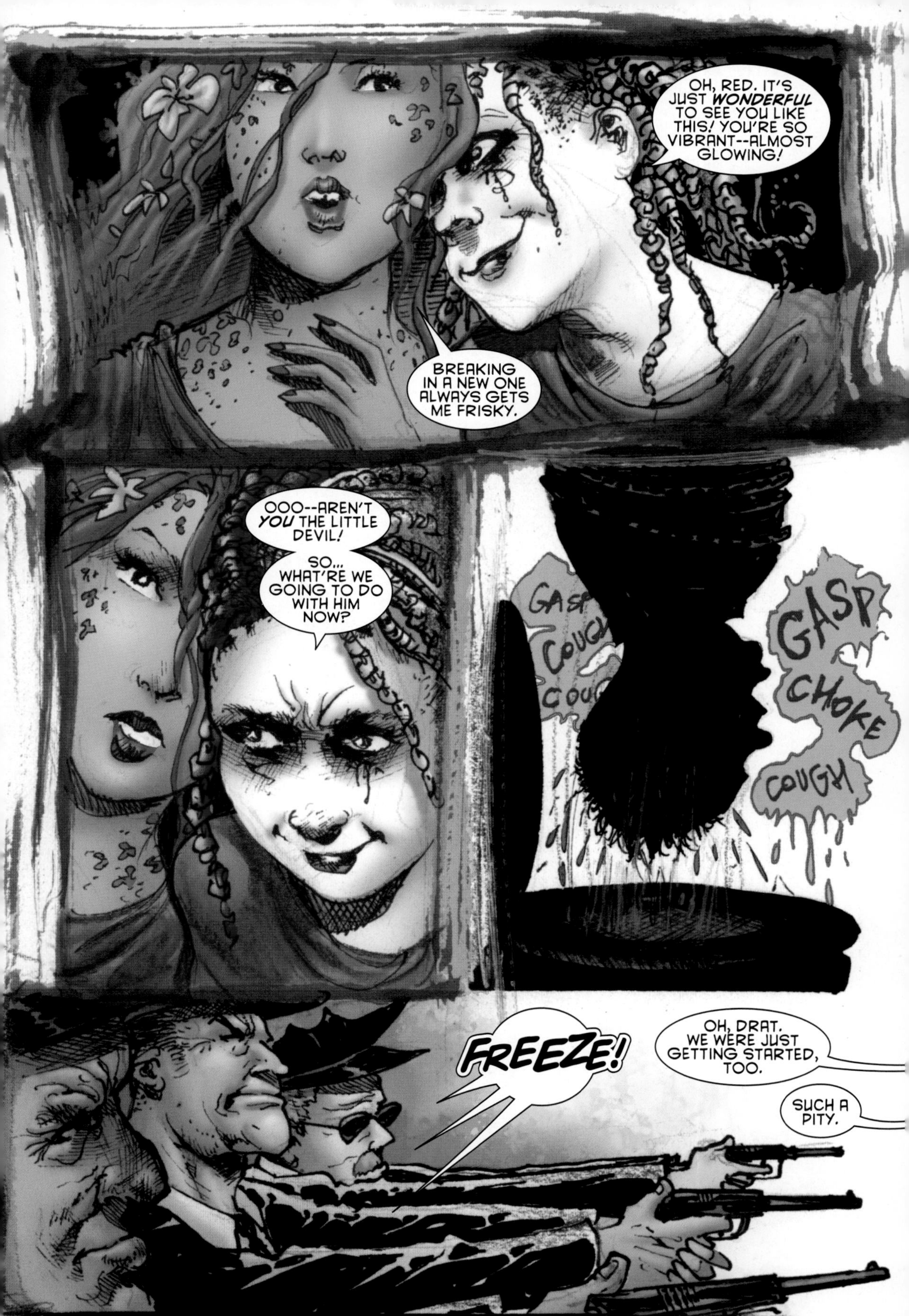
OH, RED. IT'S JUST WONDERFUL TO SEE YOU LIKE THIS! YOU'RE SO VIBRANT--ALMOST GLOWING!
BREAKING IN A NEW ONE ALWAYS GETS ME FRISKY.
OOO--AREN'T YOU THE LITTLE DEVIL!
SO... WHAT'RE WE GOING TO DO WITH HIM NOW?
GASP COUGH COUGH
GASP CHOKE COUGH
FREEZE!
OH, DRAT. WE WERE JUST GETTING STARTED, TOO.
SUCH A PITY.

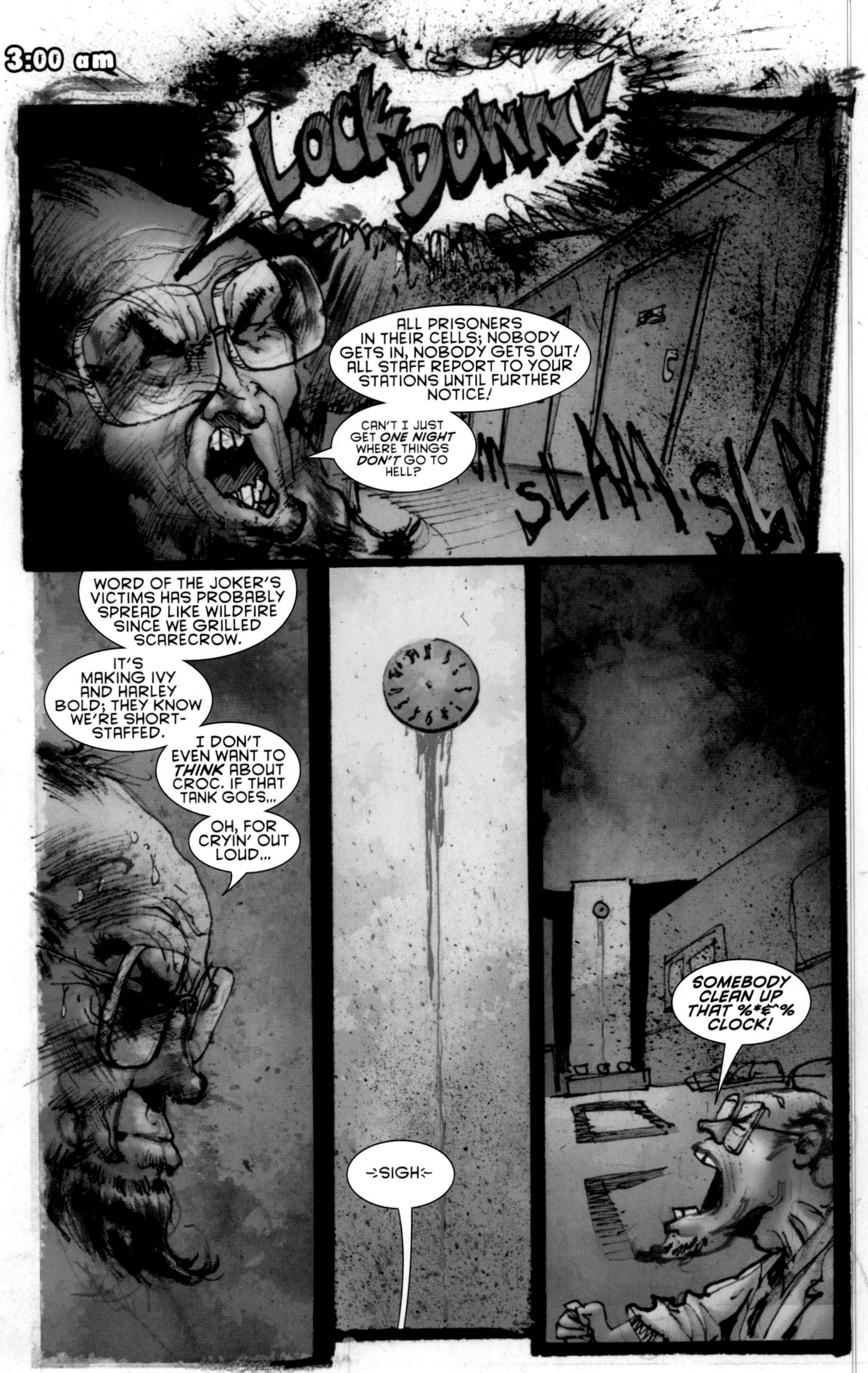

3:00 am
LOCKDOWN!
ALL PRISONERS IN THEIR CELLS; NOBODY GETS IN, NOBODY GETS OUT! ALL STAFF REPORT TO YOUR STATIONS UNTIL FURTHER NOTICE!
CAN'T I JUST GET *ONE NIGHT* WHERE THINGS *DON'T* GO TO HELL?
SLAM SLAM
WORD OF THE JOKER'S VICTIMS HAS PROBABLY SPREAD LIKE WILDFIRE SINCE WE GRILLED SCARECROW.
IT'S MAKING IVY AND HARLEY BOLD; THEY KNOW WE'RE SHORT-STAFFED.
I DON'T EVEN WANT TO *THINK* ABOUT CROC. IF THAT TANK GOES...
OH, FOR CRYIN' OUT LOUD...
SIGH
SOMEBODY CLEAN UP THAT %*£^% CLOCK!

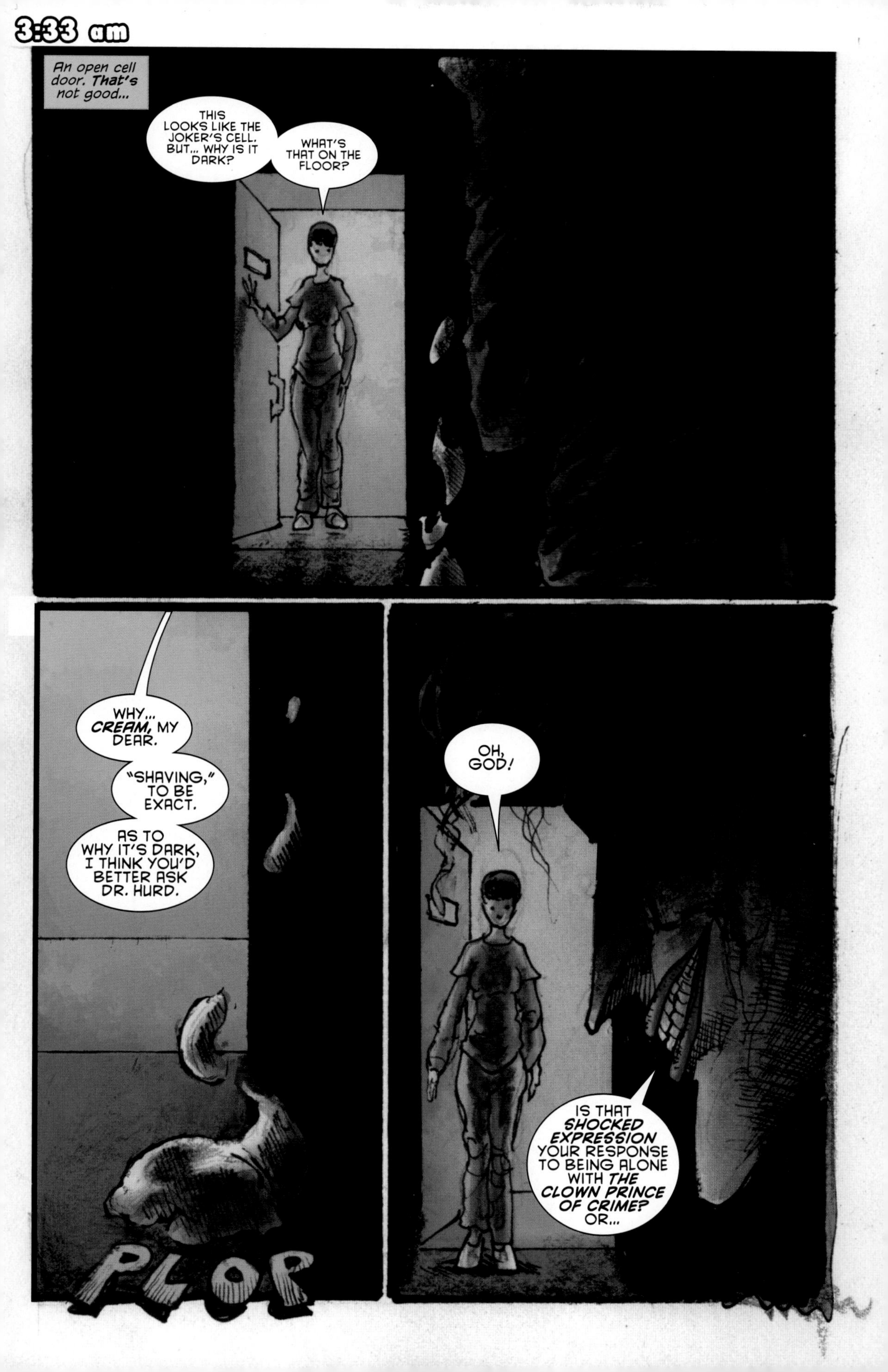
3:33 am
An open cell door. That's not good...
THIS LOOKS LIKE THE JOKER'S CELL. BUT... WHY IS IT DARK?
WHAT'S THAT ON THE FLOOR?
WHY... CREAM, MY DEAR.
"SHAVING," TO BE EXACT.
AS TO WHY IT'S DARK, I THINK YOU'D BETTER ASK DR. HURD.
PLOP
OH, GOD!
IS THAT SHOCKED EXPRESSION YOUR RESPONSE TO BEING ALONE WITH THE CLOWN PRINCE OF CRIME? OR...

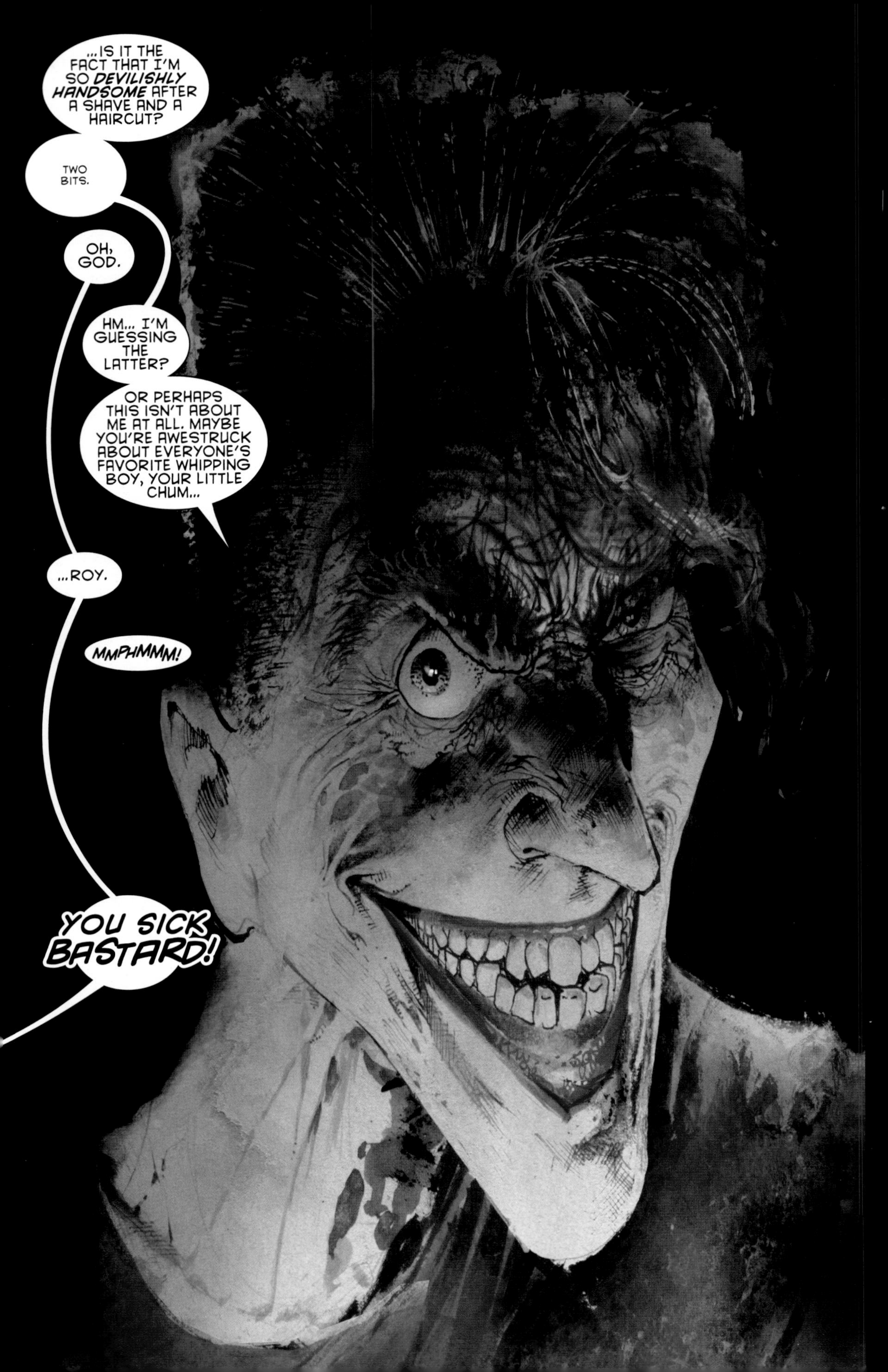
...IS IT THE FACT THAT I'M SO DEVILISHLY HANDSOME AFTER A SHAVE AND A HAIRCUT?
TWO BITS.
OH, GOD.
HM... I'M GUESSING THE LATTER?
OR PERHAPS THIS ISN'T ABOUT ME AT ALL. MAYBE YOU'RE AWESTRUCK ABOUT EVERYONE'S FAVORITE WHIPPING BOY, YOUR LITTLE CHUM...
...ROY.
MMPHMMM!
YOU SICK BASTARD!

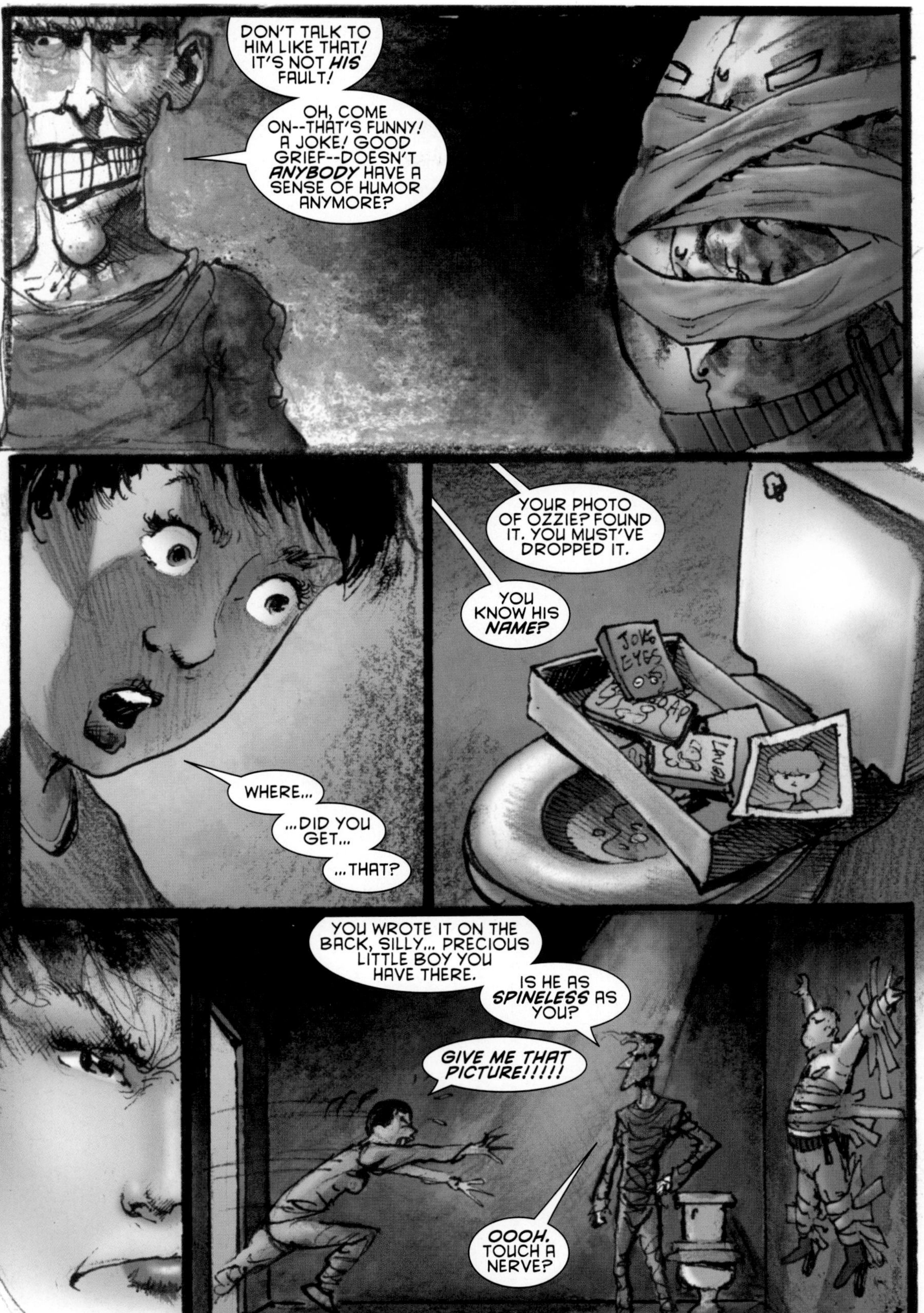
DON'T TALK TO HIM LIKE THAT! IT'S NOT *HIS* FAULT!
OH, COME ON--THAT'S FUNNY! A JOKE! GOOD GRIEF--DOESN'T *ANYBODY* HAVE A SENSE OF HUMOR ANYMORE?
WHERE...
...DID YOU GET...
...THAT?
YOUR PHOTO OF OZZIE? FOUND IT. YOU MUST'VE DROPPED IT.
YOU KNOW HIS *NAME?*
YOU WROTE IT ON THE BACK, SILLY... PRECIOUS LITTLE BOY YOU HAVE THERE.
IS HE AS *SPINELESS* AS YOU?
*GIVE ME THAT PICTURE!!!!!*
*OOOH.* TOUCH A NERVE?

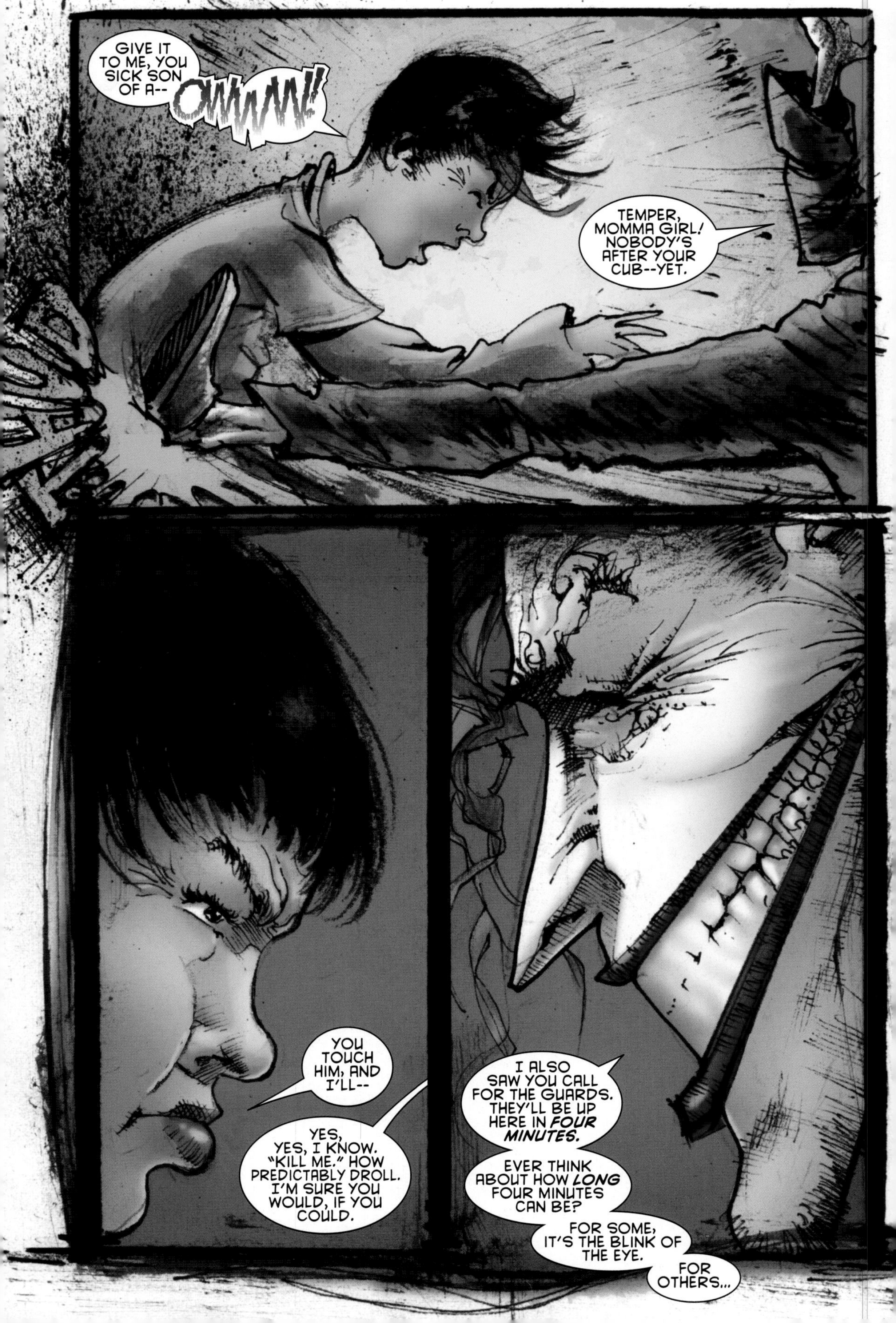

GIVE IT TO ME, YOU SICK SON OF A--
OWWW!!
TEMPER, MOMMA GIRL! NOBODY'S AFTER YOUR CUB--YET.
YOU TOUCH HIM, AND I'LL--
YES, YES, I KNOW. "KILL ME." HOW PREDICTABLY DROLL. I'M SURE YOU WOULD, IF YOU COULD.
I ALSO SAW YOU CALL FOR THE GUARDS. THEY'LL BE UP HERE IN *FOUR MINUTES.*
EVER THINK ABOUT HOW *LONG* FOUR MINUTES CAN BE?
FOR SOME, IT'S THE BLINK OF THE EYE.
FOR OTHERS...

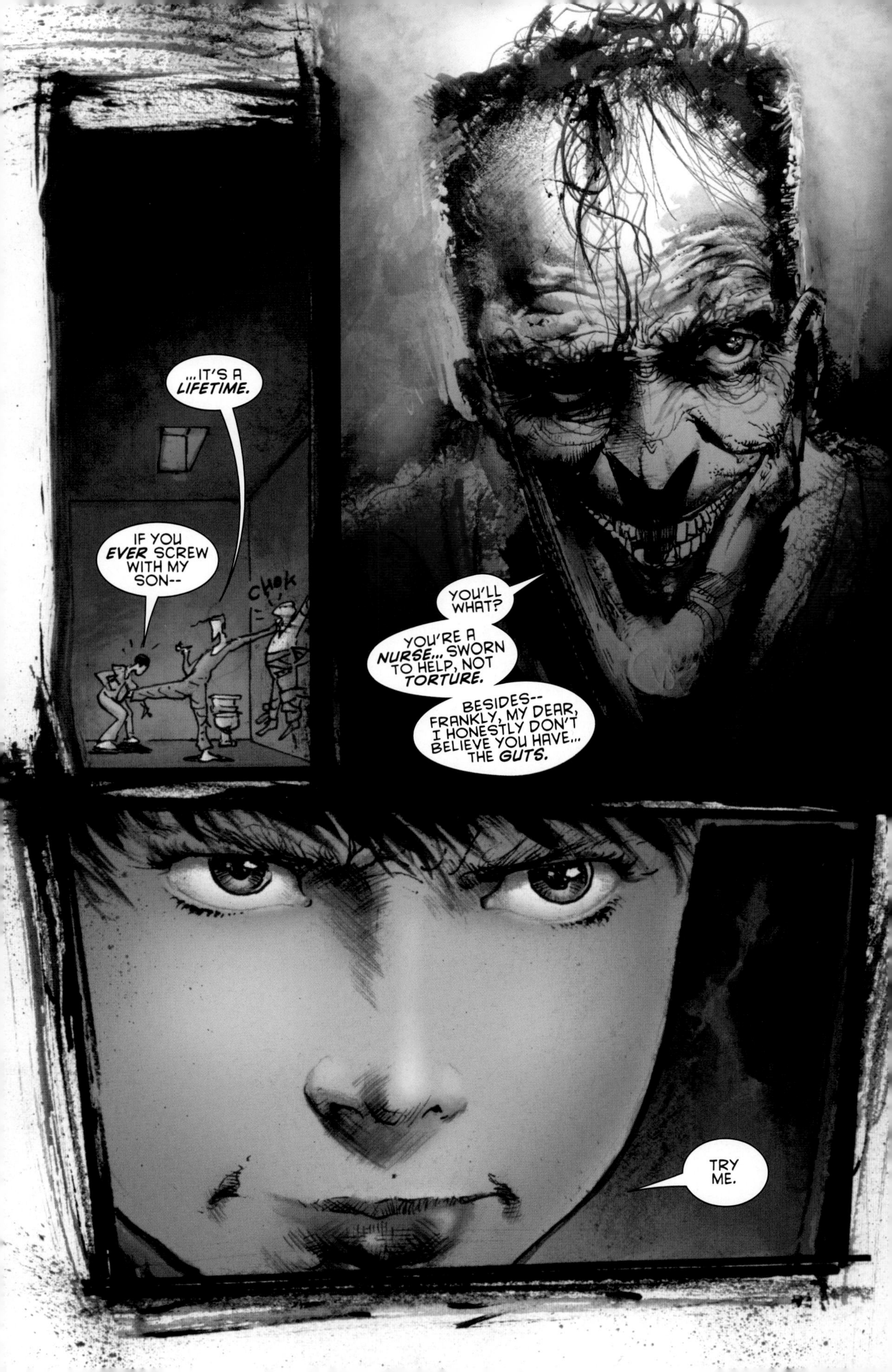
IF YOU EVER SCREW WITH MY SON--
...IT'S A LIFETIME.
CHOK
YOU'LL WHAT?
YOU'RE A NURSE... SWORN TO HELP, NOT TORTURE.
BESIDES-- FRANKLY, MY DEAR, I HONESTLY DON'T BELIEVE YOU HAVE... THE GUTS.
TRY ME.

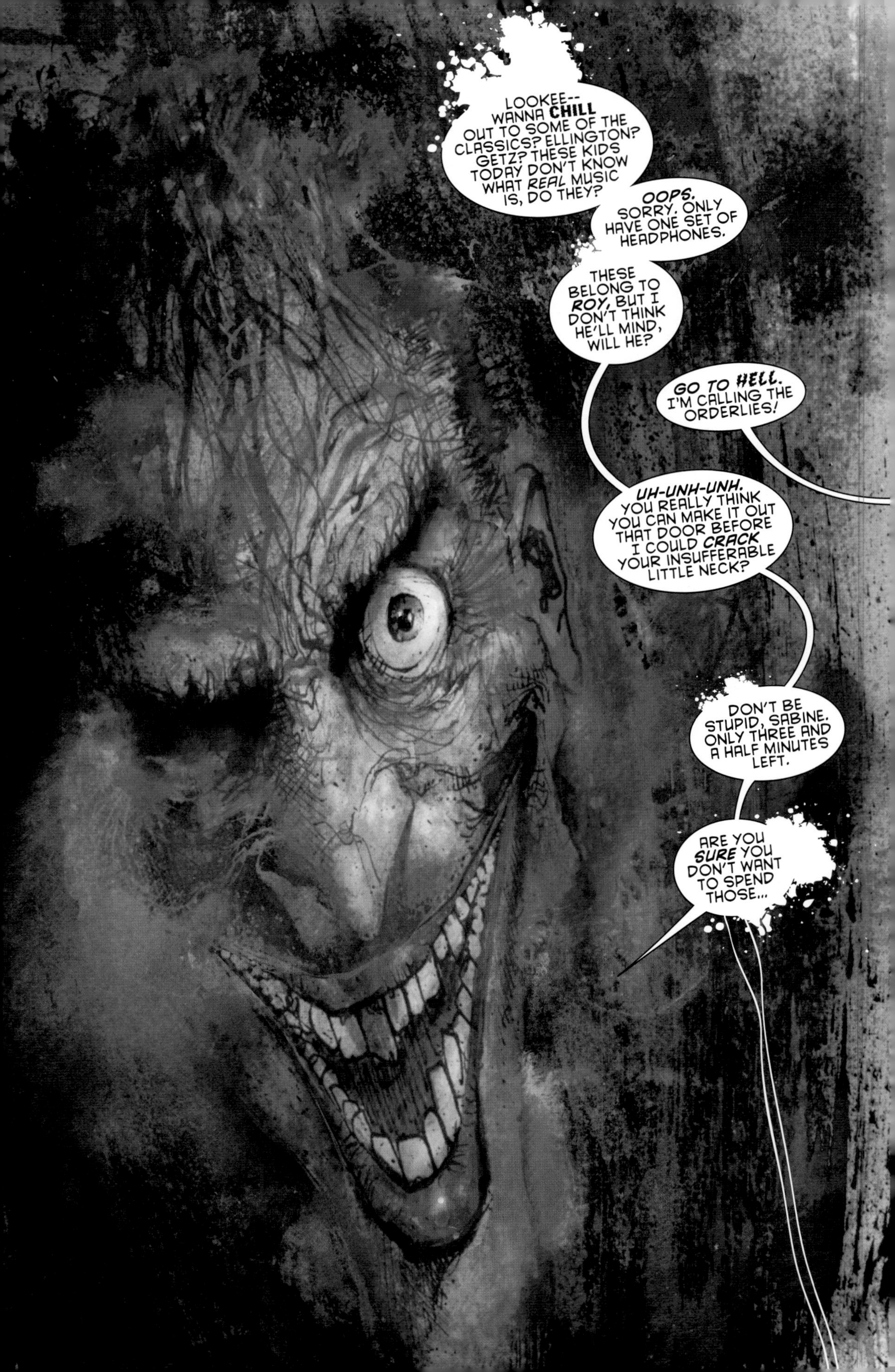
LOOKEE--WANNA CHILL OUT TO SOME OF THE CLASSICS? ELLINGTON? GETZ? THESE KIDS TODAY DON'T KNOW WHAT REAL MUSIC IS, DO THEY?
OOPS. SORRY. ONLY HAVE ONE SET OF HEADPHONES.
THESE BELONG TO ROY, BUT I DON'T THINK HE'LL MIND, WILL HE?
GO TO HELL. I'M CALLING THE ORDERLIES!
UH-UNH-UNH. YOU REALLY THINK YOU CAN MAKE IT OUT THAT DOOR BEFORE I COULD CRACK YOUR INSUFFERABLE LITTLE NECK?
DON'T BE STUPID, SABINE. ONLY THREE AND A HALF MINUTES LEFT.
ARE YOU SURE YOU DON'T WANT TO SPEND THOSE...

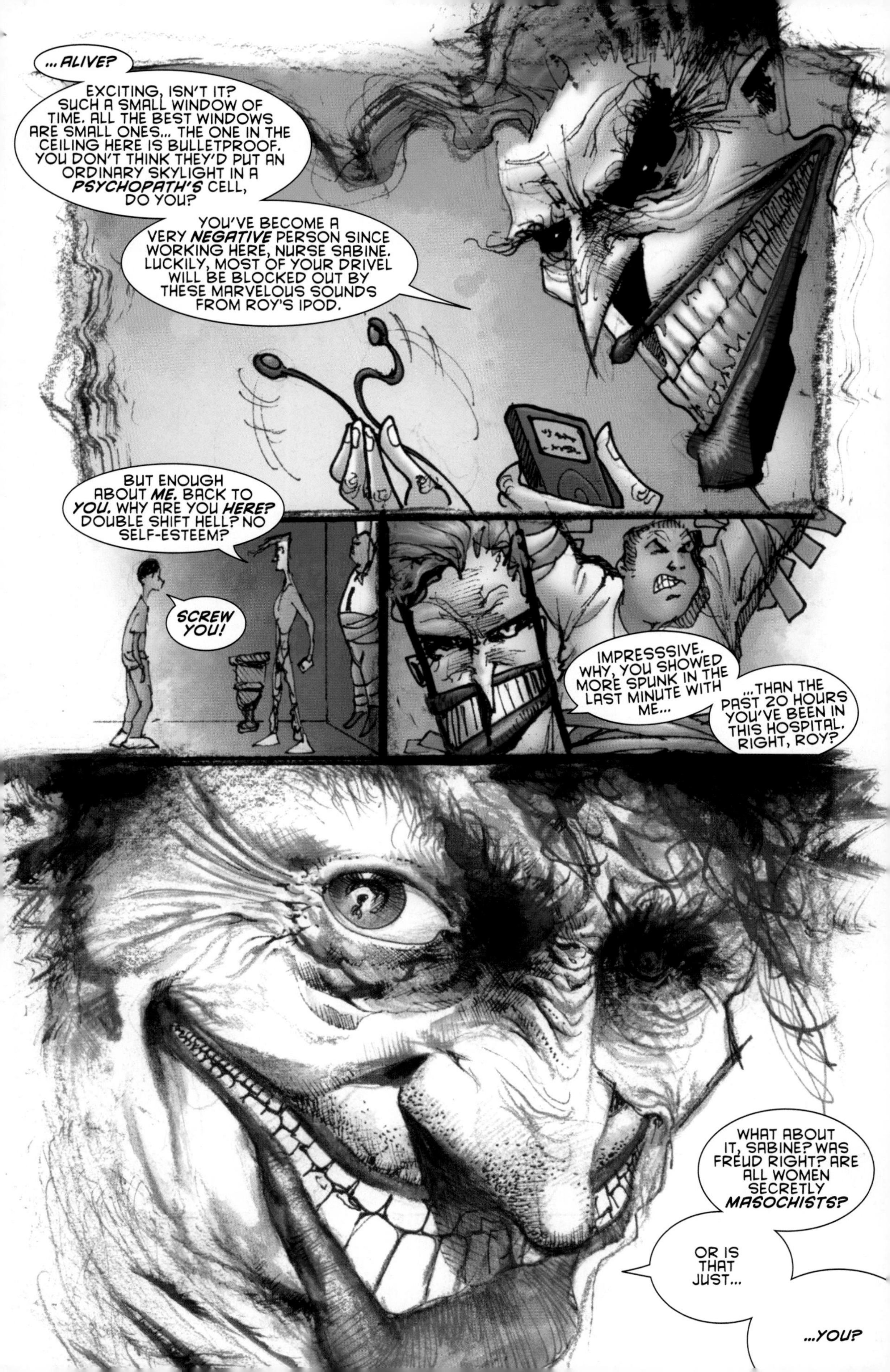
...ALIVE?
EXCITING, ISN'T IT? SUCH A SMALL WINDOW OF TIME. ALL THE BEST WINDOWS ARE SMALL ONES... THE ONE IN THE CEILING HERE IS BULLETPROOF. YOU DON'T THINK THEY'D PUT AN ORDINARY SKYLIGHT IN A PSYCHOPATH'S CELL, DO YOU?
YOU'VE BECOME A VERY NEGATIVE PERSON SINCE WORKING HERE, NURSE SABINE. LUCKILY, MOST OF YOUR DRIVEL WILL BE BLOCKED OUT BY THESE MARVELOUS SOUNDS FROM ROY'S IPOD.
BUT ENOUGH ABOUT ME. BACK TO YOU. WHY ARE YOU HERE? DOUBLE SHIFT HELL? NO SELF-ESTEEM?
SCREW YOU!
IMPRESSSIVE. WHY, YOU SHOWED MORE SPUNK IN THE LAST MINUTE WITH ME...
...THAN THE PAST 20 HOURS YOU'VE BEEN IN THIS HOSPITAL. RIGHT, ROY?
WHAT ABOUT IT, SABINE? WAS FREUD RIGHT? ARE ALL WOMEN SECRETLY MASOCHISTS?
OR IS THAT JUST...
...YOU?

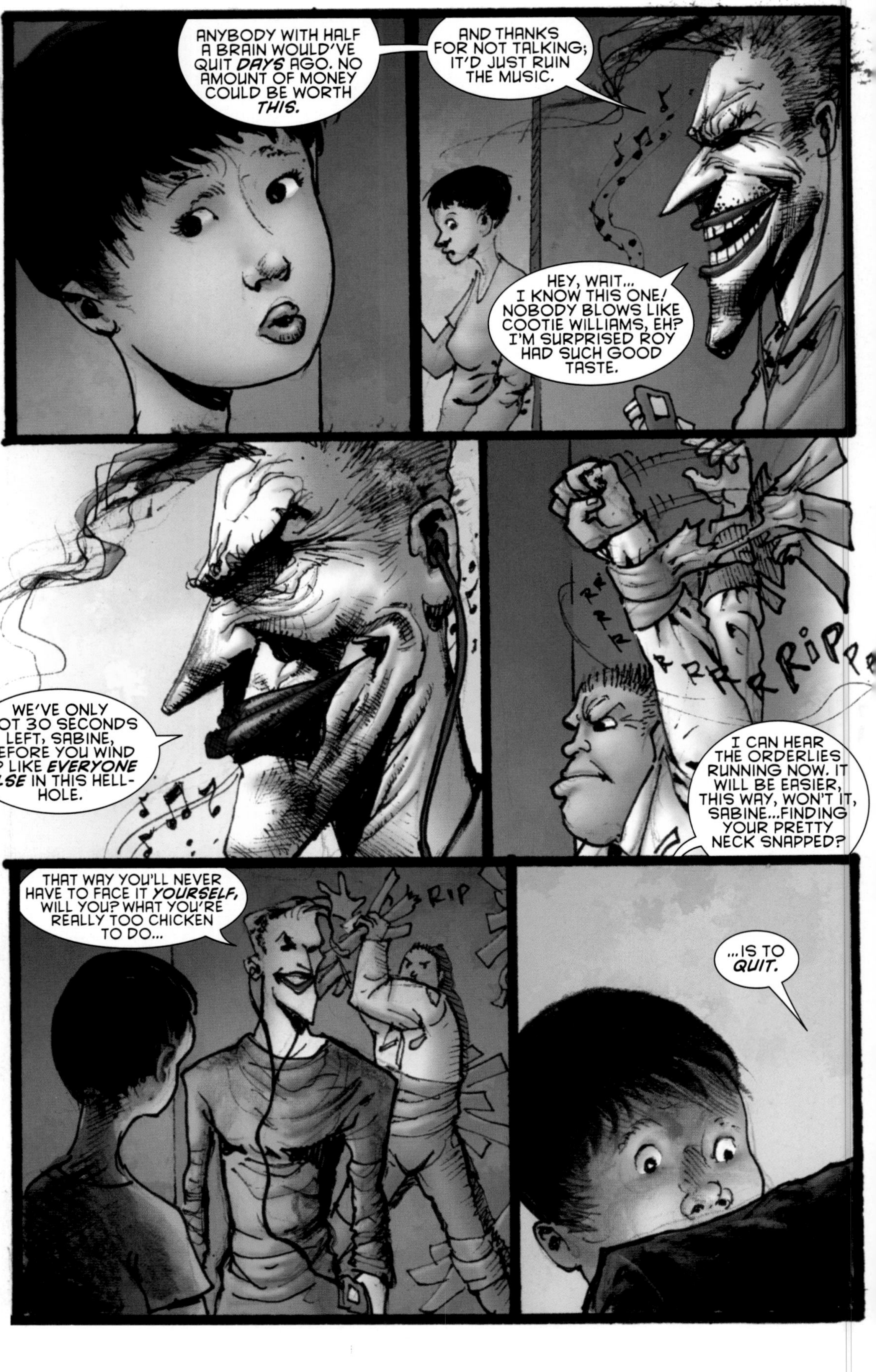
ANYBODY WITH HALF A BRAIN WOULD'VE QUIT DAYS AGO. NO AMOUNT OF MONEY COULD BE WORTH THIS.
AND THANKS FOR NOT TALKING; IT'D JUST RUIN THE MUSIC.
HEY, WAIT... I KNOW THIS ONE! NOBODY BLOWS LIKE COOTIE WILLIAMS, EH? I'M SURPRISED ROY HAD SUCH GOOD TASTE.
WE'VE ONLY GOT 30 SECONDS LEFT, SABINE, BEFORE YOU WIND UP LIKE EVERYONE ELSE IN THIS HELL-HOLE.
RRRRRRRRIPP
I CAN HEAR THE ORDERLIES RUNNING NOW. IT WILL BE EASIER, THIS WAY, WON'T IT, SABINE...FINDING YOUR PRETTY NECK SNAPPED?
THAT WAY YOU'LL NEVER HAVE TO FACE IT YOURSELF, WILL YOU? WHAT YOU'RE REALLY TOO CHICKEN TO DO...
RIP
...IS TO QUIT.

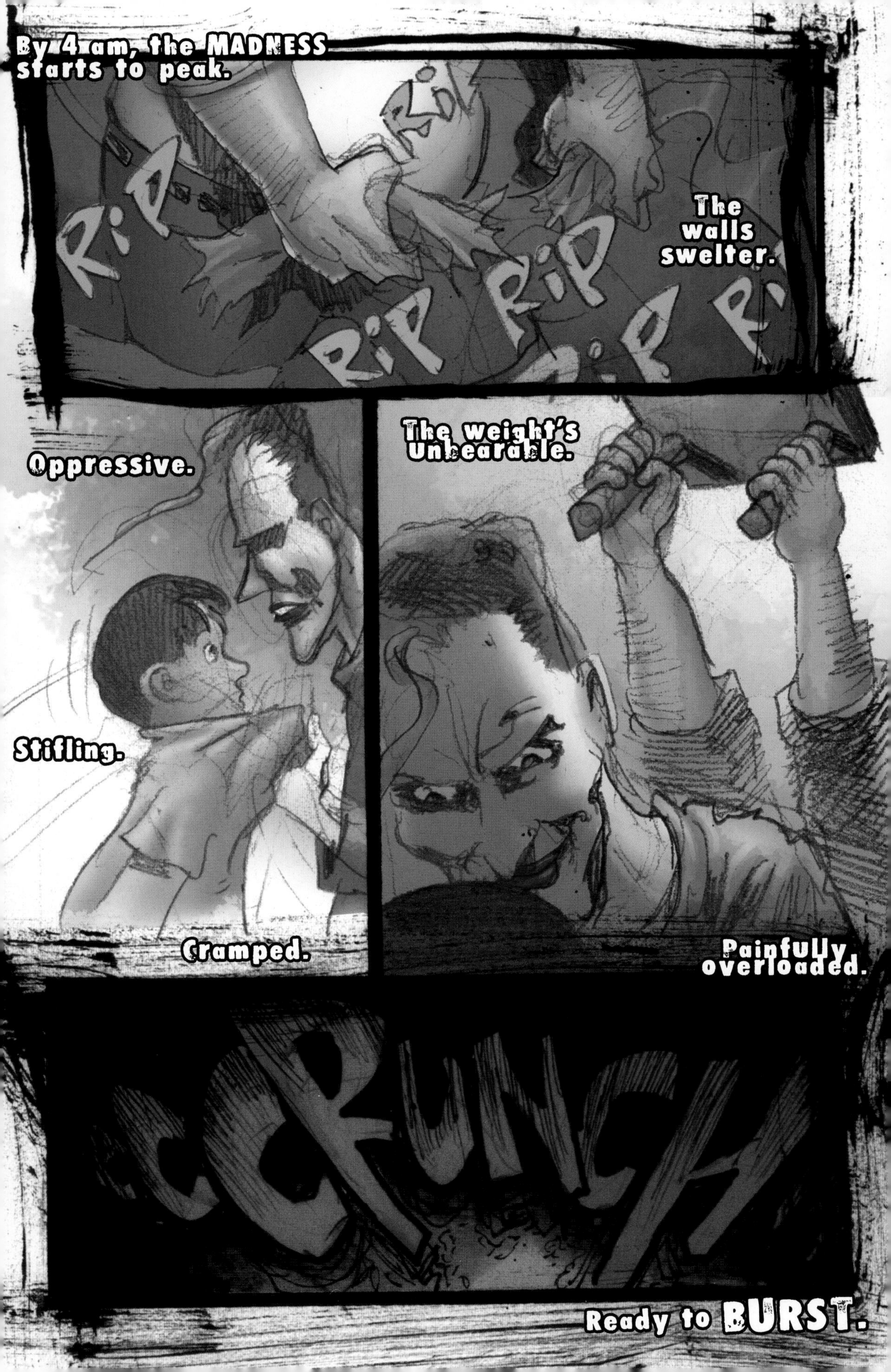
By 4 am, the MADNESS starts to peak.
RiP RiP RiP RiP RiP
The walls swelter.
Oppressive.
Stifling.
Cramped.
The weight's Unbearable.
Painfully overloaded.
CRUNCH
Ready to BURST.

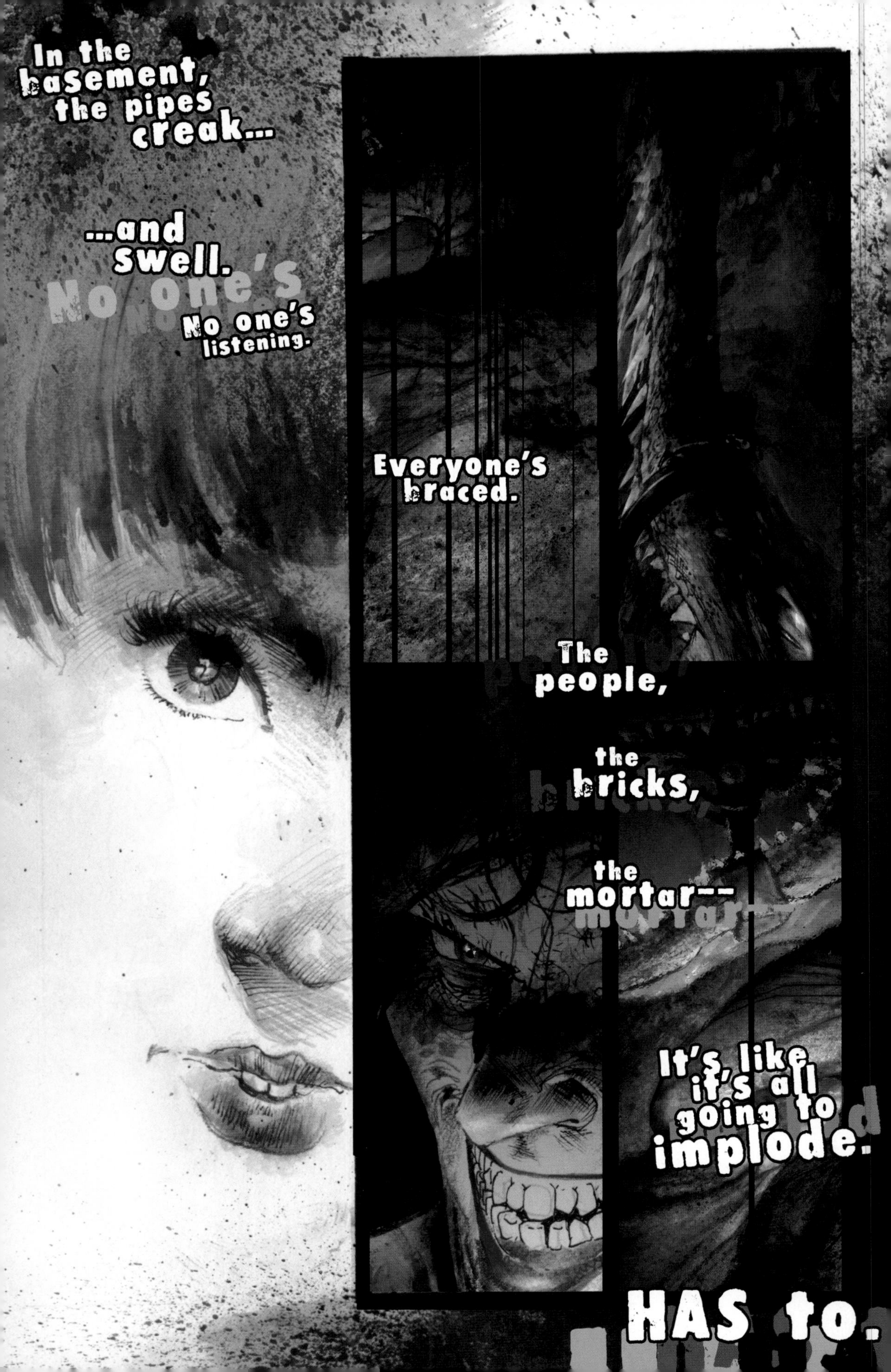
In the basement, the pipes creak...
...and swell.
No one's listening.
Everyone's braced.
The people,
the bricks,
the mortar--
It's like it's all going to implode.
HAS to.

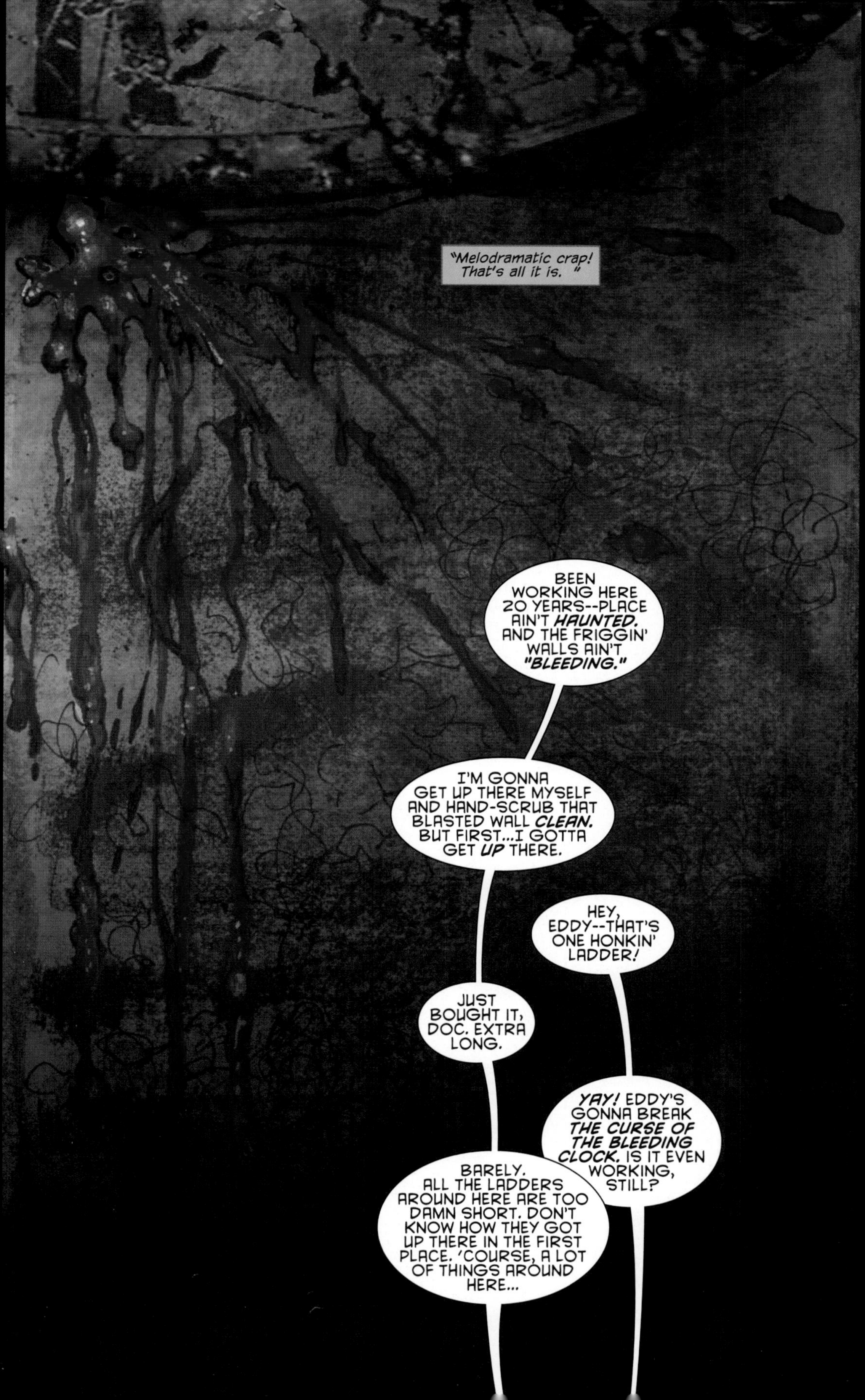
"Melodramatic crap! That's all it is. "
BEEN WORKING HERE 20 YEARS--PLACE AIN'T HAUNTED. AND THE FRIGGIN' WALLS AIN'T "BLEEDING."
I'M GONNA GET UP THERE MYSELF AND HAND-SCRUB THAT BLASTED WALL CLEAN. BUT FIRST...I GOTTA GET UP THERE.
HEY, EDDY--THAT'S ONE HONKIN' LADDER!
JUST BOUGHT IT, DOC. EXTRA LONG.
YAY! EDDY'S GONNA BREAK THE CURSE OF THE BLEEDING CLOCK. IS IT EVEN WORKING, STILL?
BARELY. ALL THE LADDERS AROUND HERE ARE TOO DAMN SHORT. DON'T KNOW HOW THEY GOT UP THERE IN THE FIRST PLACE. 'COURSE, A LOT OF THINGS AROUND HERE...

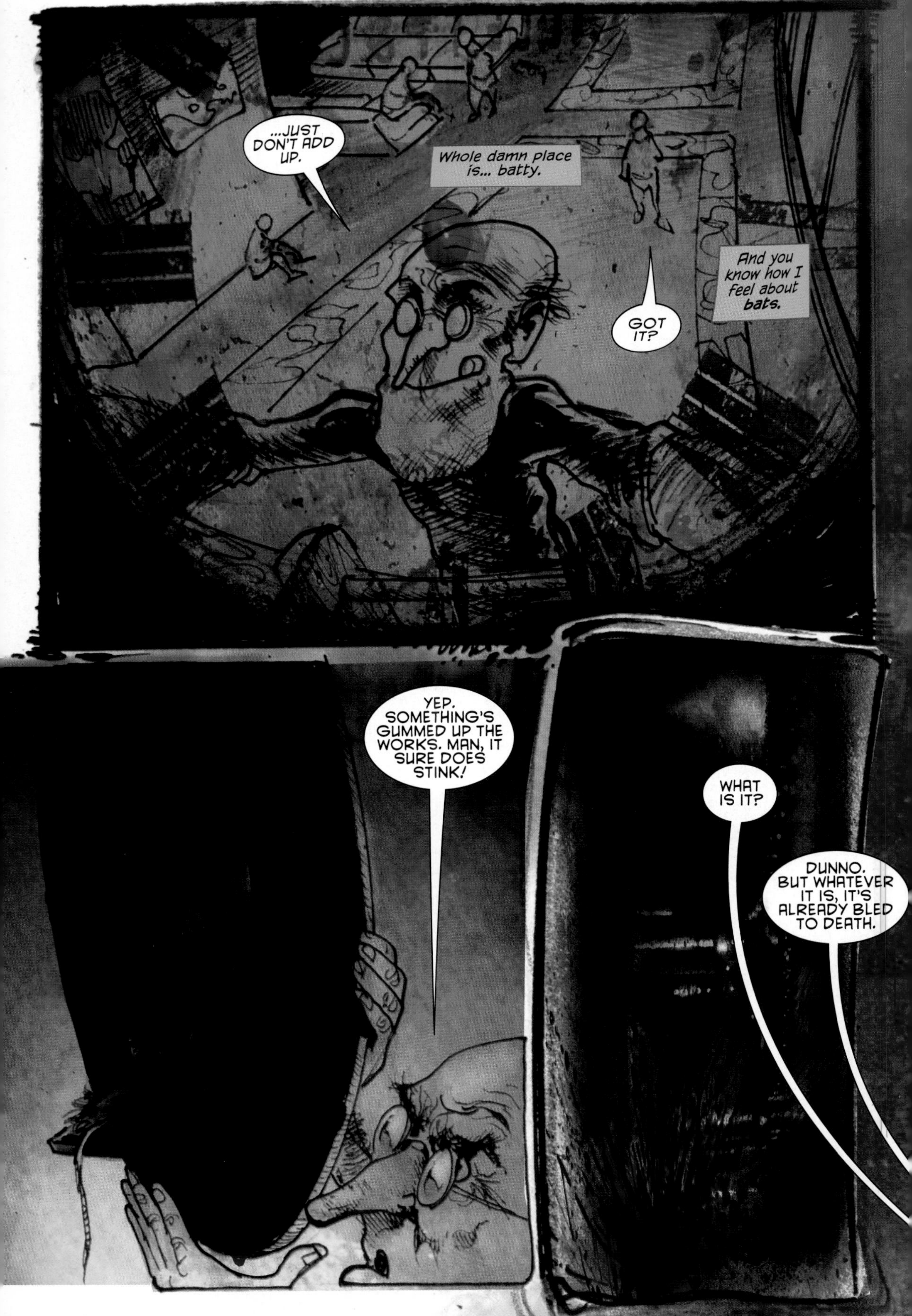
...JUST DON'T ADD UP.
Whole damn place is... batty.
GOT IT?
And you know how I feel about **bats.**
YEP. SOMETHING'S GUMMED UP THE WORKS. MAN, IT SURE DOES STINK!
WHAT IS IT?
DUNNO. BUT WHATEVER IT IS, IT'S ALREADY BLED TO DEATH.

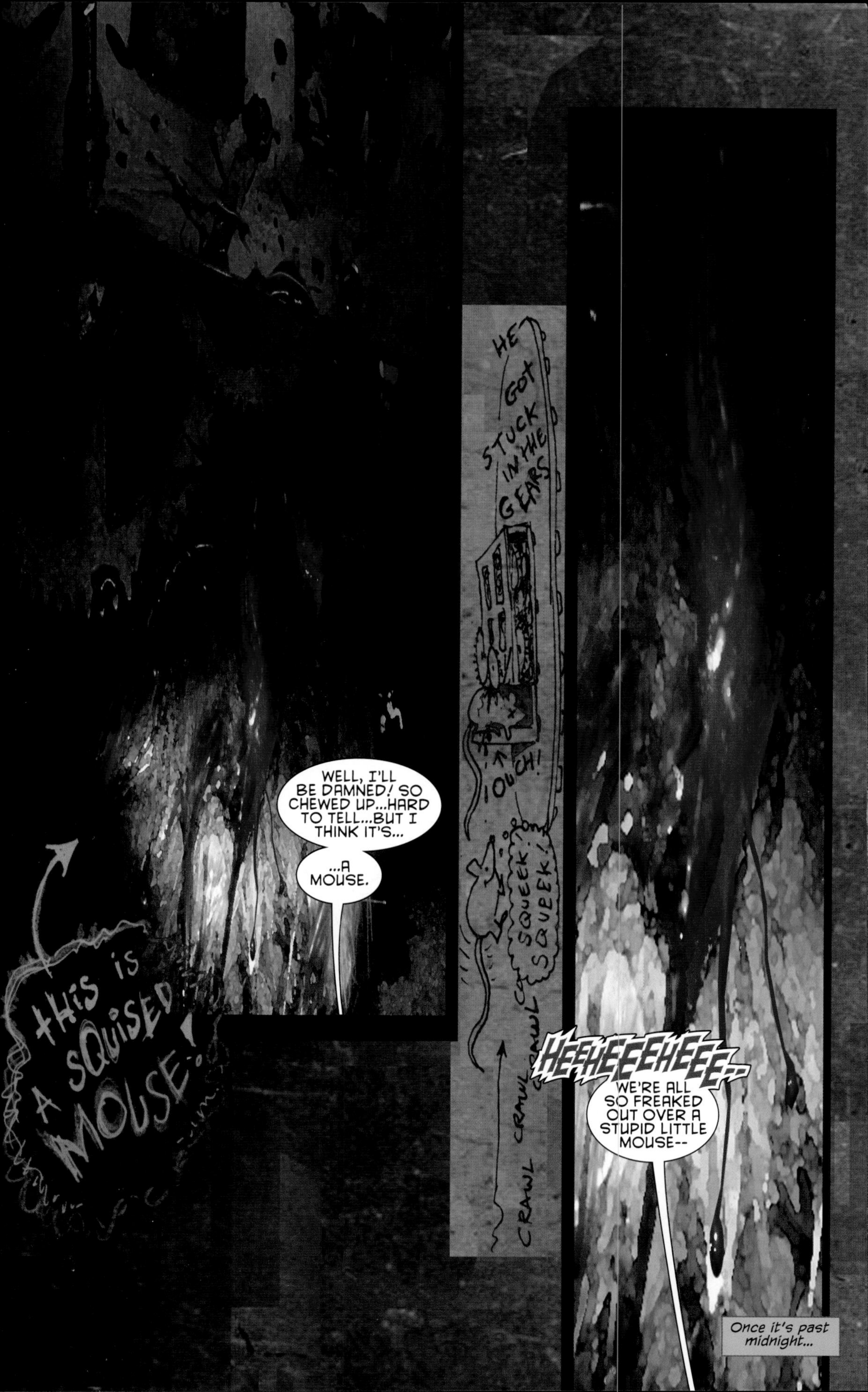
WELL, I'LL BE DAMNED! SO CHEWED UP...HARD TO TELL...BUT I THINK IT'S...
...A MOUSE.
this is a SQUISED MOUSE!
HE GOT STUCK IN THE GEARS
OUCH!
SQUEEK! SQUEEK!
CRAWL CRAWL CRAWL
HEEHEEEEHEEE--
WE'RE ALL SO FREAKED OUT OVER A STUPID LITTLE MOUSE--
Once it's past midnight...

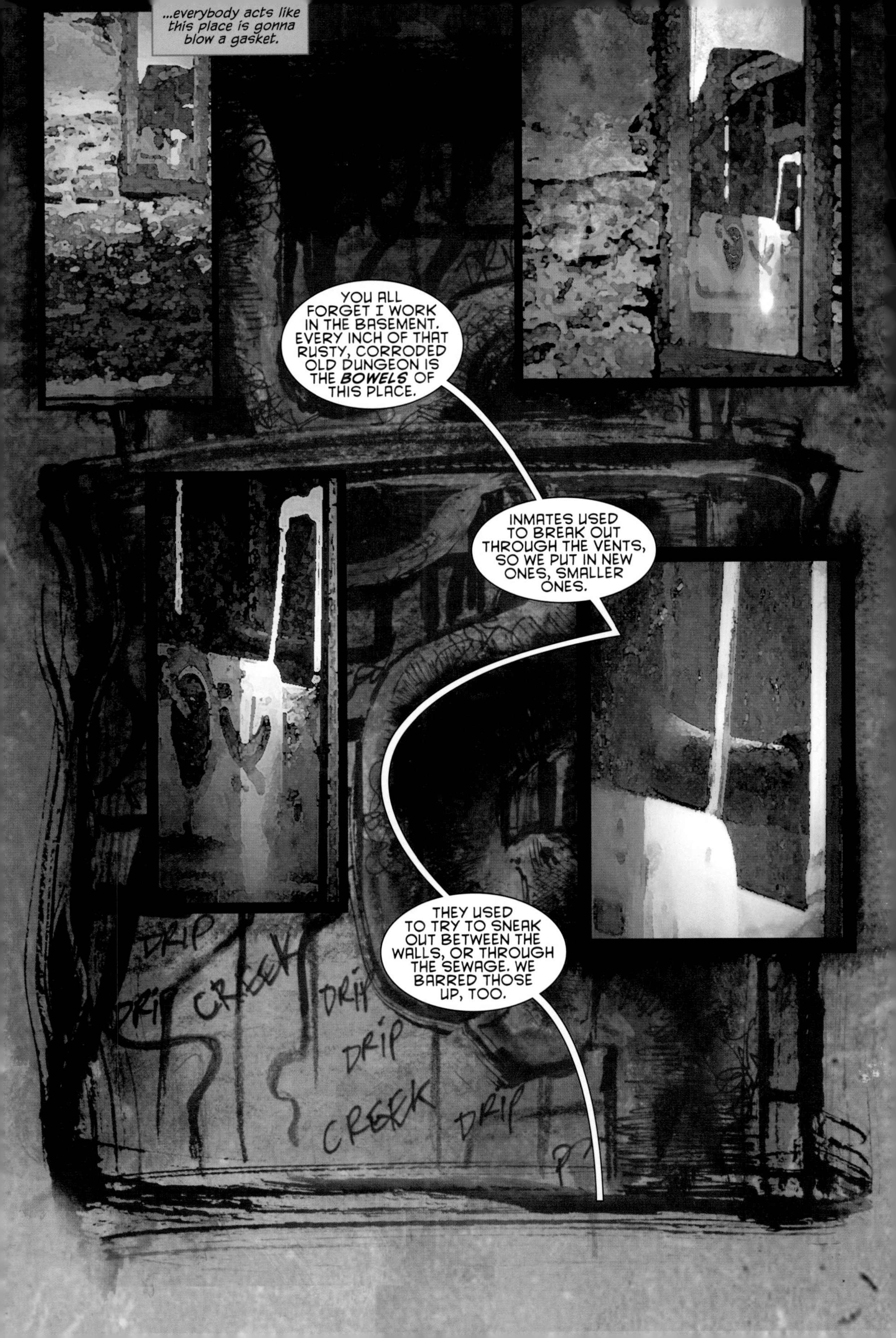
...everybody acts like this place is gonna blow a gasket.
YOU ALL FORGET I WORK IN THE BASEMENT. EVERY INCH OF THAT RUSTY, CORRODED OLD DUNGEON IS THE BOWELS OF THIS PLACE.
INMATES USED TO BREAK OUT THROUGH THE VENTS, SO WE PUT IN NEW ONES, SMALLER ONES.
THEY USED TO TRY TO SNEAK OUT BETWEEN THE WALLS, OR THROUGH THE SEWAGE. WE BARRED THOSE UP, TOO.
DRIP
DRIP
CREEK
DRIP
DRIP
CREEK
DRIP

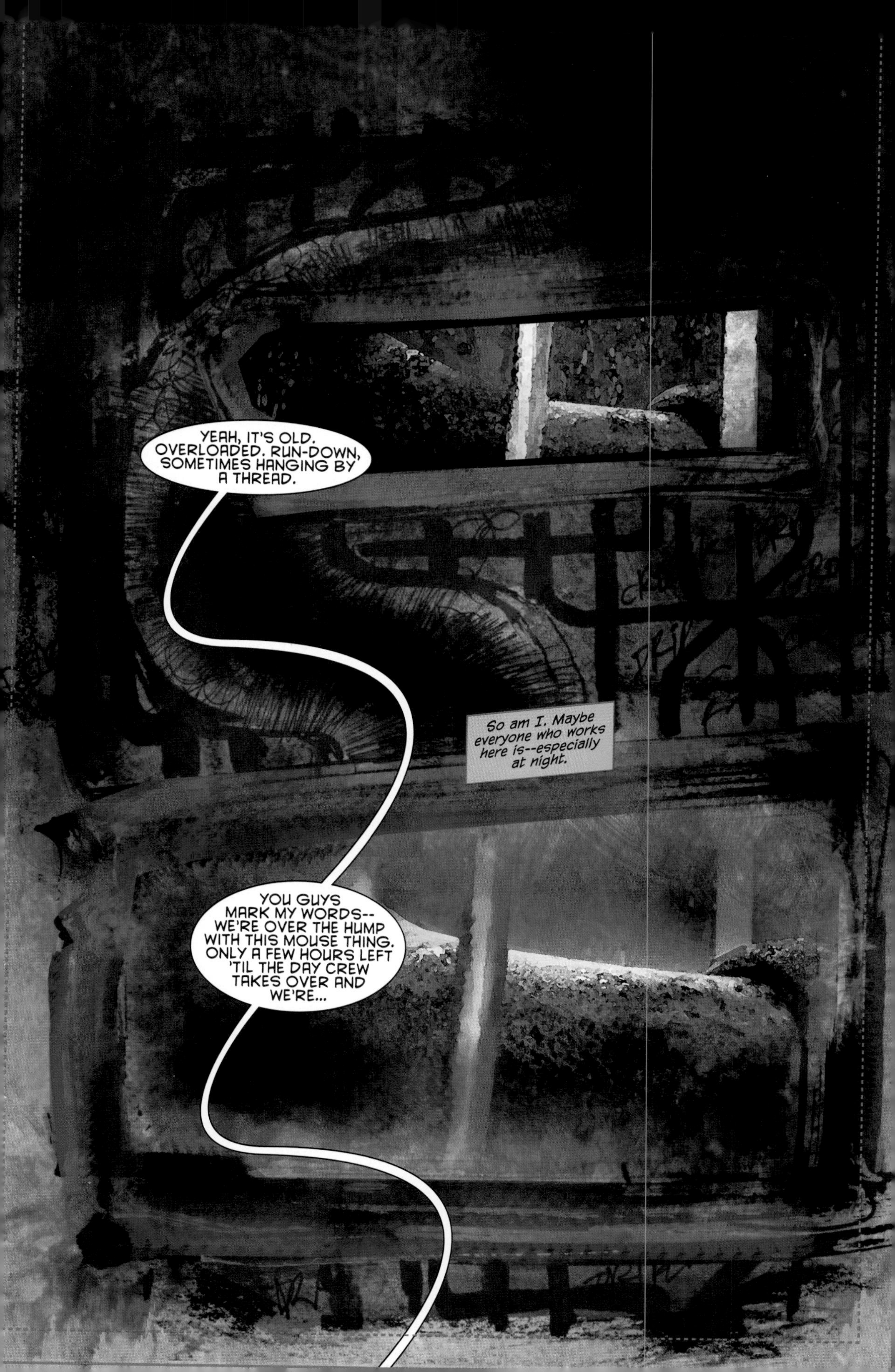
YEAH, IT'S OLD. OVERLOADED. RUN-DOWN, SOMETIMES HANGING BY A THREAD.
So am I. Maybe everyone who works here is--especially at night.
YOU GUYS MARK MY WORDS-- WE'RE OVER THE HUMP WITH THIS MOUSE THING. ONLY A FEW HOURS LEFT 'TIL THE DAY CREW TAKES OVER AND WE'RE...

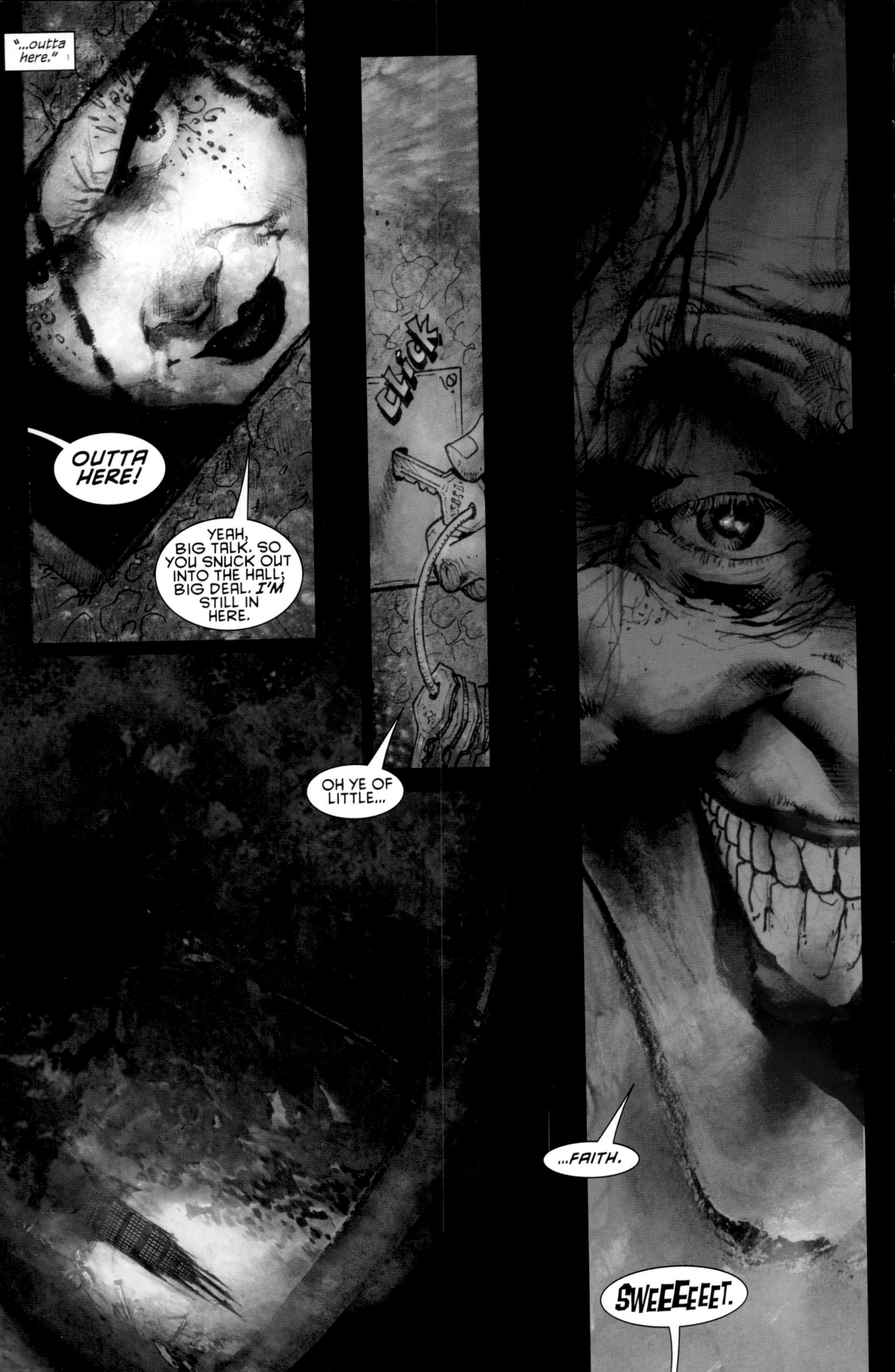
"...outta here."
OUTTA HERE!
YEAH, BIG TALK. SO YOU SNUCK OUT INTO THE HALL; BIG DEAL. *I'M* STILL IN HERE.
CLICK
OH YE OF LITTLE...
...FAITH.
SWEEEEEET.

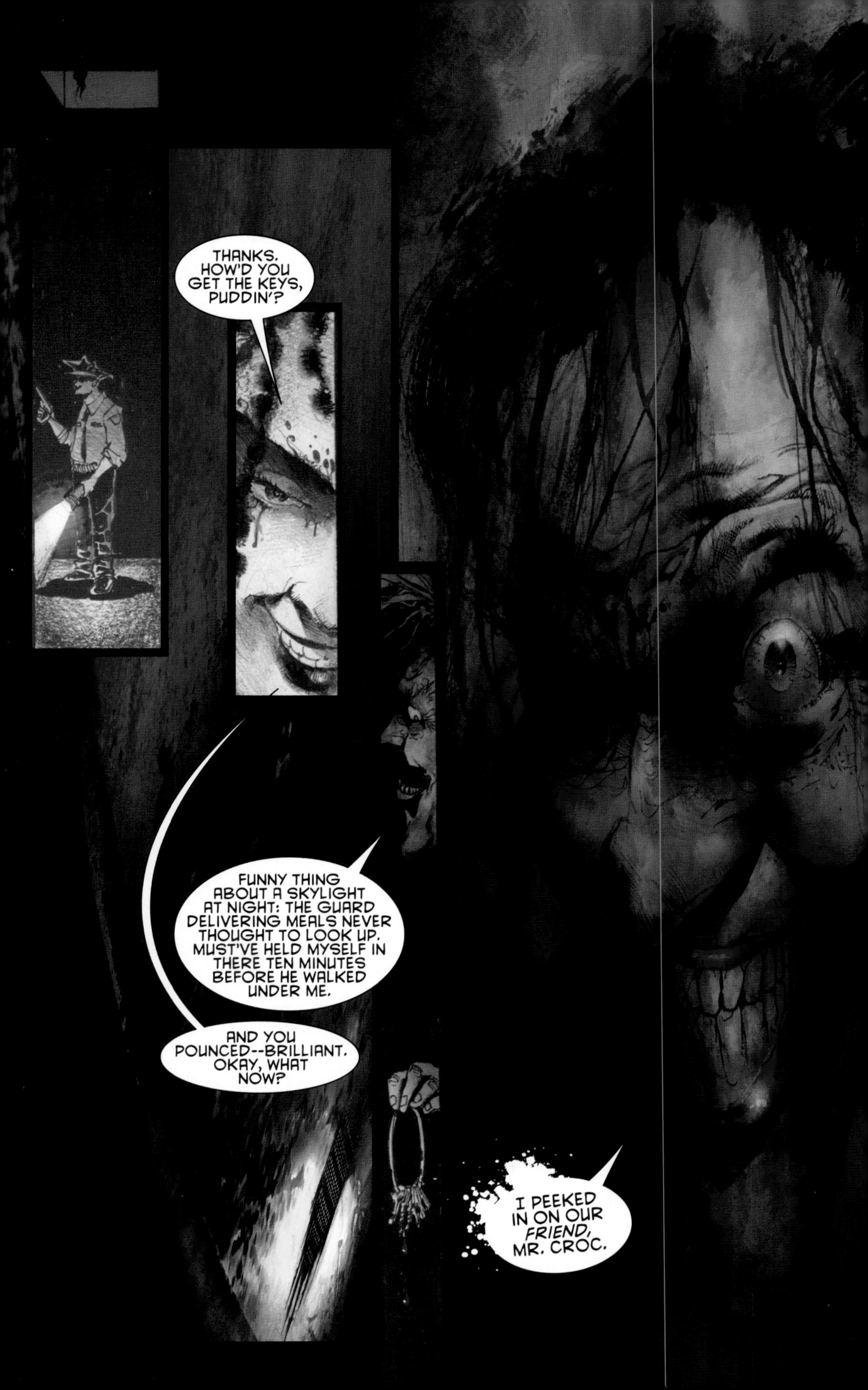
THANKS. HOW'D YOU GET THE KEYS, PUDDIN'?
FUNNY THING ABOUT A SKYLIGHT AT NIGHT: THE GUARD DELIVERING MEALS NEVER THOUGHT TO LOOK UP. MUST'VE HELD MYSELF IN THERE TEN MINUTES BEFORE HE WALKED UNDER ME.
AND YOU POUNCED--BRILLIANT. OKAY, WHAT NOW?
I PEEKED IN ON OUR *FRIEND,* MR. CROC.

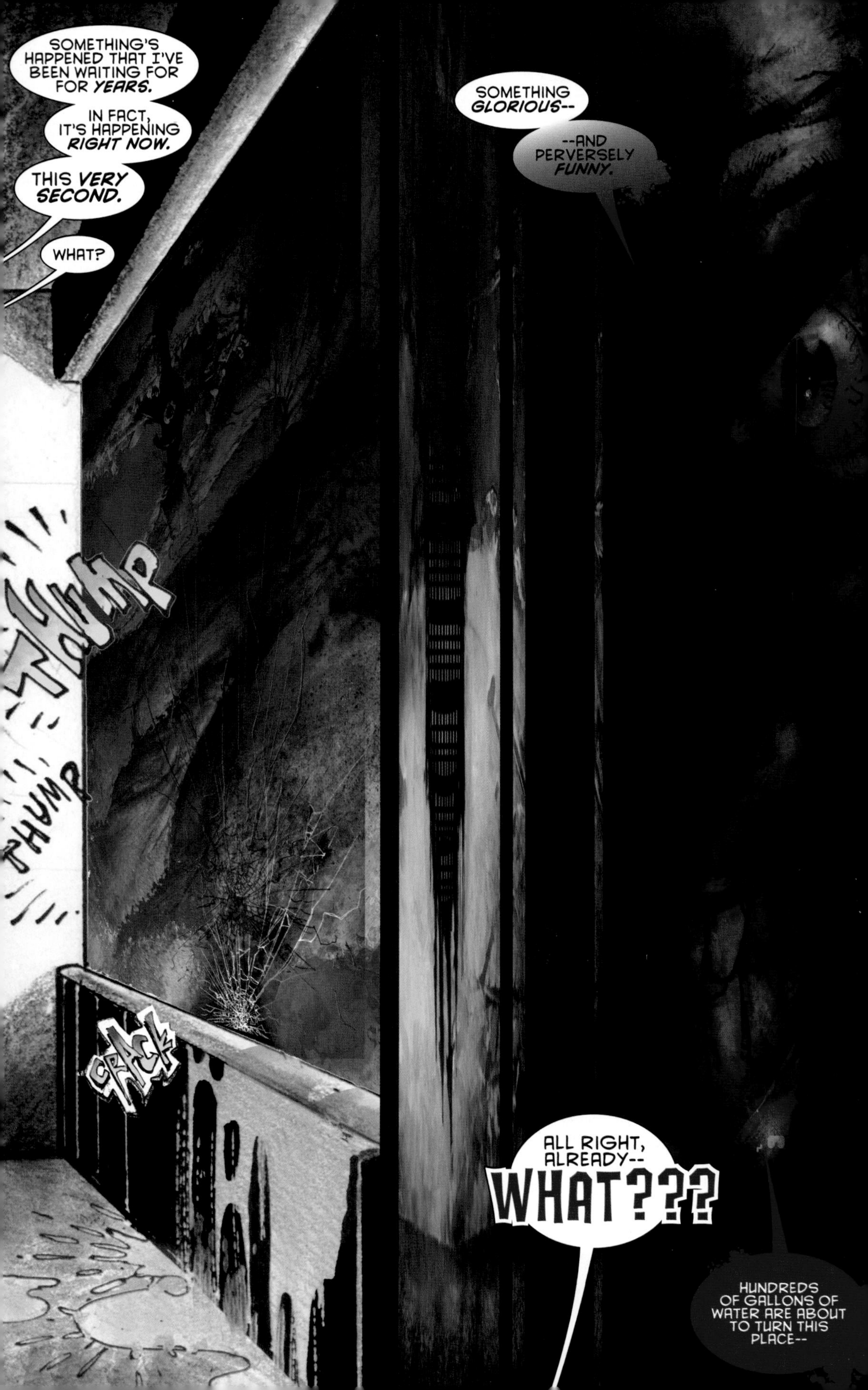
SOMETHING'S HAPPENED THAT I'VE BEEN WAITING FOR FOR *YEARS.*
IN FACT, IT'S HAPPENING *RIGHT NOW.*
THIS *VERY SECOND.*
WHAT?
SOMETHING *GLORIOUS--*
--AND PERVERSELY *FUNNY.*
THUMP
THUMP
CRACK
ALL RIGHT, ALREADY-- WHAT???
HUNDREDS OF GALLONS OF WATER ARE ABOUT TO TURN THIS PLACE--

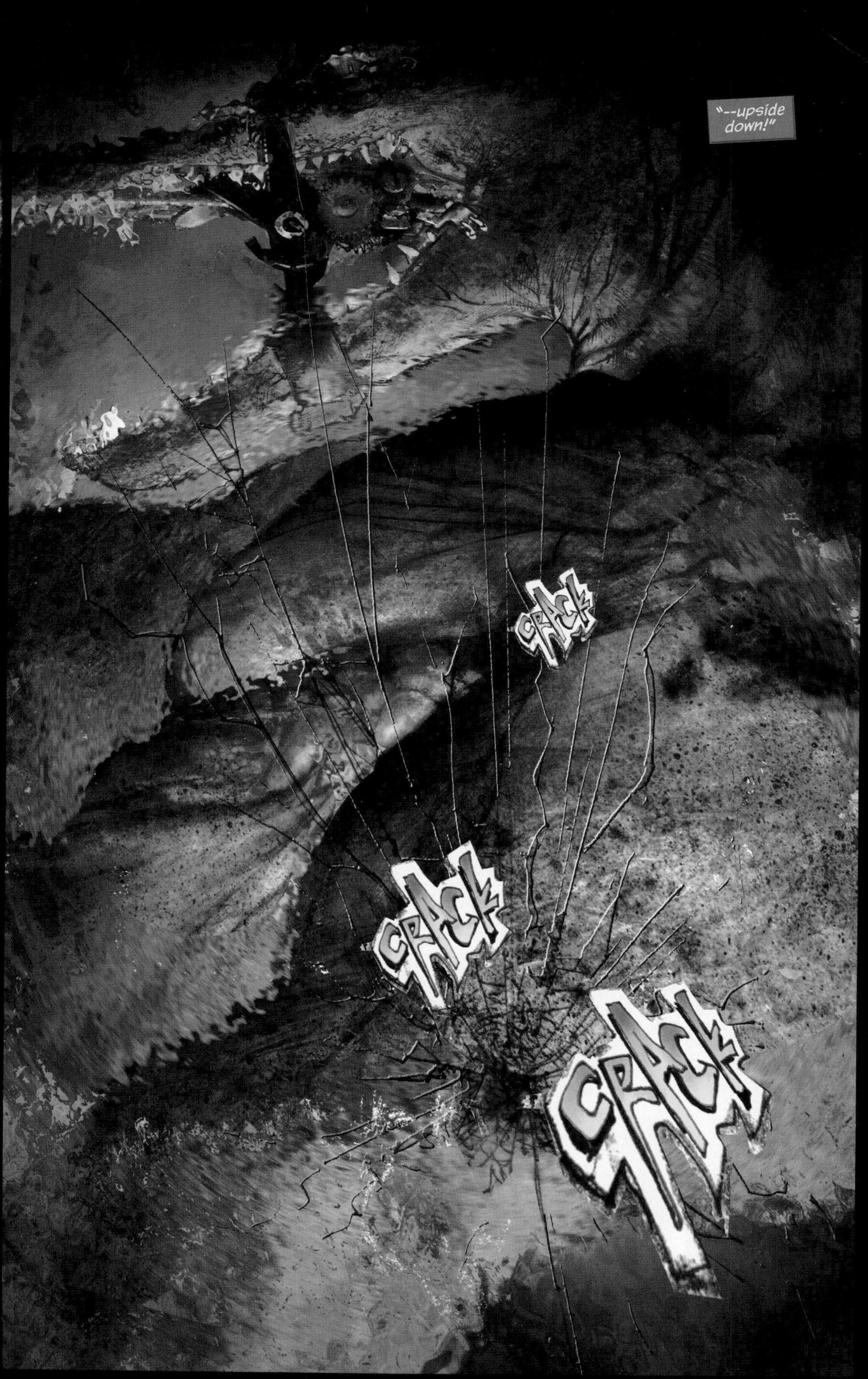
"--upside down!"
CRACK
CRACK
CRACK

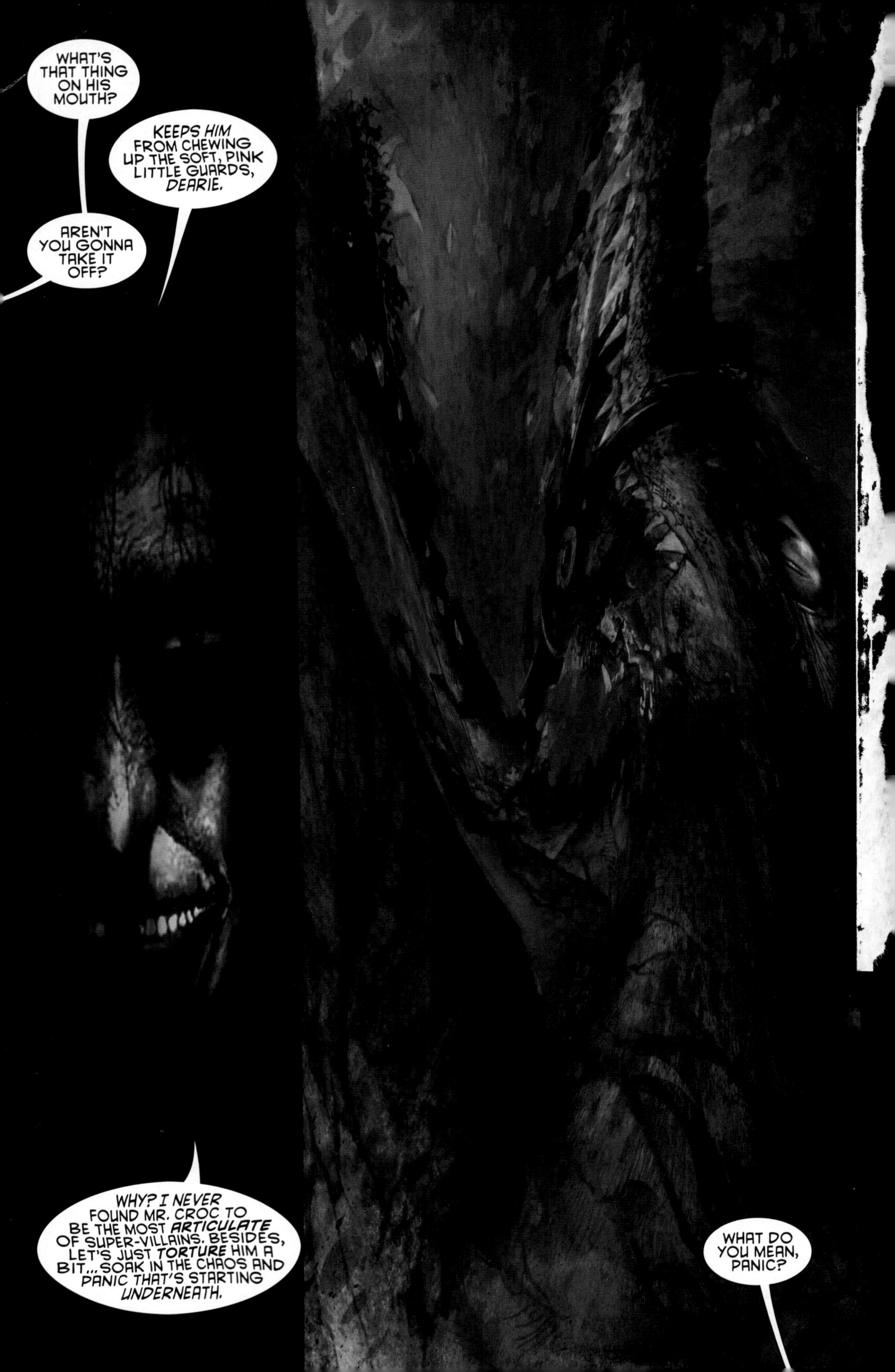
WHAT'S THAT THING ON HIS MOUTH?
KEEPS *HIM* FROM CHEWING UP THE SOFT, PINK LITTLE GUARDS, *DEARIE.*
AREN'T YOU GONNA TAKE IT OFF?
*WHY? I NEVER* FOUND MR. CROC TO BE THE MOST ***ARTICULATE*** OF SUPER-VILLAINS. BESIDES, LET'S JUST ***TORTURE*** HIM A BIT... SOAK IN THE CHAOS AND *PANIC* THAT'S STARTING *UNDERNEATH.*
WHAT DO YOU MEAN, PANIC?

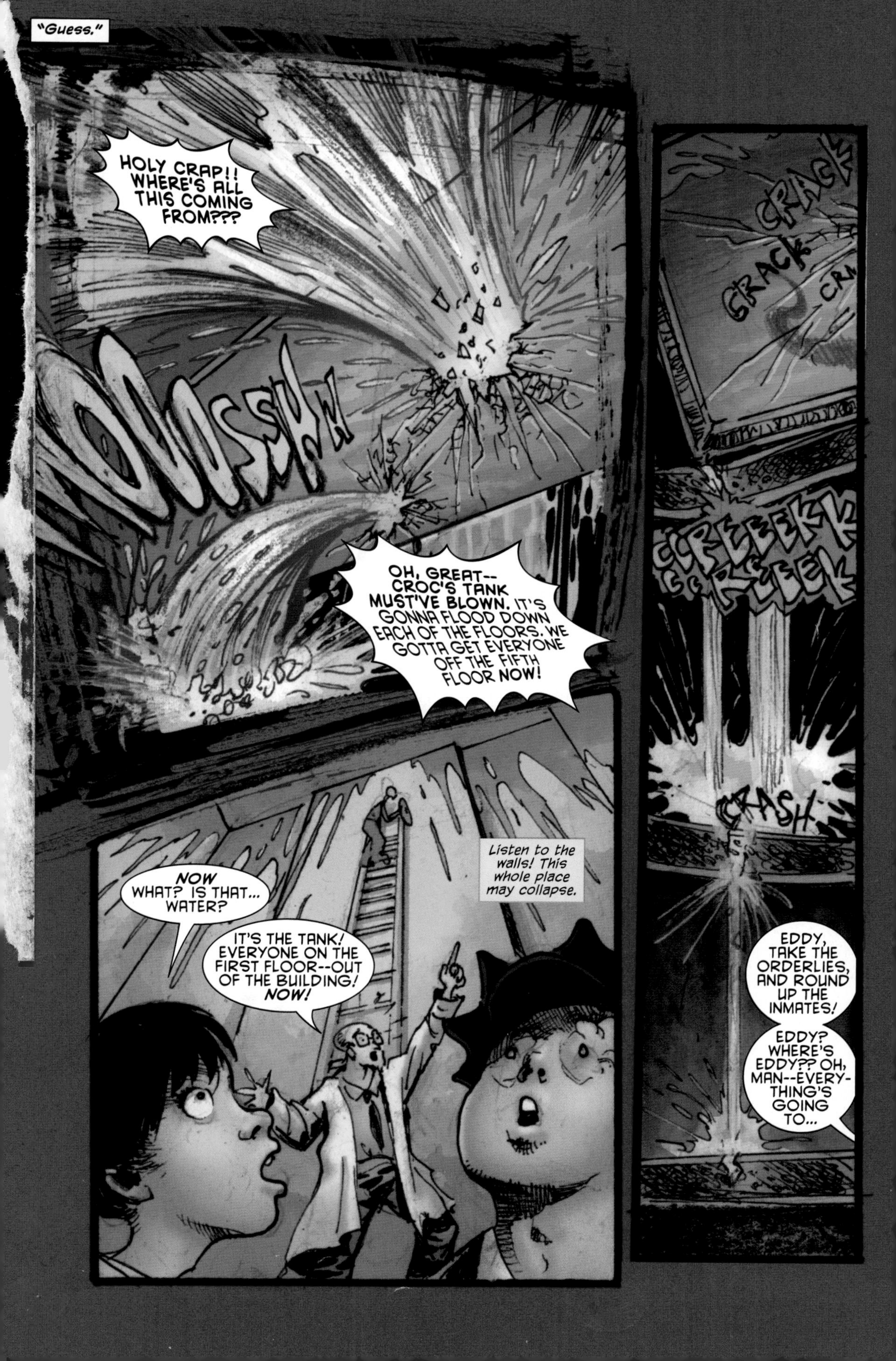
"Guess."
HOLY CRAP!! WHERE'S ALL THIS COMING FROM???
OH, GREAT-- CROC'S TANK MUST'VE BLOWN. IT'S GONNA FLOOD DOWN EACH OF THE FLOORS. WE GOTTA GET EVERYONE OFF THE FIFTH FLOOR NOW!
CRACK
CRACK
CRASH
NOW WHAT? IS THAT... WATER?
IT'S THE TANK! EVERYONE ON THE FIRST FLOOR--OUT OF THE BUILDING! NOW!
Listen to the walls! This whole place may collapse.
EDDY, TAKE THE ORDERLIES, AND ROUND UP THE INMATES!
EDDY? WHERE'S EDDY?? OH, MAN--EVERYTHING'S GOING TO...

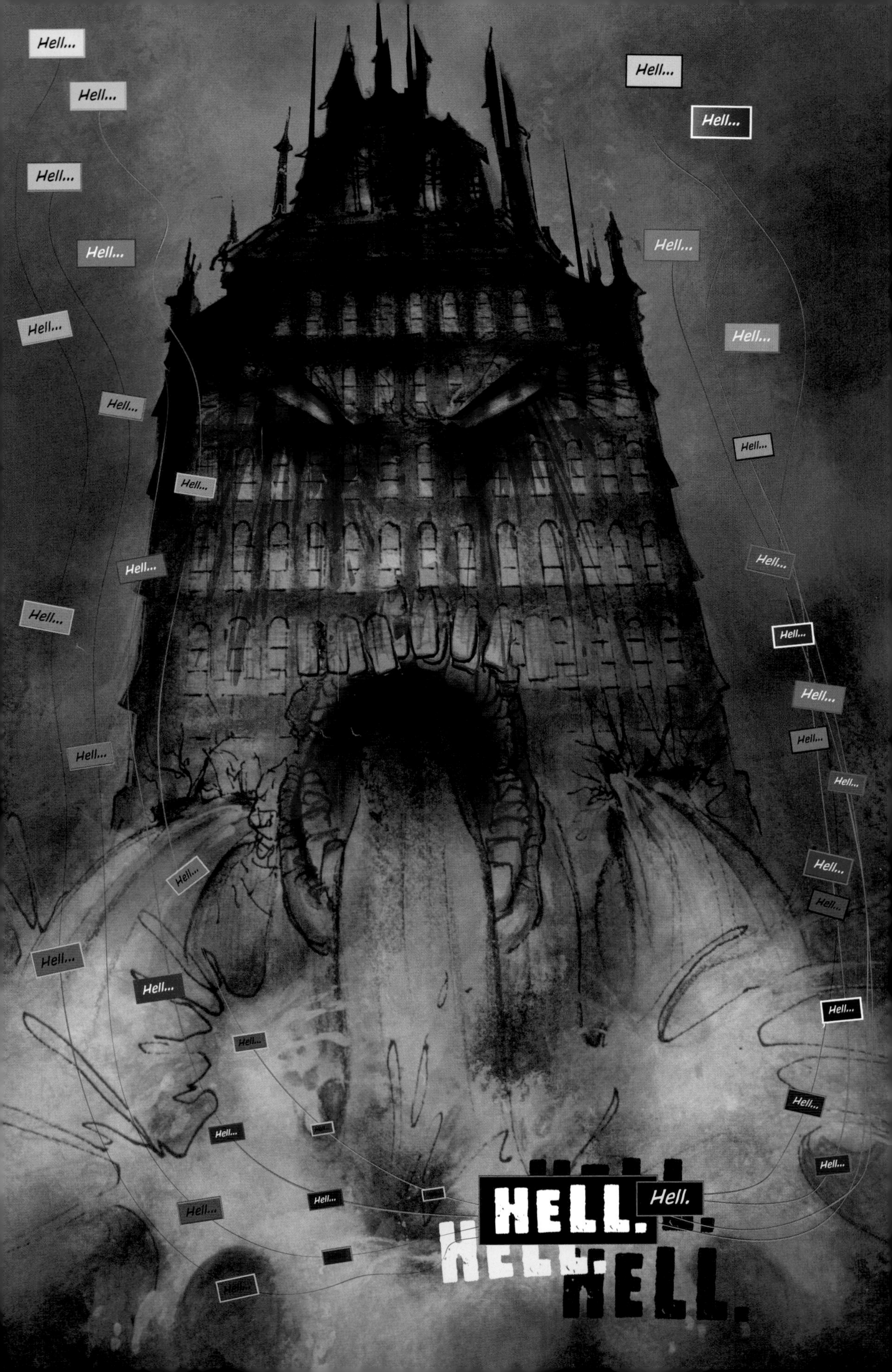
Hell...
Hell...
Hell...
Hell...
Hell...
Hell...
Hell...
Hell...
Hell...
Hell...
Hell...
Hell...
Hell...
Hell...
Hell...
Hell...
Hell...
Hell...
Hell...
Hell...
Hell...
Hell...
Hell...
Hell...
Hell...
Hell...
Hell...
Hell...
Hell...
Hell...
Hell...
Hell...
Hell...
HELL.
Hell.
HELL.
HELL.

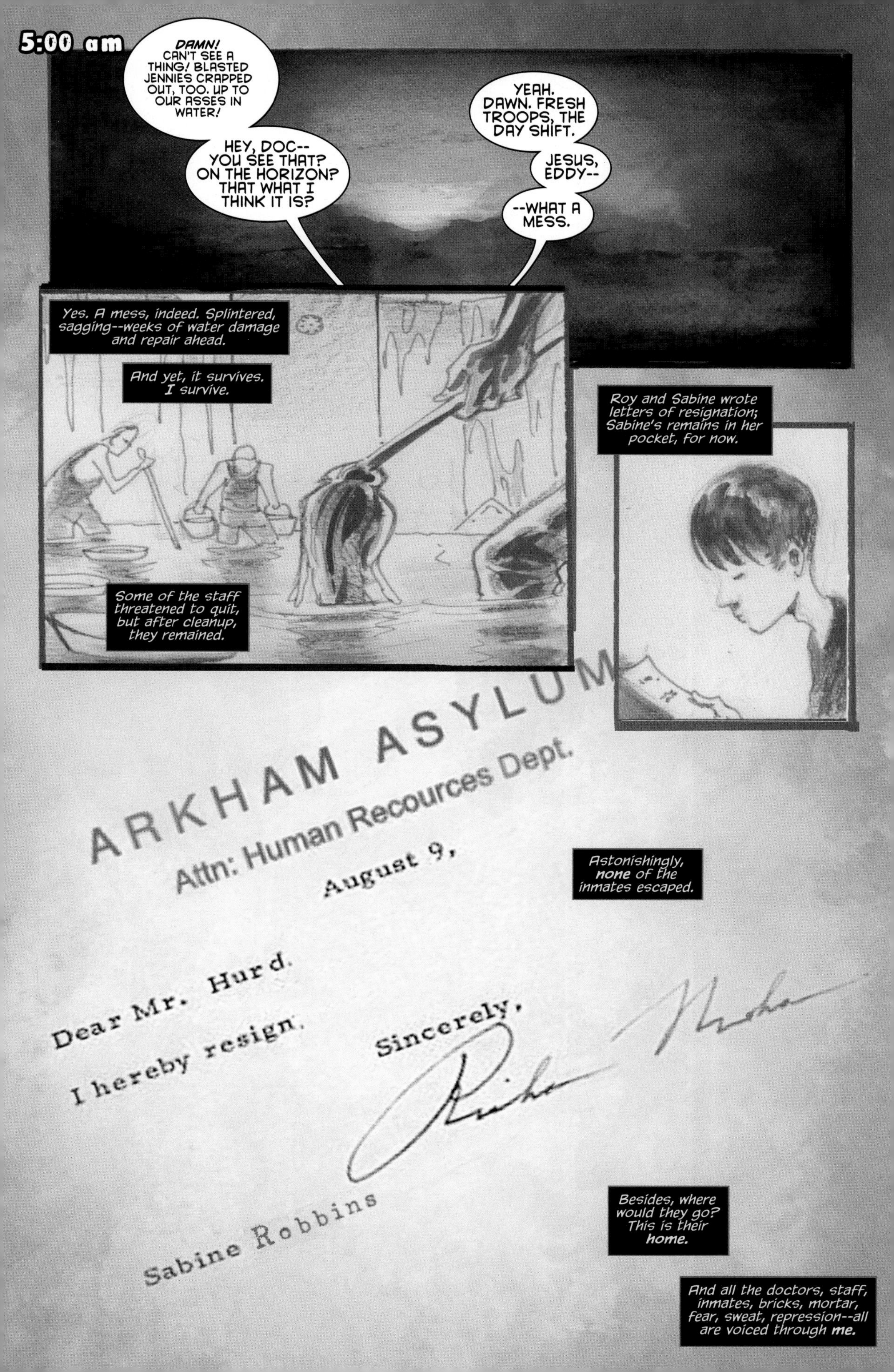
5:00 am
DAMN! CAN'T SEE A THING! BLASTED JENNIES CRAPPED OUT, TOO. UP TO OUR ASSES IN WATER!
HEY, DOC-- YOU SEE THAT? ON THE HORIZON? THAT WHAT I THINK IT IS?
YEAH. DAWN. FRESH TROOPS, THE DAY SHIFT.
JESUS, EDDY--
--WHAT A MESS.
Yes. A mess, indeed. Splintered, sagging--weeks of water damage and repair ahead.
And yet, it survives. I survive.
Some of the staff threatened to quit, but after cleanup, they remained.
Roy and Sabine wrote letters of resignation; Sabine's remains in her pocket, for now.
ARKHAM ASYLUM
Attn: Human Recources Dept.
August 9,
Dear Mr. Hurd.
I hereby resign.
Sincerely,
Sabine Robbins
Astonishingly, none of the inmates escaped.
Besides, where would they go? This is their home.
And all the doctors, staff, inmates, bricks, mortar, fear, sweat, repression--all are voiced through me.

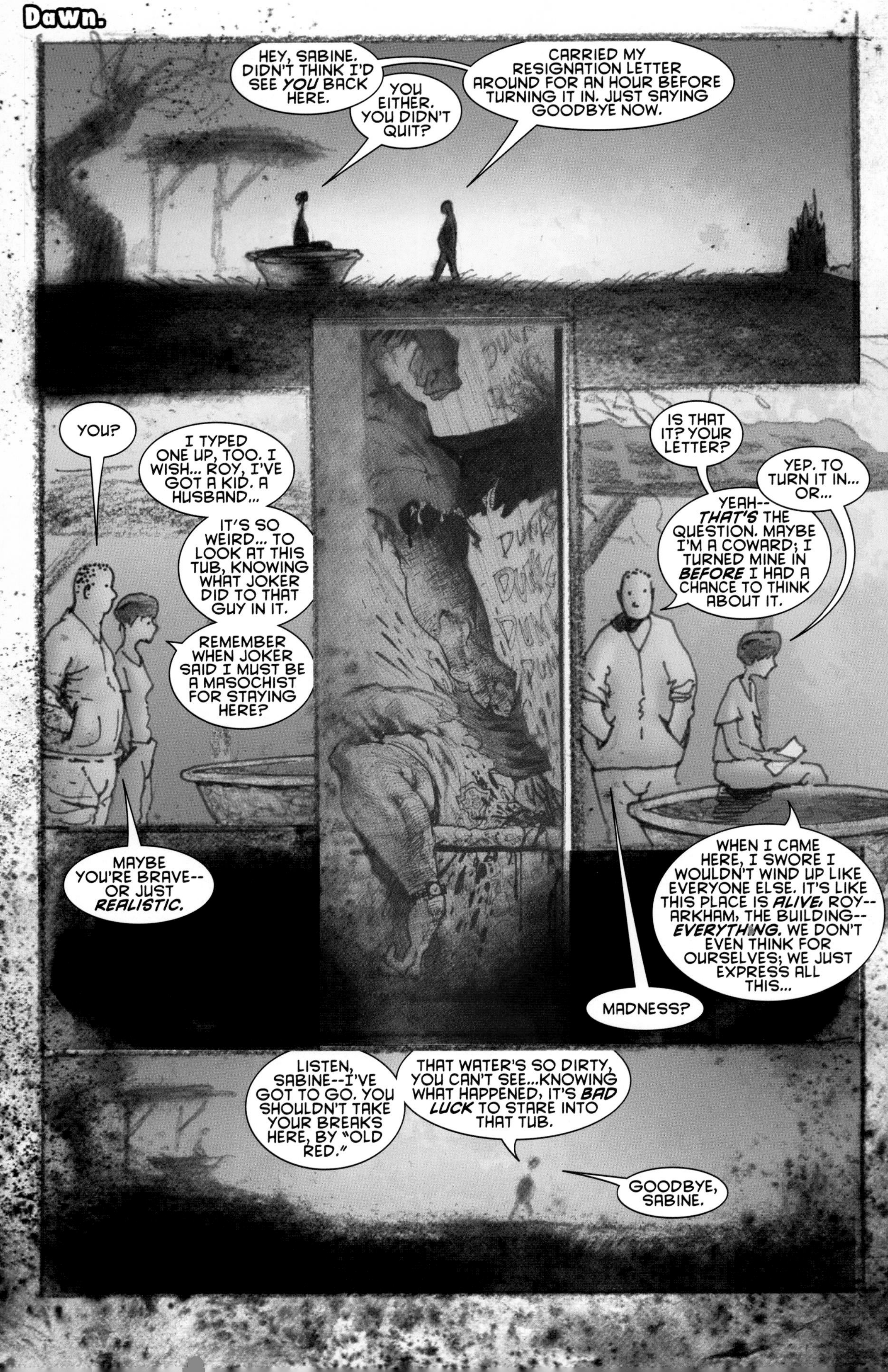
Dawn.
HEY, SABINE. DIDN'T THINK I'D SEE YOU BACK HERE.
YOU EITHER. YOU DIDN'T QUIT?
CARRIED MY RESIGNATION LETTER AROUND FOR AN HOUR BEFORE TURNING IT IN. JUST SAYING GOODBYE NOW.
YOU?
I TYPED ONE UP, TOO. I WISH... ROY, I'VE GOT A KID. A HUSBAND...
IT'S SO WEIRD... TO LOOK AT THIS TUB, KNOWING WHAT JOKER DID TO THAT GUY IN IT.
REMEMBER WHEN JOKER SAID I MUST BE A MASOCHIST FOR STAYING HERE?
MAYBE YOU'RE BRAVE-- OR JUST REALISTIC.
IS THAT IT? YOUR LETTER?
YEP. TO TURN IT IN... OR...
YEAH-- THAT'S THE QUESTION. MAYBE I'M A COWARD; I TURNED MINE IN BEFORE I HAD A CHANCE TO THINK ABOUT IT.
WHEN I CAME HERE, I SWORE I WOULDN'T WIND UP LIKE EVERYONE ELSE. IT'S LIKE THIS PLACE IS ALIVE, ROY-- ARKHAM, THE BUILDING-- EVERYTHING. WE DON'T EVEN THINK FOR OURSELVES; WE JUST EXPRESS ALL THIS...
MADNESS?
LISTEN, SABINE--I'VE GOT TO GO. YOU SHOULDN'T TAKE YOUR BREAKS HERE, BY "OLD RED."
THAT WATER'S SO DIRTY, YOU CAN'T SEE...KNOWING WHAT HAPPENED, IT'S BAD LUCK TO STARE INTO THAT TUB.
GOODBYE, SABINE.

6:00 am

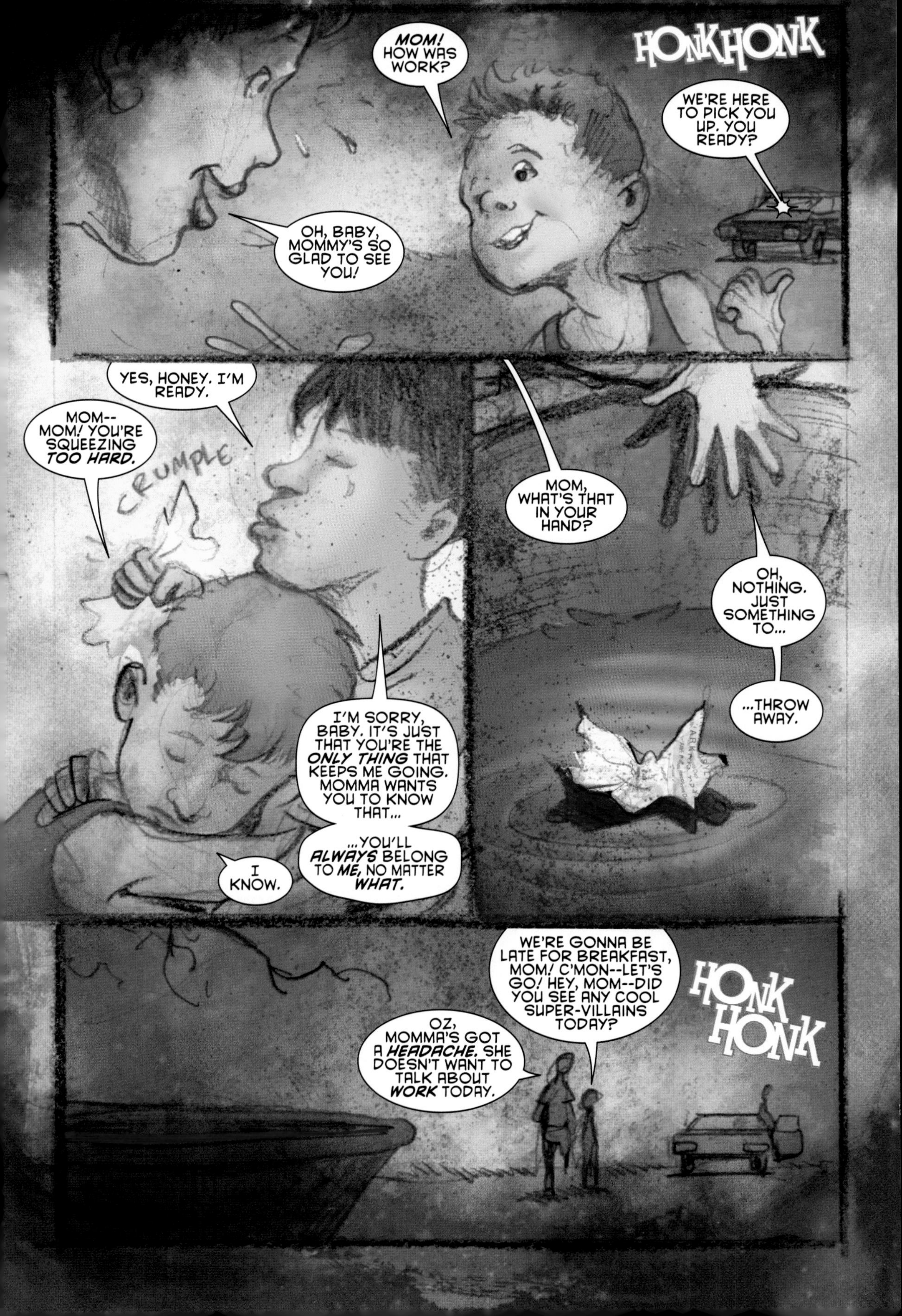

HONKHONK
MOM! HOW WAS WORK?
WE'RE HERE TO PICK YOU UP. YOU READY?
OH, BABY, MOMMY'S SO GLAD TO SEE YOU!
YES, HONEY. I'M READY.
MOM-- MOM! YOU'RE SQUEEZING TOO HARD.
CRUMPLE
MOM, WHAT'S THAT IN YOUR HAND?
OH, NOTHING. JUST SOMETHING TO...
...THROW AWAY.
I'M SORRY, BABY. IT'S JUST THAT YOU'RE THE ONLY THING THAT KEEPS ME GOING. MOMMA WANTS YOU TO KNOW THAT...
...YOU'LL ALWAYS BELONG TO ME, NO MATTER WHAT.
I KNOW.
WE'RE GONNA BE LATE FOR BREAKFAST, MOM! C'MON--LET'S GO! HEY, MOM--DID YOU SEE ANY COOL SUPER-VILLAINS TODAY?
HONK HONK
OZ, MOMMA'S GOT A HEADACHE. SHE DOESN'T WANT TO TALK ABOUT WORK TODAY.

As she drives away, I can feel that she is taking part of me with her. They **all** do.

When things go awry, you can scrub the walls, haul the bloody tub to the field, mop up, clean and power-wash, rebuild, sanitize feverishly... You can get all the nastiness out. Or try. They **always try**.

ARKHAM ASYL

Dear Mr. Herd

I hereby resign.

Sabine Henr.

But I'm still there, **inside them**. Diluting their dreams, nightmares, and hopes, every minute of the day. Not just the Asylum's horror...

ARKHAM ASYLUM

Dear Mr. Herd

I hereby resign

Sabine Henr.

...a very personal, **ordinary bloodshed**. What they **settle** for. What they **abandon** themselves to.

And for **whom**.

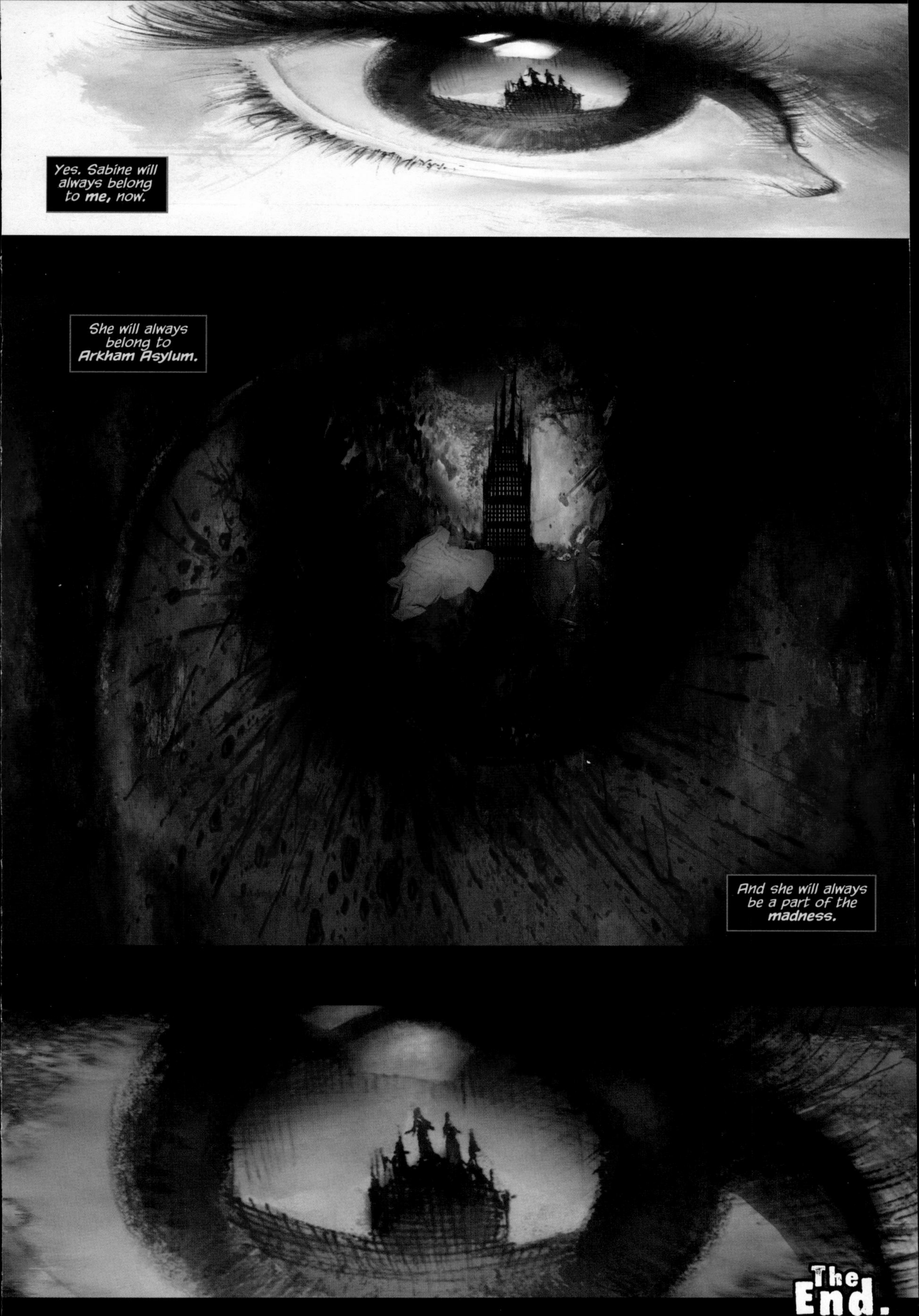

Yes. Sabine will always belong to me, now.
She will always belong to Arkham Asylum.
And she will always be a part of the madness.
The End.

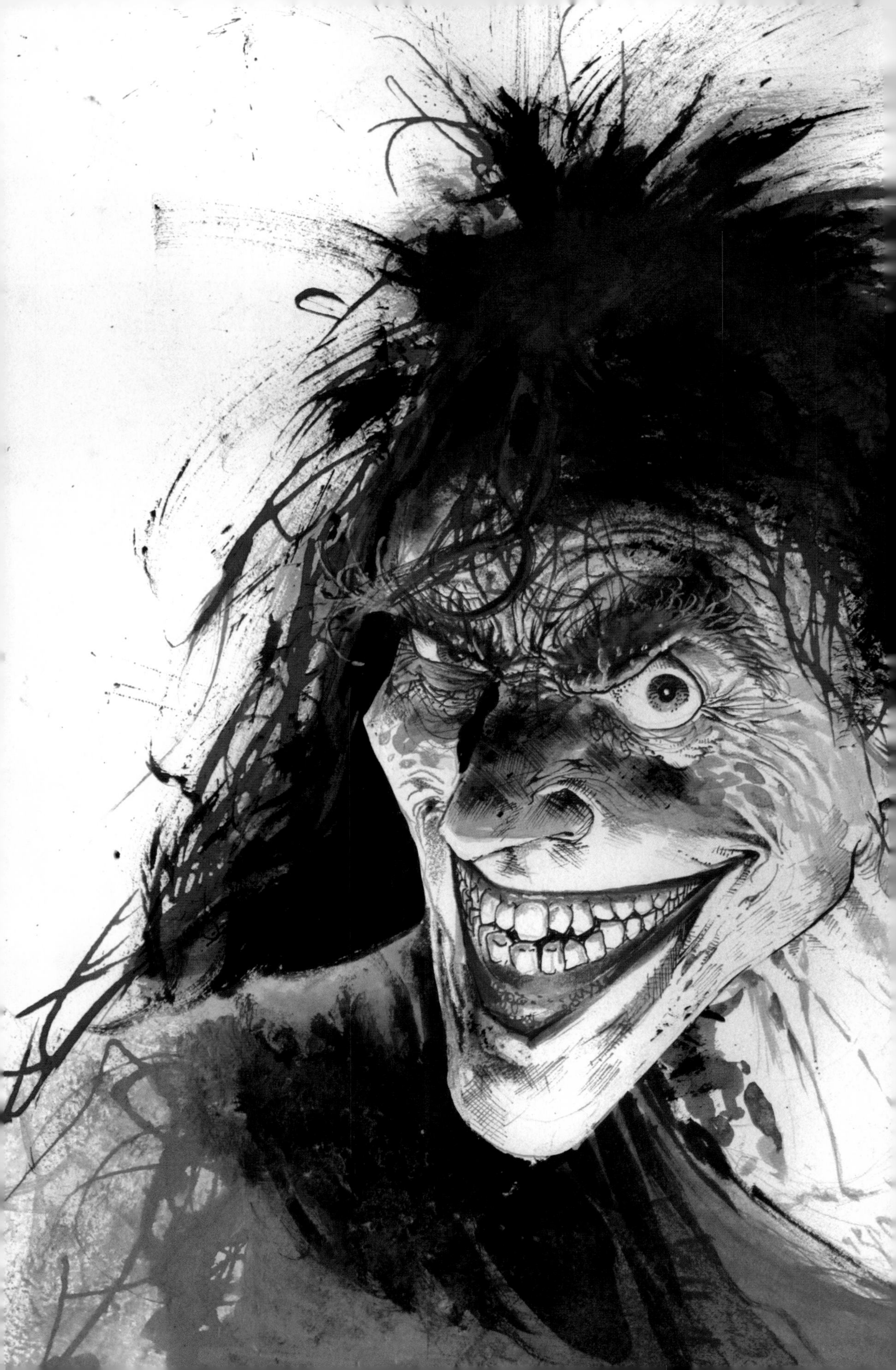

## Arkham Afterwards

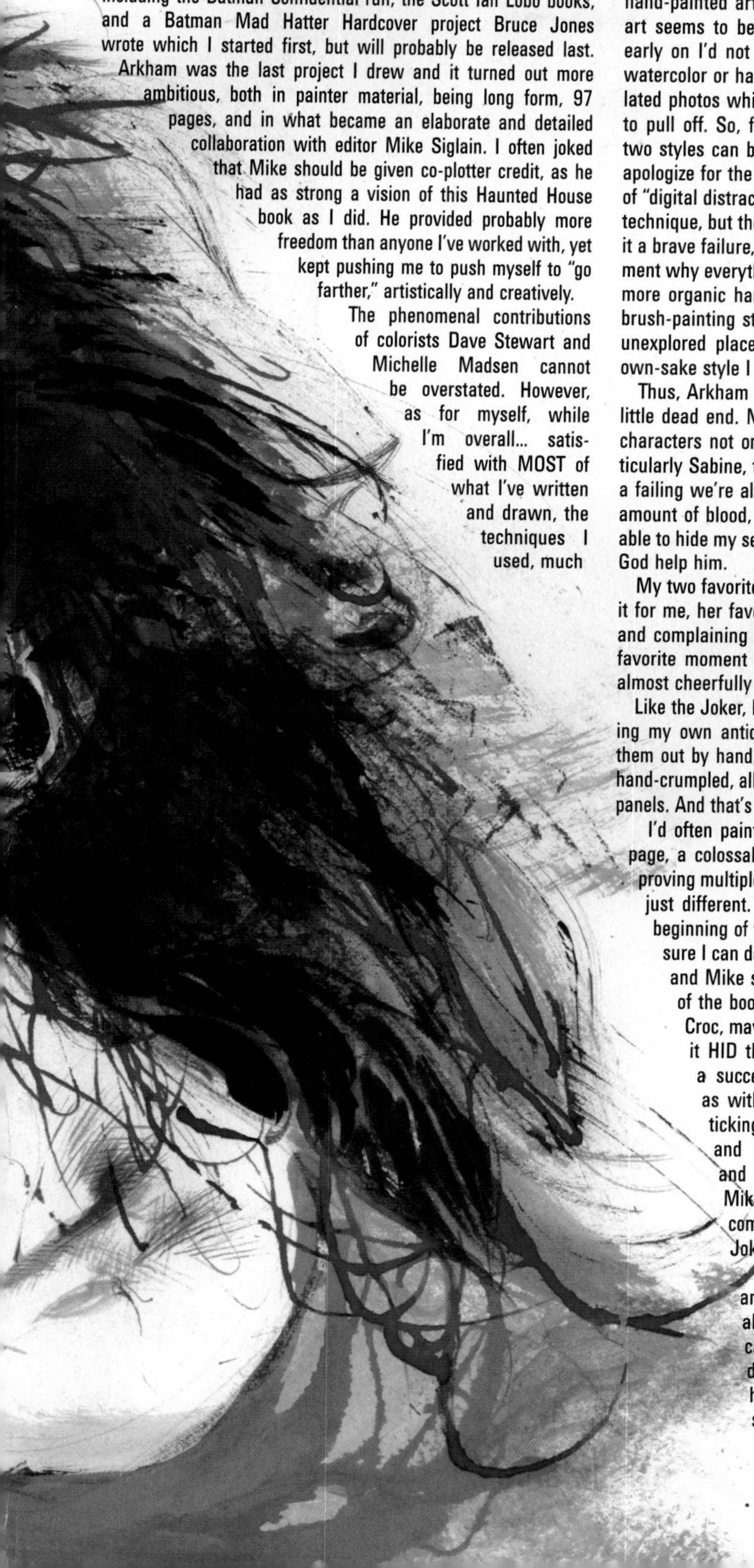

Arkham was the last of four projects I finished for DC, including the Batman Confidential run, the Scott Ian Lobo books, and a Batman Mad Hatter Hardcover project Bruce Jones wrote which I started first, but will probably be released last. Arkham was the last project I drew and it turned out more ambitious, both in painter material, being long form, 97 pages, and in what became an elaborate and detailed collaboration with editor Mike Siglain. I often joked that Mike should be given co-plotter credit, as he had as strong a vision of this Haunted House book as I did. He provided probably more freedom than anyone I've worked with, yet kept pushing me to push myself to "go farther," artistically and creatively.

The phenomenal contributions of colorists Dave Stewart and Michelle Madsen cannot be overstated. However, as for myself, while I'm overall... satisfied with MOST of what I've written and drawn, the techniques I used, much more collage, computer and photo manipulation colliding with hand-painted art, are mixed at best. The problem with digital art seems to be when it draws attention to itself. I decided early on I'd not try to hide my cartoonish hand-drawn style, watercolor or hand-painted art with digital tricks and manipulated photos which are far more realistic than I have the skill to pull off. So, for me the book was an experiment IF these two styles can be merged, without having to fight, distract or apologize for the other. On this level I think it shows the limits of "digital distraction," as in being drawn OUT of a story by the technique, but the same could be true of detailed art. I consider it a brave failure, an ambitious one, but ultimately a good argument why everything I draw after this will probably try to show more organic hand-drawn watercolor in the minimal Chinese brush-painting style or more abstract work, which is the only unexplored place left TO go after all this anal-detail-for-its-own-sake style I milked to death in this book.

Thus, Arkham is a necessary and not altogether unpleasant little dead end. Not only in plot, the dark story ends with the characters not only trapped, staff and inmates, but also, particularly Sabine, the nurse, giving up on herself. It is a choice, a failing we're all vulnerable to. To me that's scarier than any amount of blood, violence or physical carnage. I also was unable to hide my sense of humor, and Mike also encouraged this, God help him.

My two favorite lines in the book – well, my wife, who types it for me, her favorite line was the Joker being dragged away and complaining of missing Antiques Roadshow, whereas my favorite moment was the Joker's narration as he peacefully, almost cheerfully paints the severed foot in craft class.

Like the Joker, I got too carried away on this book, hand-making my own antiques jokes, aging them by computer, printing them out by hand, then spilling red paint "blood" on the box I'd hand-crumpled, all for something that would only appear in a few panels. And that's only one example.

I'd often paint as many as 6 to 15 different versions of a page, a colossal waste of time, energy and sanity, and also proving multiple pages don't always result in a BETTER page, just different. When I painted the Killer Croc page at the beginning of the book on page 9, I said to Siglain, "I'm not sure I can do a technically better splash of Croc than this" and Mike said, "Why not use it as a splash in the back of the book, then work your way up to it with hints at Croc, maybe with small inset panels." I liked this since it HID the fact that I probably could not paint such a successful Croc page, possibly ever again. But, as with the antiques jokes, and dead guards, and ticking clock, I became obsessed, overworking and reworking, and became a WORSE artist, and person, in the process. I, at last, and with Mike's help, had to step back and laugh and have compassion for myself, much as I did with the Joker. Older. Slower. Hopefully wiser.

As I watch myself age DOING this book, and have to laugh at myself, my own folly, I also TRIED to inject some humanity into these carefully guarded franchises we write and draw. I wanted to care about Sabine using her son to get through the day, to care about something in the middle of this hellish mess. Some light in the middle of the madness. To me, in a way it's either a horror story that she crumples her resignation letter, or a testament to her sacrifice for her son that she stays. To me the most chilling line in the book is when the Joker asks why she doesn't quit.

Visually, I'm all over the board and know my distorted and "wonky" view of Batman and the Joker is not for everyone. But thankfully editors like Siglain, Marts, Sattler and Dan DiDio seem to get a twisted thrill out of letting me run bad with their characters every once in a while. Then, like the Joker, I'm shoved back into my little cell and the characters are allowed to look normal again through other artists' safer, saner hands, much to the relief of the majority of fan boys, I am sure. Another dead end.

But reaching a dead end also means an opportunity for something new. Or a chance at it. I am saying goodbye in a way to the last two years at DC, but remember, I told Siglain I'd only take the Arkham job if I could not only top the Joker I drew in Batman: Secrets, but at least do a different take on him, breathe some new life into him...or die trying. So, I tried. I may have missed the mark, but I had fun trying, obsessing, and finally... moving on.

What art you'll see in the back is various raw, unfiltered versions of things, odds and ends, but most of the good stuff is buried between the covers.

sam kieth

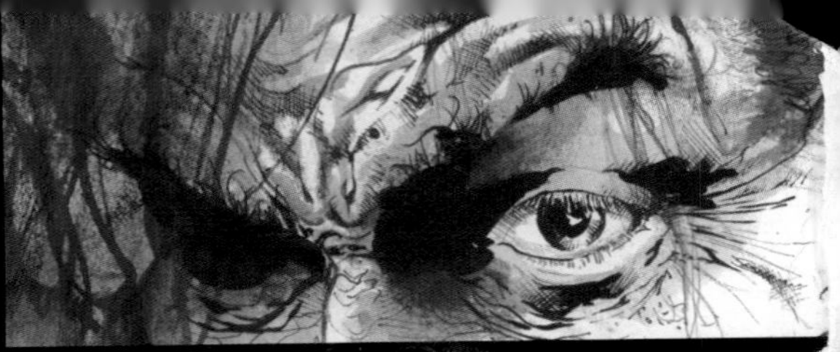

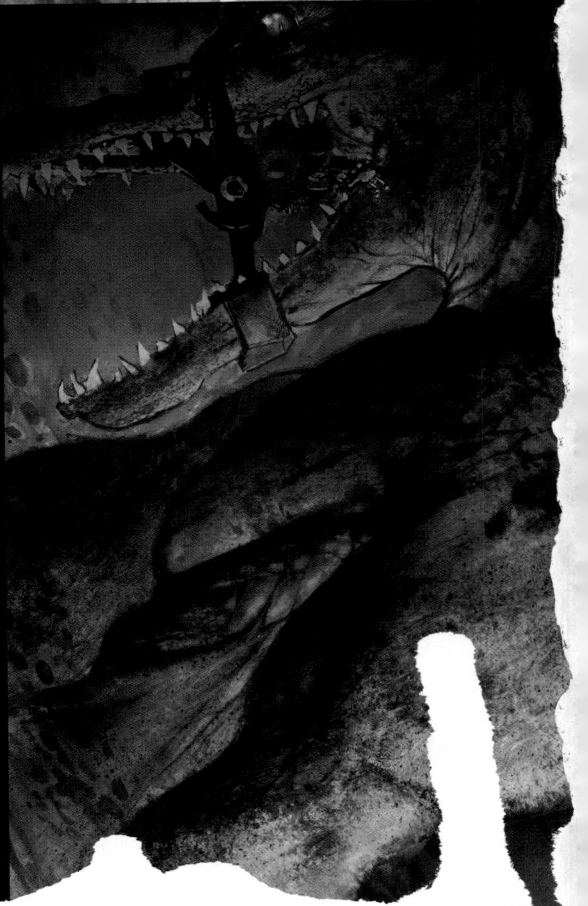

*Sam Kieth is the umpty-ninth comic artist who's done work for Marvel, DC, Image, and a long list of indie comics publishers. He drew the first five SANDMANs, and created The Maxx in '93, which became an animated series on MTV.*

*Despite writing bios of himself in the third person, he quietly lives with his wife somewhere in the mountains, writes a series of "trout books" for Oni Press, and wastes too much time making childish things out of duct tape.*

*This book is dedicated to everyone who hates their job.*

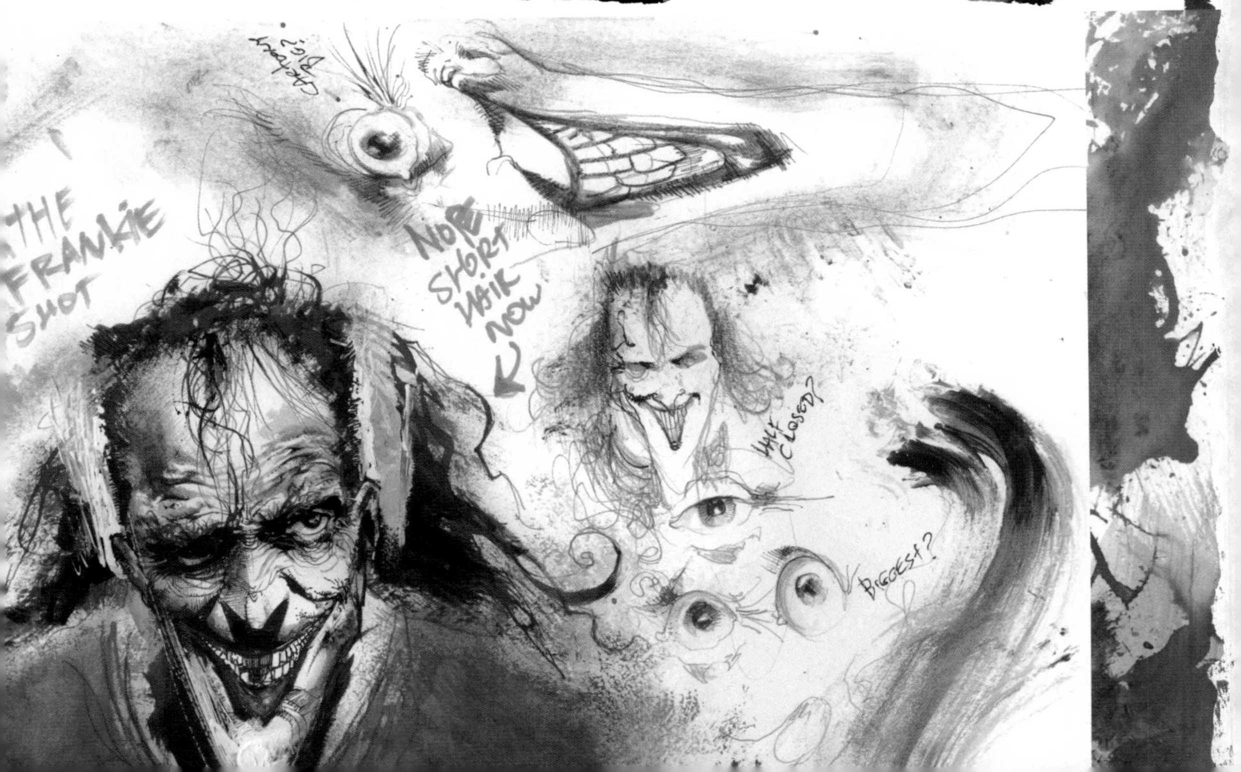
THE FRANKIE SHOT
NOPE SHORT HAIR NOW
HALF CLOSED?
BIGGEST?

COMICS KIETH
Kieth, Sam.
Arkham Asylum : madness